EYEWITNESS **COMPANIONS**

Weather

IN ASSOCIATION WITH THE
MET OFFICE

"THE ATMOSPHERE FORMS
A VAST OCEAN ABOVE US, AN
OCEAN BUT LITTLE EXPLORED...
WHERE THE LIGHTNING-FLASHES
HAVE THEIR ORIGIN."

Britain's Royal Meteorological Society, 1907

DK

LONDON • NEW YORK
MELBOURNE • MUNICH • DELHI

Senior Editor	Richard Gilbert
Senior Art Editor	Gillian Andrews
Production Editor	Maria Elia
Managing Editor	Stephanie Farrow
Managing Art Editor	Lee Griffiths
Production Controller	Imogen Boase
Publisher	Jonathan Metcalf
Art Director	Bryn Walls
US Editor	Jenny Siklós

Produced for Dorling Kindersley by
Tall Tree Ltd

Managing Editor	David John
Senior Editor	Rob Scott Colson
Editors	Kate Simkins
	Claudia Martin
Designers	Ben Ruocco
	Jonathan Vipond
Picture research	Louise Thomas
Designed by	Peter Laws
Written by	Ross Reynolds
Additional writing	John C Hammond
	Fiona Smith
	Sarah Tempest

First American Edition, 2008
in association with the
Met Office

Published in the United States by
DK Publishing, 375 Hudson Street
New York, New York 10014

08 09 10 11   10 9 8 7 6 5 4 3 2 1

DD234 November 2008

CONTENTS

CONTENTS (continued)

THE WEATHER AFFECTS US ALL, FROM THE
SIMPLE ACT OF RAISING AN UMBRELLA TO AN
AIRPLANE THAT CHANGES ITS COURSE TO AVOID
A THUNDERSTORM. BUT THE WORLD IS CONCERNED
NOT JUST ABOUT TODAY'S WEATHER—THE
CHALLENGES OF CLIMATE CHANGE WILL IMPACT
UPON ALL OF US FOR MANY YEARS TO COME.

Weather has always been elemental to the course of human history. About 12,000 years ago, retreating glaciers at the end of the last ice age allowed hunter-gatherers to migrate from Asia across the Bering land bridge and populate the Americas. With the development of farming, understanding grew of the divisions of climate and the importance of seasonal variation, which allowed farmers to plan their year. The failure of rain could cause the fall of kings. One of the world's earliest civilizations, that of the Akkadians in Mesopotamia, is thought to have collapsed in about 2100BCE due to catastrophic drought. The weather has been a crucial ingredient in some of history's most significant military campaigns, from the typhoon that scuttled the Mongol invasion of Japan in 1274, to the bad weather that put the Germans off their guard on D-Day in June 1944.

The Earth has witnessed huge changes in climate over its long life. To reveal the nature of changes hundreds of millions of years ago, scientists examine the slow break-up and drift of the continents and

SCIENTIFIC ADVANCES
The precision of observations was improved by the invention of accurate weather instruments, such as the barometer (1643).

spreading oceans, and the role that they played in creating the climate of that time. Interdisciplinary science—including glaciology and oceanography—can offer further clues to the climates over the last few hundred thousand years. The data from such disciplines becomes gradually more reliable as recent times are approached, indicating, for example, the timescale of the last ice age.

It was not until the appearance of the first civilizations that written records of the impact of the atmosphere on society were kept. Nevertheless, from the beginning of human history, some have turned their eyes to the sky to observe clouds and wind. Forecasting was, and still is, in the blood of those whose livelihood depends upon the weather. Our knowledge of what the weather was like before the Scientific Revolution of the 16th and 17th centuries is largely based on the careful, descriptive records kept by dedicated but widely scattered individuals.

WEATHER OMENS
In ancient Greece and Rome, thunderstorms were seen as bad omens. Pliny the Elder (23–79CE) wrote that they were prophetic, "direful and accursed."

MAPPING THE WEATHER
Weather forecast maps must include detailed observations of atmosphere, ocean, and land, and represent the complex interactions between them.

Early meteorologists included the Greek philosopher Aristotle (384–322BCE), who described the water cycle in his 350BCE treatise, *Meteorologica*—from which the term "meteorology" is derived. Yet it was not until the 17th century that quantitative, or scientifically measured, information became available. The development of the first thermometers and barometers occurred in the brilliant

MONITORING CLIMATE CHANGE
Nature provides an indicator of climate change in the melting rate of Arctic sea ice. As the ice retreats, habitats of animals such as the polar bear are lost.

era of the Scientific Revolution in the mid-17th century. The discovery of the fundamental physical laws by the leading minds of the day opened the way to understanding the workings of the atmosphere and oceans.

The second half of the 19th century saw the establishment of the earliest government-funded weather services, including the first storm-warning service, set up by the Paris

Observatory in 1855. The first synoptic charts, in which simultaneous observations could be viewed on a map, were created in 1860 by the English meteorologist Robert FitzRoy (1805–65) and became the standard way to display weather information.

In the early decades of the 20th century, a school of Norwegian meteorologists, led by Vilhelm Bjerknes (1862–1951), synthesized a wealth of observations to define the notion of fronts and air masses, and their impact on the weather. During the same era, English physicist Lewis Fry Richardson (1881–1953) became the first to apply mathematical techniques to weather prediction. In 1922, he attempted to use a series of differential equations to predict the weather—a method that is still used by today's supercomputer models.

Necessity is the mother of invention—the age of aviation highlighted the need for knowledge of the atmosphere some distance above the surface. By the early 1930s the first radiosondes were being used in weather balloons to transmit data. This led to a critically important grasp of the link between the upper circulation, such as jet streams, and surface weather features.

The development of electronic computers in the postwar period was an extremely significant event for forecasting. A large number of international co-operation programs

The discovery of the fundamental physical laws by the leading minds of the day opened the way to understanding the workings of the atmosphere and oceans.

and a huge expansion in computer speed and power are a key factor in the rapid progress of meteorology over recent decades.

Weather is a topic that is often used to break the ice in conversations. Nowadays, however, the talk is more likely to be of global warming and the outlook for the next century than the outlook for the next few days. This reflects an increased public awareness of a topic that is becoming more newsworthy, particularly as the occurrence of extreme weather events is more frequently being attributed to global warming. The scientists of the authoritative Intergovernmental Panel on Climate

With the world's population expanding, and industrialization keeping pace, we live in truly challenging times.

Change have stated that most of the observed warming is "very likely" to be caused by an enhancement to our planet's natural greenhouse effect due to human activity. Industrial processes are creating an unprecedented increase in greenhouse gases, which reduce the loss of the Earth's heat back into space, raising global temperatures. The global surface temperature has seen a particularly rapid increase over the last few decades, coinciding with the rapid industrial growth of the world's developing nations.

The changing climate has accelerated a program to improve understanding of the climate's physics, and to allow prediction of our future climate under different scenarios. This has become so important that the number of

LIVING WITH GLOBAL WARMING
Extreme weather events are on the increase due to rising global temperatures. In 2004, Bangladesh was devastated by the worst flooding for 15 years.

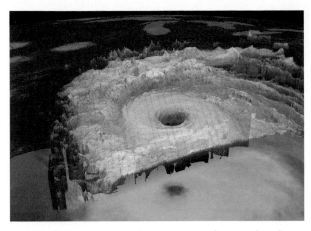

IMAGING TECHNOLOGY
Satellite imagery overlaid with computer graphics allows meteorologists to view patterns of rainfall, such as this computer image of Hurricane Katrina as it approached New Orleans in August 2005.

weather forecast centers that are now also climate forecast centers has increased substantially.

Discovering what the future holds for the world's climate will require continuing scientific research into the weather's enormous complexity. This will be tackled by using increasingly sophisticated computer models. We live in a time of rapid change in our environment. Thankfully, the international community is beginning to accept the results of collaborative scientific research on the future of climate and weather. With the world's population expanding, and industrialization keeping pace, we live in truly challenging times. While the world will continue to keep an eye on the weather, it will be increasingly important to keep an even closer eye on the changing climate.

History of weather

FROM THE EARLIEST MIGRATIONS TO THE RISE OF THE GREAT EMPIRES, THE COURSE OF HUMAN HISTORY HAS HINGED ON THE WEATHER. THE CLIMATE HAS ALWAYS DETERMINED WHERE AND WHEN HUMANS HAVE THRIVED—INDEED, CLIMATE CHANGE POSES THE GREATEST THREAT TO HUMAN SOCIETY OVER THE COMING DECADES.

Over the course of its history, the Earth's climate has undergone dramatic changes. Volcanic activity over millennia changed the mix of gases in the atmosphere, allowing complex life-forms to evolve, which in turn affected the climate by emitting or absorbing greenhouse gases such as methane and nitrous oxide, and in the case of humans, producing vast amounts of carbon dioxide through industrial processes. In addition, fluctuations in the source of our energy, the Sun, have tipped the planet into and out of ice ages. Only a few thousand years ago, the world was in "deep freeze," with extensive ice sheets extending from the poles and much lower sea levels. In fact, much of today's natural landscape was fashioned during the last glacial period and the millennia that followed.

Weather extremes have shaped the course of human history in dramatic ways. When the last ice age began and sea levels fell, the first humans began

ARAB SEAFARERS
The Arab spice trade of the Middle Ages sparked maritime innovations in the use of wind and sea currents on long voyages.

their exodus from Africa. In more recent times, large migrations, such as the mass emigration that followed the Irish Potato Famine in the 1840s, have been partly forced by weather conditions. Battles have been won and lost—and history determined—in many instances because of the weather.

As scientific understanding of weather developed in the 16th and 17th centuries, and instruments such as the barometer were invented, farmers and seafarers began using the weather to their advantage.

Today, we are faced with the effects of man-made climate change, and devastating consequences if industrial society does not change the polluting ways in which it produces energy. The tragic conflict in Darfur, East Africa, for example, has arisen over dwindling areas of arable land, caused by reduced rainfall.

Climate is inextricably linked to our past and our future. Whatever we do to shape the world we live in, the weather will always play a vital role in deciding our fate—and that of our planet.

HIGH FLYER
British meteorologist James Glaisher used a hot-air balloon to measure atmospheric conditions in the 1860s, and broke the world record for altitude.

RECONSTRUCTING THE PAST

Scientists can piece together the story of weather by analyzing the data locked in natural indicators, such as tree rings and ice cores. Some of this evidence stretches back hundreds of millennia. A comparison of these findings with recorded events shows how short- and long-term changes in weather have shaped human history.

WRITTEN IN THE RINGS

The evidence of tree rings gives a surprisingly accurate picture of temperature change over time. Trees form annual growth rings that can be seen when the trunk is cut through horizontally. The width of these rings in any year can indicate fluctuations in temperature and rainfall. A wide ring suggests plentiful growth during a mild year; a narrow ring, limited growth in a cooler year. As trees may live for several millennia—some Bristlecone pines, for example, are known to be 8,500 years old—their records often stretch back to a time when human records of weather were scarce or unreliable. Scientists who analyze the data of tree rings are known as dendrochronologists. They take evidence from several trees across a region, and collate the results for an accurate picture of the climate of a particular period.

CIRCLES OF LIFE
The width of each ring in a tree trunk shows how good growing conditions were each year.

DEEP-FROZEN DATA

Ice cores drilled from thick polar ice caps can provide evidence of temperatures dating back hundreds of thousands of years—far longer than the data in any tree. But information from air trapped in the ice has the disadvantage of becoming "fuzzier"—less detailed—as it gets older.

FROST FAIRS
During the Little Ice Age, the rivers and lakes of Europe regularly froze over in winter. This painting depicts a "frost fair" on the Thames River, London, in the 18th century.

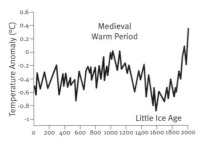

TREE RING DATA
Data from studies of tree rings in the Ural mountains of Russia shows how average temperatures have varied over the centuries.

Near the top of the cores, the air samples can be dated to a particular year, but further down, the ice compacts under pressure and individual years can no longer be distinguished.

ABRUPT CLIMATE CHANGE

From tree rings and ice cores, we know that some changes in the climate occurred over relatively short periods and may have been "forced" by particular natural events. A massive influx of glacial meltwater into the North Atlantic some 12,900 years ago, for example, may have changed ocean circulation and abruptly reversed the general warming of the period.

In more recent times, the period from the 10th to 14th centuries in Europe, known as the Medieval Warm Period, was characterized by relatively warm conditions, possibly linked to increased solar activity. During the Little Ice Age, some two centuries later, there were severe winters across the northern hemisphere, this time potentially linked to a decrease in solar activity.

EVIDENCE FROM ICE CORES

The ice caps of Antarctica and Greenland have an average thickness of about 1¼ miles (2 km) and are, in effect, frozen thermometers. Ice cores can be drilled and cut for detailed analysis, providing scientists with samples of air that was trapped when the snow fell. Researchers measure levels of carbon dioxide and oxygen isotopes in the trapped air, which indicate the snow's temperature and ocean volume when it formed. This makes it possible to map changes in the climate over the past 400,000 years. We now know, for example, that during the last ice age, polar temperatures were 18°F (10°C) lower than they are today.

Prehistoric climates

The Earth has witnessed dramatic changes of climate over the 4.6 billion years of its history. Some changes were related to prolonged periods of volcanic activity, while others were forced by the slow tectonic movements of continents and ocean basins.

MOLTEN PLANET

For the first 100 million years of its history, the Earth was a scene of violent volcanic activity. The primitive atmosphere was composed mainly of gases expelled from volcanoes, when eruptions generated massive volumes of carbon dioxide. They also sent huge amounts of volcanic ash and dust high up into the atmosphere.

Prolonged periods of volcanism had a powerful influence on climatic temperatures. If small particles enter the stratosphere, they tend to remain there for long periods of time. As they

VOLCANIC ATMOSPHERE
The earliest atmosphere consisted of carbon dioxide, nitrogen, and hydrogen issued from volcanoes, a process known as "outgassing."

absorb solar radiation, these particles can warm the atmosphere. In contrast, dust veils reduce the amount of sunshine reaching the Earth's surface and have a cooling effect.

SWAMP CLIMATES AND ICE AGES

The early stages of the Carboniferous Period (354–290 million years ago) were characterized by warm and damp conditions—caused by landmasses shifting closer to the equator. Swamp forests released huge amounts of oxygen into the atmosphere. Peat was formed when the vegetation died.

FOSSIL FERN
This plant originally grew in the giant swamps of the Carboniferous Period, when much of the world was covered in forests of club mosses and ferns.

SUPERCONTINENT
Pangaea formed about
300 million years ago.
Other supercontintents
may have existed
before it.

GLACIER WORLD
During the Earth's ice ages,
glaciation was far more extensive
than it is today, and shaped
mountains and valleys.

Over time
the peat was
compressed and turned to coal and oil,
which are now burned as fuel, releasing
carbon dioxide into the atmosphere.

The Carboniferous Period ended in
a cold period, known as the Karoo Ice
Age, as the level of insulating gases in the
atmosphere fell. Ice ages have recurred
periodically in the Earth's history, caused
variously by changes in the atmosphere,
the Earth's orbit, volcanism, and the
position of the continents.

DRIFTING CONTINENTS

Prior to the Jurassic Period (206–142
million years ago), there was just one single
continent, called Pangaea ("all Earth"). It
started to divide during this period, and
the continents have been slowly drifting
ever since. This gradual motion, which has
opened up the world's ocean basins,
transforms climate over time, by shifting
ocean currents and moving landmasses
into warmer or colder latitudes.

EXTINCTION EVENT

There have been several mass extinctions
of life during the Earth's history. The most
recent, about 65 million years ago, was
probably caused by an asteroid collision,
which ended the heyday of the dinosaurs.
The impact would have transformed the
world's climates by sending huge amounts
of dust into the atmosphere, causing global
dimming and acid rain. The force of the
collision would also have triggered waves
of volcanic and seismic activity.

Religion and folklore

Before the era of scientific understanding, religion and folklore
played a critical role in perceptions of day-to-day weather conditions
and the seasons. A belief in the power of deities was commonplace,
and observations formed the basis of many useful weather predictions.

AZTEC BELIEFS

The Aztec (or Mexica)
civilization that thrived
in the Valley of Mexico
between the 13th and
15th centuries worshipped
a large pantheon of
deities, including
Centeotle, the god of
maize, and Tlaloc, who
was thought to control
the weather. Aztec
society was based
on agriculture, so was
susceptible to drought
and flood. People
believed that Tlaloc
determined these
conditions by sending
down lightning bolts and
different types of rain that would either
ruin crops or produce bumper harvests.
Hurricanes were thought to be a sign of
the gods' anger. Priests performed child
sacrifices in an attempt to appease them.

GOD OF RAIN
The Aztec god of rain, Tlaloc, was
depicted wearing a net of clouds
and shaking a thunder rattle.

NORSE MYTHOLOGY

Between the 8th and 11th centuries,
Norse, or Viking, sailors from
Scandinavia made a series of daring
voyages of discovery, reaching as far as
Greenland and North America. They
attributed the storms they encountered
on their journeys to Thor, the god of
thunder. They believed thunder was
the noise made by Thor as he raced
through Middle Earth (the realm of
mankind) on his chariot. Lightning
flashes were produced whenever he
threw his ax-hammer to slay his enemies.
Another important Norse god was Frey,

the god of rain, sun, and fertile
earth, whom the Vikings
prayed to in the spring
for plentiful crops. Frey
was especially venerated
by peasants and farmers.

THE MAYPOLE

To mark the end of winter
and to look forward to a fertile
and productive planting and
growing season, villagers
across Europe have long
danced around a maypole
in celebration of the
annual festival of May Day.
The earliest accounts of
maypole dancing date from
the 14th century, although
the ceremony itself is thought to date back
to a Roman festival in honor of Flora, the
goddess of fruit and flowers. During
medieval times, May Day was a public
holiday involving much merriment,
although in Sweden, maypole dancing
occurred on Midsummer's Day.

GOD OF THUNDER
The word "thunder" comes from the name Thor, the
god of thunder, after whom Thursday is also named.
Representations of Thor's hammer were worn by
Vikings for good luck and protection.

WEATHER DANCE
Rain dancers in Niger in West Africa attempt to summon a cloudburst during a period of drought by appealing to the spirit world.

MAY DAY CELEBRATIONS
The maypole is a centuries-old tradition, but holding ribbons while dancing around it is a 19th-century addition to the ceremony.

RAIN DANCING

Around the world, many cultures have performed ritual dances in an attempt to invoke rain during times of drought. The tradition lives on in the arid southwest of the United States, where peoples including the Hopi still perform a dance in spring to attract rain during the planting season.

In Romania, a dancing ritual called Paparuda takes place in the spring and at times of drought. Similar customs are also observed in parts of West Africa.

WEATHER LORE

The 16th century ushered in the "Age of Sail," as four-masted ships carried European settlers to the New World. Through careful observation, sailors developed a body of maritime weather wisdom embodied in sayings, which were the most reliable forecast tool available. "Rainbow to windward, foul falls the day, rainbow to leeward, rain runs away," for instance, is an accurate observation, since rain clouds are always in the direction of the rainbow. "When halo rings Moon or Sun, rain's approaching on the run" is also accurate: today we know that the chance of rain within 24 hours is high after a Moon halo. The halo is caused by ice crystals in high cirrostratus clouds, which indicate an approaching warm front.

SAILORS' OBSERVATIONS
Much of the world's weather lore originated between the 16th and 19th centuries, when large, ocean-going ships made voyages to the Americas.

Climates in ancient times

Cave paintings by neolithic man give us the earliest indications that the climate in some parts of the world was quite different from today's. Later, in a small area around ancient Greece, brilliant civilizations flourished and gave us our first insight into the workings of weather.

WET NORTH AFRICA

Stunning cave paintings of giraffes, hippos, and rhinos, among other current-day savanna animals, have been preserved in caves in the Tassili-n-Ajjer mountains of southeastern Algeria. The paintings suggest a much wetter climate sometime between 8000 and 4000BCE when it is believed they were made. The network of wadis—dry channels that once carried water—in today's parched desert were formed during this period.

The ancient kingdoms of Egypt were totally dependent on the flow of the Nile River, which creates a band of fertile land through the yellow-brown desert. The Old Kingdom, a period in which the pharaohs first came to rule, grew and flourished from 2686 to 2181BCE. Each summer, the river would flood, covering the land with nutrient-rich silt, vital for a successful

WETTER TIMES
Cave paintings in southern Algeria date from 2900BCE. Ostriches, gazelles, and domestic cattle are depicted, none of which now live in the region, which has become a desert.

harvest. The floods were so regular and important that the Egyptians based their calendar around them. Occasionally, the floods would fail, which often led to political unrest. Tomb reliefs depicting people dying of hunger indicate that the Old Kingdom was brought to an end by 20–30 years of drought, which led to a repeated failure of the floods. Evidence, including concentrations of iron oxide in silt deposits, suggests an abrupt change to significantly drier conditions around 2150BCE over a massive region stretching from Tibet to the Mediterranean.

FARMER-BUILDERS
The pyramids of Giza were built when the Old Kingdom was at the height of its power— ordinary Egyptians would work on the tombs while their farms were flooded by the Nile River.

THE TOWER OF WINDS

The octagonal Tower of the Winds was built in Athens' marketplace between 100 and 50BCE by Andronicus of Cyrrhus. Friezes depict the weather associated with the winds from eight points of the compass. Boreas, the north wind, is a man blowing a chilly wind through a shell; Zephyros, a westerly wind, is shown as a man scattering flowers. The tower included the first ever wind vane in the form of a bronze Triton mounted at the top.

THE FIRST METEOROLOGIST
Aristotle described many atmospheric phenomena. Many of his theories about their causes, such as "nature abhors a vacuum," were wrong, but they remained influential for some 2,000 years.

CLASSICAL THINKERS

In the 6th century BCE a brilliant school of philosophy was founded in the ancient Greek city-state of Athens. Scholars endeavored to understand the workings of the whole universe—including the human body and the weather and climate. The philosopher Aristotle (384–322BCE) wrote the world's first text on atmospheric phenomena, *Meteorologica*, which was divided into four books. A total of 15 of the 42 chapters were devoted to the science of the atmosphere, including the formation of clouds and mist, of dew and frost, and the origin of rain, snow, hail, and wind. One of Aristotle's pupils, Theophrastus, wrote about winds and weather-signs, an indication that, in these early days, there was a keen interest in prediction based on observations of the sky.

DROUGHT AND DECLINE IN PERU

The Moche civilization developed in what is now northern Peru, from 100 to 700CE. Elaborate ceramics and gold work attest to a sophisticated culture based on farming. Fields were irrigated by a complex system of canals.

Late in the 6th century, however, archaeological evidence suggests that a "super El Niño" (see pp.166–67) may have resulted in a period of around 30 years of rain and flooding followed by an equally long period of drought. This led to severe famine as the Moche fields and irrigation systems were destroyed. The Moche believed that their crops were guaranteed by the sacrifices they made to the gods. The failure of the crops meant a failure of their very belief system—the archaeological evidence suggests that the culture did not recover from these catastrophic events.

MOCHE POTTERY
At its height, the Moche civilization produced sophisticated pottery, including portrait vases such as this. Some were linked to human sacrifices made by priests, invoking divine help for crops and harvests.

Medieval climate changes

Changes in the climate, both long- and short-term, led to the founding and abandoning of cities in the medieval world. A prolonged period of warmer weather led to settlements as far north as Greenland. In Japan, timely storms protected the islands from invaders.

MAYAN DOWNFALL

The Mayan civilization developed in Central America in the middle of the 3rd century. At its peak it extended from the Yucatán peninsula in present-day Mexico, south to Guatemala and Honduras. The southern part of the Mayan empire declined sharply sometime during the 8th and 9th centuries. Advanced cities, some of which contained large stone pyramids, were abandoned and soon consumed by the jungle, to be hidden and forgotten for centuries.

Evidence taken from lake-bed sediments and pollen cores shows that there was a severe and prolonged drought at the time of the Mayan decline. This is a possible explanation for why the Maya abandoned their cities.

NORSE ADVENTURERS

The Viking king Eric the Red led a small expedition to what is now Greenland in 982 after he had been expelled from Iceland. On the southern tip of the island and up the southwest coast, he discovered land and a climate that were suitable for cultivating crops and keeping livestock, and he returned three years later with a party of settlers to establish two colonies on the island. Conditions were still relatively harsh, with a very short growing season, and Eric may have tricked some settlers into coming with him by exaggerating the fertility of the new land

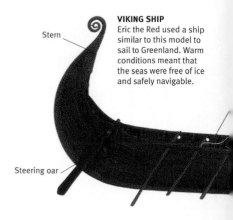

VIKING SHIP
Eric the Red used a ship similar to this model to sail to Greenland. Warm conditions meant that the seas were free of ice and safely navigable.

Stern

Steering oar

he called "green." Nevertheless, communities in the area thrived at first, trading dairy products and furs for goods from Europe.

It is believed that a deterioration of the climate after some 500 years of benign conditions, known as the Medieval Warm Period, led to the decline and eventual abandonment of Greenland by the Vikings. During these years, temperatures were high over the whole of the North Atlantic.

LOST CIVILIZATION
The ruined temples of the Mayan city of Tikal lie in the jungle of present-day Guatemala. Tikal was the largest of the classical Mayan cities that were abandoned more than 1,000 years ago when the seasonal rains failed.

ail made
om wool

PROTECTED BY THE WEATHER
This 13th-century Japanese engraving depicts the Buddhist monk Nichiren summoning the kamikaze typhoon to protect Japan from the Mongol invaders.

Prow

SEASONS FROM THE BOOK OF HOURS
This triptych from a medieval illuminated manuscript shows the changing seasons in northern Europe. During the Medieval Warm Period, there were vineyards in southern England.

DIVINE WIND

Between 1274 and 1281, the Mongol emperor Kublai Khan, who had conquered China and commanded a vast empire, undertook a number of invasions of Japan. Samurai warriors from rival Japanese clans joined together to repel the invaders, who had to sail from China across the Sea of Japan.

During the first invasion in 1274, the samurai fought so fiercely that the Mongol forces sought refuge in their warships offshore, where a typhoon blew up overnight and destroyed their fleet.

A later attempt to invade Japan, in 1281, is thought to have involved one of the largest fleets in history. Fate was against the invaders once more and the navy was cut to pieces by another typhoon. The Japanese called the storm "kamikaze," meaning "divine wind." They believed that the kamikaze had been sent to protect them by the gods.

Warfare and exploration

The weather was the deciding factor in several historic events during the 15th and 16th centuries. Two famous victories had dramatic consequences for English history, while Christopher Columbus was fortunate to avoid tropical storms on his voyage across the Atlantic.

VICTORY IN A QUAGMIRE

On October 25, 1415, at Agincourt in northern France, a French army of 25,000 knights and foot soldiers confronted a force of just 6,000 English and Welsh soldiers led by King Henry V of England. However, the huge numerical advantage counted for nothing on the day, partly because of heavy rain the night before the battle.

The battlefield turned into a quagmire, to the disadvantage of the French, many of whom wore heavy armor. Foot soldiers and cavalry became bogged down in mud, greatly slowing their maneuvers and making the cavalry easy targets for the English longbowmen. The result was a famous English victory. But for the inclement weather, the smaller army may well have been overrun.

MIRED IN THE MUD
This English painting commemorates the victory at Agincourt. On the right, longbowmen take aim at the French cavalry bogged down in mud.

TRADE WINDS AND EMPIRE

In the late 15th century, the Spanish monarchs Ferdinand and Isabella sponsored exploratory expeditions across the Atlantic in search of new trade routes to China. On August 3,

SHIPS WRECKED
The Spanish Armada was battered by storms off the east coast of England. Of the 130 ships that left Spain, just 67 made it home.

PLANTING THE FLAG
Columbus places the standard of the Spanish crown on an island in the Bahamas. The trade winds carried him a long way, but not quite as far as he thought—Columbus himself thought he may have landed on an island in Japan.

1492, Christopher Columbus set sail on such a mission from southern Spain. Previous attempts to sail west via the Azores had been hampered by the westerly headwinds found there, so Columbus set a course for the Canaries. From there, his fleet sailed successfully in the reliable northeast trade winds right across the tropical Atlantic, and landed on a Bahamian Island on October 12, 1492. His fleet had taken advantage of the tailwind provided by the trade winds and was lucky to avoid tropical storms at that time of year. On Columbus's voyage home, a terrible storm on the more northerly route of their return track, within the westerly wind belt, helped carry them back to Europe.

STORM DAMAGE

In the summer of 1588, the Spanish undertook a well-armed expedition involving some 130 vessels. Their aim was to rendezvous with a massed Spanish army in northern France, and invade Britain. After the fleet had met with the waiting army near Calais, the English sent fire ships into the Armada, which scattered northward up the east coast of England. The Armada was forced to sail right around the British Isles to find a route back to Spain. Though some destruction was wreaked by the English navy, most of the damage suffered by the Armada was due to the bad storm it encountered to the north and west of Scotland, and west of Ireland.

The Scientific Revolution

Huge scientific advances took place during the 17th and 18th centuries, which saw the first awakening of a truly scientific interest in nature. During this period, reliable instruments were developed to measure the atmosphere, which was key to understanding weather phenomena.

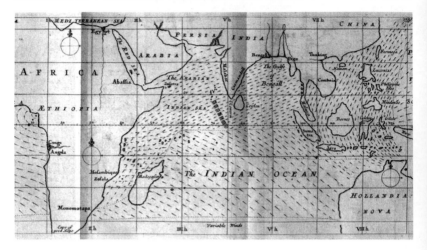

IMPROVED UNDERSTANDING

Italian scientist Evangelista Torricelli built the first barometer in 1643 to prove the existence of atmospheric pressure and discredit the Aristotelian dictum that "nature abhors a vacuum." Torricelli's ideas were confirmed in 1648 by French mathematician Blaise Pascal, who had a mercury barometer taken to the top of the Puy de Dome, a mountain in central France. The instrument showed clearly that pressure decreased with height as it moved up within the fluid envelope of the atmosphere.

Another breakthrough was made by Edmond Halley, an English meteorologist perhaps best known for the comet named after him. In 1686,

SCIENTIFIC TREATISE
This illustration from Torricelli's treatise *Experience of Emptiness* depicts an experiment demonstrating atmospheric pressure.

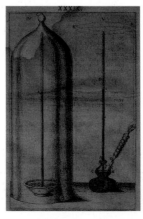

EARLIEST WEATHER MAP, 1686
Edmond Halley used data taken from ships' logs to draw the first weather map. It shows the trade winds and monsoons that blow across subtropical oceans.

he published a map of surface winds across the world's subtropical oceans. He also understood the influence that solar heating patterns have on atmospheric motion, and the way in which the uneven temperature of the Earth's surface causes warm air to rise, in turn causing air to circulate.

THE LAWS OF PHYSICS

One of the most important events of the Scientific Revolution was the formulation of the laws of physics, which laid the foundations for the meteorological sciences. Two giants of the Royal Society, a scientific body founded by the English King Charles II in 1662, made advances that were critical to the understanding of atmospheric phenomena:

Isaac Newton formulated his Law of Gravitation and Laws of Motion, and Robert Boyle established the mathematical relationship between the pressure, volume, and temperature of a gas.

KEEPING RECORDS

The British led the way in keeping records of weather phenomena during this period. English polymath Robert Hooke took observations of temperature and pressure, publishing his readings in 1664. The earliest rainfall records for a substantial period were taken by Richard Towneley in Lancashire. He used a gauge of his own design and kept records from 1677 to 1704.

Many clergymen started to keep weather diaries. William Derham, a rector in Upminster in Essex, observed and then logged weather data from 1697 to 1716. Thomas Barker kept records in Lyndon, Rutland, from 1736 to 1798.

EARLY METAL THERMOMETER
This German thermometer from 1748 measures the lengths of four lead rods to determine the temperature. Later, liquid mercury was used, a method first proposed by German engineer Daniel Fahrenheit in the 1720s.

Casing containing lead rods

Casing inscribed with significant temperatures, such as body heat

Temperature dial

Tripod stand

MERCURY BAROMETER
This is a reconstruction of a barometer made by Robert Hooke while working for the Royal Society In the 1660s. It converts the rise and fall of mercury into circular motion so that it can be represented by a needle on a dial.

Column of mercury

Mechanism turns the rise and fall of the mercury into the circular motion of a needle

Dial showing the likely weather

ANDERS CELSIUS

In 1742, Swedish astronomer Anders Celsius (1701–44) formulated his temperature scale. The original version set the boiling point of water at sea level at 0 degrees and the freezing point at 100 degrees. This scale was reversed a year after his death. Celsius also established that the boiling point goes down as atmospheric pressure reduces.

Weather in the modern era

The 19th century saw the expansion of the weather-observing
network to many parts of the world. It was a century in
which many dramatic events turned on the weather, and
scientists were increasingly able to understand why.

NAPOLEON'S RETREAT

In the late summer of 1812, Napoleon's
Grande Armée of about half a million
troops began its march to capture Tsar
Alexander's Moscow. Battles were won
on the eastward journey, culminating
in the arrival on September 14 of the
much-depleted army of 100,000 at an
abandoned Moscow. Napoleon retreated
westward with his army on October 19.

Extreme cold took its toll on the
poorly provisioned soldiers. On
December 8, just 25,000 troops, all
that remained of the Grande Armée,
arrived at Vilnius in Lithuania.

THE SUMMER THAT NEVER WAS

On April 10, 1815, the volcano
Tambora in Indonesia erupted, sending
so much dust and ash into the air that it
was completely dark for two days as far
away as 370 miles (600 km). Over the
following months, the fine dust spread
through the upper atmosphere right
around the globe, reflecting back some
of the Sun's radiation and cooling the

VOLCANIC SUNSET
British artist JMW Turner was famed for his sunsets. The
colors he observed in this painting were caused by ash
in the atmosphere after Tambora erupted in 1815.

planet. The year 1816 started well
enough in North America, but declined
into a cool spring followed by an
exceptionally poor summer. There were
frosts and snowfall into May and June
over parts of New England, where the
corn crop was just 10 percent the normal

ANEMOMETER
The anemometer was invented to measure wind speed. Wind drives the hemispheric cups and its speed is recorded on the meter.

Spinning cups

Cylindrical meter

a substantial destruction of crops. The idea that volcanic eruptions could have such an effect was not new. The American polymath Benjamin Franklin postulated that the cool summer of 1783 was related to the eruption of Mt. Laki in Iceland that year.

IRISH FAMINE

In late September 1845, the *Dublin Evening Post* reported the discovery of a disease of the potato crop across parts of Ireland. A mold with airborne spores known as the "late blight" was destroying the potato crop, a disaster to a poor country where potatoes were the staple. In 1845, 40 percent of the crop perished. In 1846, the entire crop was lost. About 1.5 million people died in the Great Famine, and Ireland's population declined from 8.3 million to 6 million in just a few years, partly due to emigration, principally to North America.

The British government immediately set up an inquiry to find the cause of the blight, but it wasn't until 1882 that the culprit—a fungus that thrives in mild, rainy weather conditions—was identified.

yield. Fruit and other food harvests were also extremely poor, and many settlers in New England and eastern Canada were forced to move west in search of better conditions.

It was not only North America that suffered—parts of Europe witnessed an extremely poor summer, too. The Swiss government declared a state of emergency to aid its starving population. Ireland experienced 142 cold, wet days out of 152 "summer" days, which led to

JOHN DALTON

English scientist John Dalton (1766–1844) has been described as the "father of modern meteorology." He correctly worked out that air is a mixture of different gases, not a compound of elements. Dalton's rigorous methods transformed meteorology from a study based largely on folklore into a serious scientific discipline.

UNDER-PREPARED
Poorly equipped and underfed, three-quarters of what remained of Napoleon's army perished during the retreat from Moscow as the temperature plunged to -15°F (-26°C) on November 14 and -33°F (-36°C) on December 6.

Weather and world affairs

The 20th century saw unprecedented change, and not always for the good; world wars ravaged vast swathes of the globe, and there was a growing realization that human activity had begun to change the climate. For the first time, weather affected events on a global scale.

WEATHER AND WAR

The battles in Belgium and northern France during World War I left millions dead on both sides. The Battle of Passchendaele in Flanders in 1917 was a planned offensive by the British that

LIQUID MUD
Stretcher bearers struggle through knee-deep mud during the Third Battle of Ypres at Passchendaele in 1917. Many soldiers drowned in the mud.

turned into a costly failure due to weather conditions. The British decided to commence the attack on October 19 despite worsening weather. Rain had started to fall over northern Belgium on October 4, followed by three days of torrential rain that soaked into ground that had already been churned up. The tracts of sodden, sticky mud became extremely arduous for soldiers, and the artillery could not move forward quickly enough and in sufficient numbers to lend bombardment support for the advance. The whole event was a disaster. A soldier who was present later wrote that "it was necessary to advance with the greatest of care, lest we should become hopelessly bogged…."

DUST BOWL

In the 19th century, a great number of settlers moved to the High Plains in the Midwest, where they were offered land

NORMANDY LANDINGS

Perhaps the most critically important weather forecast ever made was that on which the Supreme Commander of Allied forces, General Eisenhower, decided to launch the invasion of Normandy in June 1944, toward the end of World War II. One of the largest amphibious assaults ever attempted, this ambitious plan saw 156,000 Allied troops cross the English Channel into German-occupied France. The weather prediction was a combined effort of British and American meteorologists and correctly determined that the landings could go ahead. The window of opportunity was small, however, with rough seas preventing the use of landing craft and cloud cover obscuring air targets right up until the day of the invasion, D-Day, itself.

to farm. The settlers coped with occasional droughts in the early years, but plowing the soil-binding shortgrass proved disastrous when both a prolonged drought and the notorious High Plains winds struck.

The drought began in 1930. Without modern techniques to prevent erosion, dust storms blew away vast amounts of good topsoil. By 1940, 2.5 million people had moved away from the region to seek a better life elsewhere—to California, for example. John Steinbeck's classic novel *The Grapes of Wrath* chronicles the hardships suffered by these migrants as they sought work in California at the height of the Depression.

D-DAY
Allied troops land on a Normandy beach on June 6, 1944. Meteorologists were consulted to ensure conditions would be favorable on the day.

THE SCIENCE OF METEOROLOGY

The modern scientific methods now used in meteorology were not properly understood until the 17th century. Since then, advances in understanding and instrumentation have produced a series of leaps forward in weather forecasting.

THE ROLE OF TELEGRAPHY

In the 1830s, the American painter and inventor Samuel Morse developed the electric telegraph. This was the first ever system of high-speed long-distance communication. It enabled the development of what has become an enormously sophisticated international network of advanced weather-prediction centers all around the globe. In 1835, Morse showed that signals could be transmitted along a wire, and in 1838 he demonstrated that a print could be made of the message at the receiving end. In 1843, facilitated by government funding, the first signals were successfully transmitted from Baltimore to Washington.

The invention of the telegraph allowed widely scattered, simultaneous weather observations to be transmitted, as quickly as possible after they were taken, to one central office so that an up-to-date chart showing the current state of the atmosphere could be drawn. To predict the weather scientifically, it is essential to first gather good observations and represent them on a weather map.

ROBERT FITZROY

Robert FitzRoy (1805–65) was an admiral in the British Royal Navy who captained HMS *Beagle* on its famous second voyage with Charles Darwin on board. FitzRoy compiled weather records taken at sea that led to the founding of the UK Meteorological Office, one of the world's first, in 1854.

PIONEERS OF OBSERVATION

Pioneering work was carried out on both sides of the North Atlantic by individuals including US lawyer-turned-meteorologist James Espy, who in 1831 organized a committee to collect weather data. Espy published his convection

Spark gap

Key for sending messages

Tape for printing messages

Inker

MORSE CODER

An early telegraphic receiver, dating from the 1830s, featuring a key for sending messages in Samuel Morse's code, and an inker for receiving them.

theory of storms in 1841, and was appointed National Meteorologist by Congress in 1842. His work described the sequence that meteorologists should follow, from data collection and collation, and research on various phenomena, to predicting the future state of the atmosphere.

BALLOON OBSERVATION

For prediction, it is not only the weather at the surface that is important. Just as critical is knowledge of what is happening throughout the depth of the atmosphere. The first people to provide this information were pioneers in hot-air ballooning, who were

FLOATING TO THE STARS
The chart (right) shows the path James Glaisher's balloon took on its record-breaking flight from Wolverhampton to Ludlow. Many miles up, Glaisher had an unprecedented view of shooting stars (below).

interested in taking observations of temperature and pressure during their ascents and descents.

One such individual was James Glaisher, who was Superintendent of Meteorology and Magnetism at the Royal Greenwich Observatory in London from 1838 to 1874, and founded the Royal Meteorological Society in 1850. Glaisher became renowned for his balloon ascents during the 1860s.

He and a colleague, aeronaut Henry Coxwell, broke the world altitude record on September 5, 1882 when they ascended to 7 miles (11 km) from a gasworks in Wolverhampton, England. From meteorological data taken during this and other ascents, Glaisher deduced that the lapse in temperature with height was about 2°F (1°C) for each 330 ft (100 m) of ascent.

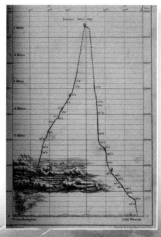

Mapping the weather

The invention of telegraphy enabled the collection of several observations at one site, where clear, up-to-date weather maps could be produced. Modern meteorologists rely on the latest information to give them an accurate picture of current conditions.

VICTORIAN ORGANIZATION

The British meteorologist James Glaisher was the first to organize the simultaneous collection of weather data from different locations. In 1849, he arranged for London's *Daily News* to print 50 observations taken at 9:00 a.m. on the previous day at train stations around the UK. Glaisher then used this data to draw his own weather maps. Two years later, the Great Exhibition at the Crystal Palace, London, provided a showcase for the Electric Telegraph Company. It organized the collection by telegraph of a range of weather observations from 64 sites around the UK and France that were presented each day at 9:00 a.m. to provide the world's first same-day weather map. By 1861, Admiral Robert FitzRoy (see p.40) had organized a twice-daily submission of data to London for publication. In the same year, *The Times* newspaper began to print a daily weather forecast, and by 1875 the Meteorological Office had issued the world's first weather chart for the UK in the same newspaper. Military leaders around the world began to recognize the value of weather maps in tracking storms and planning operations. France began a daily weather service in 1863 and the US followed suit in 1871.

THE VIEW FROM SPACE

The next big advance in data gathering came nearly 100 years later in April 1960, when the US launched the first weather satellite, TIROS I, which orbited the Earth once a day. In 1964, a satellite that

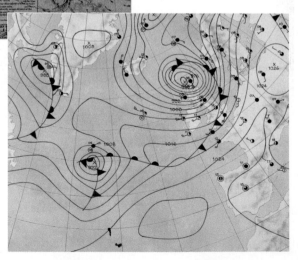

EARLY MAP
A weather map of the US from 1872, produced by the US War Department. Isobars, which link areas of the same pressure, show the locations of highs and lows.

SYNOPTIC CHART
This synoptic chart, produced in the UK in the 1970s, provides a summary of selected observations taken at the same time. In addition to isobars, it also shows the location of warm and cold fronts.

URBAIN LE VERRIER

Urbain Le Verrier (1811–77) was a French mathematician best known for accurately predicting the existence of the planet Neptune, through observation of the orbit of Uranus. He made his observations from the Paris Observatory, where he rose to become director. In this capacity, Le Verrier first warned the French Government in 1863 that France was becoming dangerously dependent on the UK for its weather information. He established a daily bulletin from 18 cities in France and neighboring countries, and in July 1863, he instituted a French storm-warning service. As part of this service, a daily weather map was produced from September 1863.

kept pace with the Earth's rotation was launched. There are now five of these "geosynchronous" satellites in orbit at the Earth's equator. They appear from the surface to be stationary above one point, and always provide images from the same region. This allows meteorologists to make animated sequences of moving weather systems.

MODERN MAPS

Weather maps today are generated by computers and can display a huge variety of different data to suit the individual forecaster and the occasion. Paper copies of maps are becoming increasingly rare, and forecasters will look at data in map form on computer monitors, where they can interact with them, modifying the forecast where necessary. Many weather services in poorer parts of the world still rely on the production of synoptic charts by hand.

SATELLITE IMAGERY
This infrared image of Hurricane Rita was taken for the US Navy on September 22, 2005 from a geosynchronous satellite. Images such as this were used to make animations tracking the cyclone.

Military meteorology

Weather often plays a key role in military operations, but its impact on such events has lessened over the years. This is because of improvements in understanding of weather phenomena and advances in the ability to monitor and predict weather patterns.

ZEPPELIN RAIDS
Germany first used airships for bombing raids during World War I. Cold weather made the frames brittle and the airships became unsafe, so the raids were eventually abandoned.

WEATHER BALLOONS
Aerial warfare led to advances in meteorological sampling devices, such as weather balloons.

EARLY AIR ATTACKS

The first aerial bombing raids were made by German Zeppelins in 1915, during World War I, opening a period of some three and a half years of attacks, latterly by fighter planes. Many of the airships were shot down, and some suffered from weather-related problems. Coastal features were sometimes shrouded in fog, making it difficult to spot targets. Low cloud was also a common hazard across northwestern Europe.

Added to these problems was the effect of wind direction on the airships' speed and navigability, and the fact that the craft was intensely cold for the crew. Build-up of ice on the Zeppelin also affected its stability.

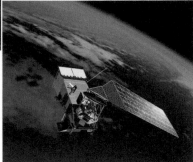

GROWING SUPPORT

The establishment of national air forces in several countries during World War I led to demands for better forecasts for flying operations. In turn, this led to the growth of a network of high-altitude weather balloons, mainly during and after World War II. The large-scale operations of World War II were a great stimulus to extending the geographical range of observations in the UK, US, and Germany, and improving understanding of the relationship between airflow at higher levels of the atmosphere and surface weather features. The achievements of forecasters, given the often sparse data they had to work with, were outstanding. This was epitomized in the forecast for the D-Day landings (see p.39). Other theaters of World War II, such as the conflicts in the Far East and across the central and western Pacific, demanded widely differing meteorological knowledge and skills.

GULF WAR
Sandstorms were a prominent feature of the first Gulf War (1990–91), often damaging equipment that was not built for such conditions.

MODERN WARFARE

Technology has revolutionized military weather analysis and forecasting. Specialist military satellites provide high-resolution imagery so that ground operators can monitor weather features that will affect combat zones. Infrared satellite imagery provides night-time coverage.

Weather predictions made by inputting the data into powerful computers can provide information on, for example, the location and thickness of different layers of cloud, the extent and intensity of dust or sandstorms, the speed and direction of low-level winds, and even detailed sea-state conditions for marine landings.

Weather and society today

Over the coming years, climate change may become an urgent issue for many countries. Concerns over fossil-fuel production have increased pressure to utilize renewable energy sources, and economic problems may be intensified by extreme weather or seasonal anomalies.

CLIMATE AWARENESS

Since the turn of the 21st century there has been a scientific consensus that the use of fossil fuels is contributing toward rising global temperatures. The Earth is warming, precipitation is increasing and changing its distribution across the globe, the frequency of frost and snow days is decreasing, and sea levels are rising. In 1988, the World Meteorological Organization and the United Nations Environment Programme established the Intergovernmental Panel on Climate Change to consider "the scientific, technical, and socioeconomic information relevant for the understanding of the risk of human-induced climate change." The panel's reports have provided key input for initiatives such as 1997's Kyoto Protocol, which laid a framework for reducing worldwide greenhouse gas emissions.

WEATHER AND THE ECONOMY

It has been estimated that about 30 percent of the US economy is directly affected by weather conditions, while the UK Met Office suggests that about 70 percent of businesses in Britain face some degree of risk associated with adverse weather. A cool, wet summer can affect agricultural production

RECLAIMING DESERTS
Many countries are using modern and traditional techniques to "take back" desert land and make it fertile, such as this project in Israel.

SOMETHING IN THE AIR
Wind power is one possible solution to the problem of diminishing fossil fuels, but it is more effective in some locations than others.

MONEY MATTERS
Stock markets are sensitive to weather. Crop failures may drive up prices, for example, or cargo lost in storms may result in insurance payouts.

and influence the price of grain, for example. With an increasing trend toward biofuels to power vehicles, this could increase the cost of transport, and affect all industries reliant on transport.

Weather-related disasters, such as the bush fires in Australia in 2007 and 2008, caused by an ongoing drought in the region, can put huge pressure on government budgets. Widespread flooding across parts of southern and central England during July 2007 brought chaos to farming and transport in those areas.

POWER PROVIDER

The price of oil is critically important to the operation of the global economy. It can occasionally be influenced by dramatic weather events, such as hurricanes in the Gulf of Mexico, which can damage offshore rigs. Price can also be used as a political tool by governments of oil-rich countries.

The need is growing for low-carbon and sustainable power. The atmosphere and oceans have the capacity to supply a substantial portion of our energy needs if governments are prepared to invest in

research to develop the resource. Wind and tidal energy production is growing, but is not suitable everywhere. Solar energy is also viable, although there is significant seasonal and geographical variation in its availability.

DARFUR: CLIMATE CONFLICT

The conflict in Darfur in western Sudan began in 2003, and is estimated to have claimed up to half a million lives. Arab militias backed by the government attempted to control dwindling areas of fertile land by driving away the local African farmers. The root of the conflict lies in slow desertification—rainfall has fallen by some 30 percent over the last four decades.

How weather works

WEATHER SYSTEMS ARE CONSTANTLY CIRCULATING WITHIN THE EARTH'S ATMOSPHERE, TRANSPORTING ENERGY FROM ONE PART OF THE PLANET TO ANOTHER, AND PRODUCING CLOUDS AND PRECIPITATION. THE WEATHER IS EVER-CHANGING, BUT FOLLOWS IDENTIFIABLE PATTERNS ON BOTH LARGE AND SMALL SCALES.

The complex patterns of weather on the Earth are a consequence of the uneven heating of the planet by the Sun. The differences in heating can be measured on a large scale of thousands of miles, varying according to latitude and season. These differences determine the climates found around the globe. Variations can also be found on a small scale down to just a few feet—depending on factors such as the heat absorbency or topography of the Earth's surface—and have a significant influence on local weather conditions. The uneven heating of the Earth sets the air in the atmosphere in motion, and it is this motion that drives day-to-day weather variations, from the quiescent conditions of an anticyclone to the rage of a typhoon rushing across the western Pacific.

On a global scale, weather systems carry heat away from lower latitudes towards higher latitudes. As air is

PREVAILING WINDS
Winds blow towards areas of low pressure. The prevailing wind in an area reflects patterns in the global movement of air.

heated it expands, rises, and tends to move toward the poles, displacing colder air, which causes large-scale air circulation and creates areas of high and low pressure. The warmer air carries water vapor with it, which condenses as it rises to form clouds. The rain that soaks you today may well be formed from cloud droplets that condensed out of water vapor that evaporated many days ago, several thousand miles away.

Variations in the weather can also be caused on a more local scale. The growth of fluffy fair-weather clouds in summer, for example, is caused by a thermal plume of warm air that has risen from the ground as the surface is heated by the summer Sun. The rising bubble of warm air takes heat up into the atmosphere to warm it locally and produce clouds.

The weather is generally unchanging near the Equator, but becomes changeable around the poles. It is more vigorous and disturbed in winter than summer as it responds to variations in heating patterns on the global scale.

TOPOGRAPHIC VARIATIONS
Weather changes according to topography. There are tropical forests at the foot of Mount Kilimanjaro in Tanzania, while at its summit is a permanent ice cap.

THE EARTH'S ENERGY SOURCE

The Sun provides the Earth with a near-constant supply of energy, which reaches the planet in the form of radiation. Variations in this energy supply across the globe, and across time, determine the Earth's weather patterns.

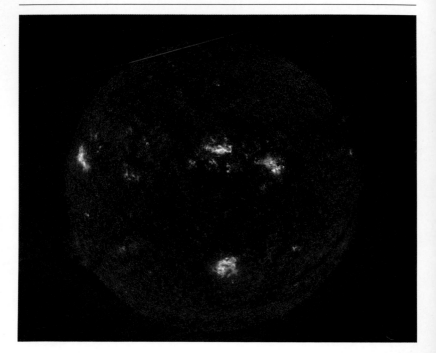

SOLAR RADIATION

All the energy that reaches us from the Sun has traveled through the near-vacuum of space as electromagnetic radiation. Weather patterns on the Earth are determined by how much of this radiation reaches different parts of the planet. This heats the atmosphere unevenly, causing the movement of air that drives all changes in the weather.

Variations in the heating of the atmosphere are caused by a number of factors. These include the

THE ACTIVE SUN
The Sun's activity causes clouds of free electrons and protons, called plasma, to flare out of its atmosphere. Tiny variations in its activity can affect the weather.

proximity of a region to the equator, atmospheric pollution, and the degree to which different surfaces, such as the sea, snow, and vegetation, reflect or absorb the Sun's radiation.

SPOTS ON THE SUN

A clue to the variation in solar activity is the number of sunspots—cooler regions on the Sun's surface. The number of sunspots varies in a cycle that peaks about every 11 years, alternating between the Sun's northern and

DARK SPOT
Sunspots are cooler areas of the Sun's surface, but they are associated with intense solar activity, such as solar flares.

THE ELECTROMAGNETIC SPECTRUM

Electromagnetic radiation travels in the form of waves of differing lengths. Radio waves may be many feet long, while the waves that we can see are shorter than the width of a pinhead, and gamma waves are the length of an atom's nucleus. As its length shortens, a wave's frequency increases. The solar radiation that reaches the Earth is concentrated around the visible part of the electromagnetic spectrum.

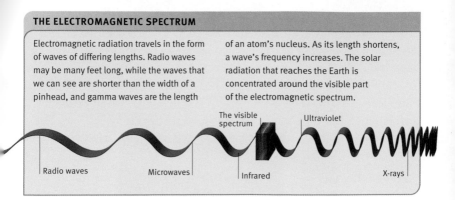

Radio waves   Microwaves   The visible spectrum   Infrared   Ultraviolet   X-rays

southern hemispheres, so a complete cycle is 22 years long. Sunspots are about 3,100°F (1,700°C) cooler than the rest of the Sun's surface, which is about 10,300°F (5,700°C). However, the area around a sunspot is hotter, and the more sunspots there are, the brighter the Sun is. The Sun's total energy output usually varies by 0.1 percent between the maximum and minimum of the cycle, but occasionally it has dropped by more than this. A notable drop in sunspots lasted from 1645 to 1715. Known as the Maunder Minimum, this period of reduced solar activity may have been the cause of the unusually cool conditions on the Earth during that period.

SEASONAL VARIATION

Seasons are the result of the 23.5-degree inclination of the Earth's rotational axis in relation to the plane around which it orbits the Sun. This angle means that at opposite ends of the year—December and June—one

THE SOLSTICES

On June 20/21, every point north of the Arctic Circle faces the Sun for a full 24 hours. On December 21/22, it is the Antarctic's turn to experience constant daylight. These dates are known as the solstices.

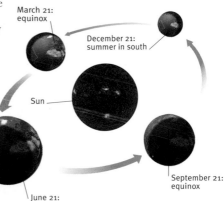

March 21: equinox

December 21: summer in south

Sun

September 21: equinox

June 21: summer in north

hemisphere is tilted toward the Sun while the other is tilted away, creating a substantial difference in solar heating between winter in one hemisphere and summer in the other. The Earth's orbit is such that we are closest (or at "perihelion") to the Sun during early January and most distant (or at "aphelion") in early July. This means that solar radiation is stronger in the southern hemisphere's summer than in the northern hemisphere's summer.

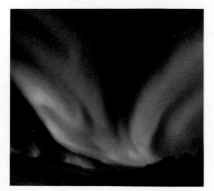

AURORA BOREALIS

When plasma from the Sun, known as solar wind, reacts with the Earth's atmosphere, it can create light shows in the skies at the poles. In the northern hemisphere this phenomenon is called the Aurora Borealis, or Northern Lights.

Composition of the atmosphere

The Earth's atmosphere was created around 4.6 billion years ago, when our planet was born as part of the Solar System, and has continued to evolve ever since. Today, the composition of the atmosphere is changing as rapidly as ever due to industrial activity.

PRIMITIVE ATMOSPHERE

Scientists believe that the Earth's earliest atmosphere was composed of hydrogen and helium. Heat from the Earth's still-molten crust and the Sun, plus the solar wind, dissipated this atmosphere. Around 4.4 billion years ago, the Earth had cooled to form a crust. Volcanic activity caused "outgassing" from the planet's interior, releasing gases such as water vapor, carbon dioxide, methane, and sulfur dioxide. This second atmosphere was retained by the Earth's gravity.

About 3 billion years ago, cyanobacteria—primitive, single-celled organisms—began flourishing in the

EARLIEST LIFE FORMS
Primitive cyanobacteria colonies produced oxygen and calcium carbonate as waste products of photosynthesis. The calcium carbonate built up solid mats called stromatolites, which are still found in saltwater lakes and lagoons.

seas, and may have played a critical role in adding oxygen to the atmosphere, creating the Earth's third, or modern, atmosphere. Cyanobacteria absorb carbon dioxide and release oxygen as a product of photosynthesis. The atmosphere has continued to evolve and today is principally composed

THE WEATHER LAYER

When viewed from the stratosphere, the troposphere can be clearly seen as the upper limit of cloud cover. All weather activity takes place in the troposphere.

Other 0.1%
Nitrogen 78%
Argon 0.9%
Oxygen 21%

GAS COMPOSITION

Gases in a dry atmosphere include nitrogen, oxygen, and argon. In addition to these, about 0.25 percent of the atmosphere is water vapor. Humid air near the surface is about 4 percent water vapor.

DESCENDING FROM THE STRATOSPHERE

On August 16, 1960, Colonel Joe Kittinger of the US Air Force threw himself out of a helium balloon floating 19½ miles (31.33 km) above New Mexico. Kittinger experienced temperatures as low as -94°F (-70°C) during his world-record skydive. He was in freefall for four minutes, 36 seconds, and reached a maximum speed of 614 mph (989 kph) before opening his parachute at 18,000 ft (5,500 m). Kittinger wore a pressurized suit for the jump to protect him from the extreme conditions.

of nitrogen and oxygen, with traces of argon, carbon dioxide, neon, methane, krypton, and hydrogen, as well as water vapor.

STRUCTURE OF THE ATMOSPHERE

Meteorologists split the atmosphere into layers according to temperature, which changes with height depending on gas composition. The furthest layer is the exosphere, about 430 miles (700 km) up. At its edge, the atmosphere dwindles to nothing as its lightest gases (mainly hydrogen) drift into space. Below is the thermosphere, where temperatures can be raised as high as 27,000°F (15,000°C) as solar radiation heats oxygen.

The next layer is the mesosphere, which absorbs little of the Sun's rays, so temperature decreases with height up to the mesopause, where the temperature can drop to -130°F (-90°C). Below this is the stratosphere, where the temperature stays uniform or increases with height. This warming is due to the absorption of ultraviolet sunlight by ozone.

The innermost layer, known as the troposphere, stretches from the Earth's surface up to about 6 miles (10 km) at high latitudes and 11 miles (18 km) at low latitudes. This layer contains all the weather systems and 75 percent of the atmosphere's gases. It is characterized by falling temperatures, down to -112°F (-80°C) at the top of the troposphere. The troposphere is "unstable" (see pp.232–33), since warmer air tends to rise up through the cooler air above it, in contrast to the "stable" stratosphere.

Exosphere
430–500 miles
(691–800 km)

Thermosphere
54–430 miles
(87–690 km)

Meteorites
burn up in
thermosphere

Mesopause

Mesosphere
31–54 miles
(50–87 km)

Stratopause

Stratosphere
11–31 miles
(18–50 km)

Tropopause

Troposphere
0–6/11 miles
(0–10/18 km)

ATMOSPHERIC LAYERS
Temperature falls as you ascend through the troposphere, then rises through the stratosphere, falls through the mesosphere, and rises again through the thermosphere.

Heating the atmosphere

Surprisingly, as the Sun shines through the atmosphere, it does not heat the air much at all. The mixture of gases that compose the atmosphere are mainly "transparent" to the Sun's rays. It is in fact the trace gases in the air that are important in heating the Earth and its atmosphere.

UNEVEN HEATING

The incoming solar supply is concentrated most over the low, tropical latitudes and least across the higher polar regions of the globe. Furthermore, the Sun's rays that flow into high latitudes have a longer path-length through the atmosphere than those in lower latitudes. This is one reason why different temperature patterns are found in different parts of the world.

THE GREENHOUSE EFFECT

Most of the relatively short-wave radiation given off by the Sun passes through the atmosphere and heats the Earth. The Earth then radiates this energy back out as long-wave radiation. Some of the atmosphere's trace gases, such as

METHANE PRODUCERS
Paddy fields are a major source of methane, one of the greenhouse gases that absorb the Earth's long-wave radiation.

carbon dioxide, methane, and water vapor (the "greenhouse gases"), intercept the long-wave radiation that is emitted by the Earth and atmosphere.

The planet loses heat by radiating it into space. Greenhouse gases absorb a significant amount of the outgoing radiation that is constantly flowing from the Earth's surface and the atmosphere.

HEATING UP
When radiation emitted by the Earth is absorbed by greenhouse gases, it is reflected back down, heating the surface of the Earth.

Incoming solar radiation

Some radiation deflected by atmosphere

Some long-wave radiation lost into space

Greenhouse gases absorb long-wave radiation

Long-wave radiation trapped by greenhouse gases

TROPICAL CUMULUS
Cumulus clouds can be seen forming over a tropical island. The Sun heats the land quicker than the sea, and warm air rises to form clouds.

Absorbed gases are warmed and re-radiated in all directions, including back down to the Earth. The temperature in the lower atmosphere is much higher than it would be without this "blanketing" effect. In fact, the greenhouse effect is critical to life on the Earth. The surface is some 54°F (30°C) warmer than it would be without it.

BRIGHT AND DULL SURFACES

When the Sun's energy reaches the Earth's surface, some of it is absorbed and some is reflected. The proportion of radiation that is reflected depends on how bright a surface is (known as the surface's "albedo"). This value varies from less than 10 percent for watery surfaces to up to 90 percent for fresh snow. Not only does water have a low albedo—which means it will absorb some 90 percent of the sunlight falling on it—it is also transparent, so any heating tends to spread down through it.

LAND AND SEA

Differences in the levels of absorbtion and reflection of land and sea can result in interesting local phenomena, such as small clouds forming over islands when adjacent areas are cloud-free.

Slightly darker patches on the island, with a lower albedo, can become warmer than other areas, generating cumulus clouds. As the island heats more quickly than the sea, a local sea breeze may set in as the cooler marine air flows onto the heated land. This flow can lead to a spine of cumulus cloud along a peninsula, where the sea breezes have converged along the land axis and driven the air upward to make the cloud line.

THE ALBEDO EFFECT

If a surface is dull (has a low albedo), most of the solar radiation falling on it will act to warm it up. Dark objects heat up more than bright ones, so a black road may become much hotter than the lighter surfaces either side of it. Very high temperatures produce a layer of warm air just above the surface, capped by cooler air. Light is bent as it travels from the warm air to the cool, causing a mirage that makes the dull road seem shiny.

How energy is transferred

Energy flows as heat from one place to another in three different ways.
Radiation transfers heat through any medium by electromagnetic
waves, convection by means of currents within a fluid, and conduction
from one body to another through physical contact.

TRANSFER THROUGH RADIATION

Radiation is given off by every body
of matter in the universe. How
much is emitted by a body, be it
a planet, a star, or a mass of
gas, depends on that body's
temperature. Radiation
is the only means of
transferring energy that
does not need a medium
to transport it from one
place to another. All the
heat the Earth receives
from the Sun travels
through the near-vacuum
of space as radiation.
This radiation is the engine
for all the Earth's weather.

The Earth and its
atmosphere emit long-wave
infrared radiation into space,
enabling weather satellites to
produce images at nighttime. Because
clouds are generally colder than the
cloud-free surface, they stand out on
infrared satellite pictures, allowing
meteorologists to monitor cloud
cover at night.

THE RADIATING EARTH
A composite satellite image shows infrared and visible
radiation. Clouds at different heights are colored white
and blue over the cooler water below them.

TRANSFER THROUGH CONVECTION

Convection is the process of transferring
heat within a fluid by motion within the
fluid. This is a very important means of
heat transportation in the atmosphere,
the ocean, and the Earth's interior.

Once the surface of the Earth has
been heated by solar radiation, the
warmth can be absorbed into the ground
or transported up into the atmosphere
as a "thermal"—a plume of warm
air that rises from the surface. The
thermal lifts up into the troposphere,
and cools as it ascends.

Thermals are used by birds to help
them ascend with minimum effort.
Pilots of glider planes also seek them
to exploit the extra lift that rising air

FIRE CLOUD
A forest fire can produce "pyrocumulus" clouds. A
rapidly rising thermal carries heat away from fire, and
water vapor condenses to form cloud as the air rises.

CONDUCTION AND CONVECTION

Boiling water in a pan on a gas ring gains heat through the pan's base by conduction. The heat is then mixed vigorously through the water by the motion of the water. This is convection. Radiation does not play an important role in heating the water, but acts to take heat away from the pan—you feel the radiation when you hold your hands near the pan. If you touched the pan, you would be scalded by conduction.

Water at the bottom is heated by conduction

Convection carries heat throughout the water

USING CONVECTION
Turkey vultures climb to great heights by flying a spiraling path within a thermal, a convection current that carries heat from the land into the atmosphere.

Long, broad wings allow the bird to catch as much of the rising air as possible

Warm air rises above warmer land

Darker areas of land heat up more quickly, warming the air above them

provides. Birds and pilots learn to recognize the places thermals are likely to be found—warm patches of land across a darker, plowed field, perhaps, or a south-facing slope that receives direct sunlight all day.

Convection not only transports warmth into the air via thermals, but also by the secondary process of evaporation. As the Sun warms the Earth, moisture at the surface evaporates. The water molecules with the greatest kinetic energy turn into water vapor, cooling the surface of the Earth. The water vapor is carried upward in thermals. The air cools until it reaches a level where the water vapour in it starts to condense, when water molecules with the least energy turn into liquid, warming the air. This condensation results in the formation of clouds. If the air does not cool sufficiently to condense, the thermal will not produce cloud.

TRANSFER THROUGH CONDUCTION

Conduction involves the transfer of heat by physical contact. Of the three modes of heat transfer, it is the least important to the atmosphere and weather because air is a very poor conductor. However, heat can be transferred by conduction to the lowest layer of the atmosphere by strong surface heating. The process of conduction can be felt working on a hot summer's day at a sandy beach. The sand can become intensely hot, and enough of this heat transfers by conduction from sand to foot to make it uncomfortable to walk across it.

GLOBAL ENERGY TRANSFER

The large-scale currents of air in the atmosphere and water in the oceans are driven by differences in temperature at the Earth's surface. Currents carry heat by convection from low to high latitudes, cooling the tropics and warming higher latitudes.

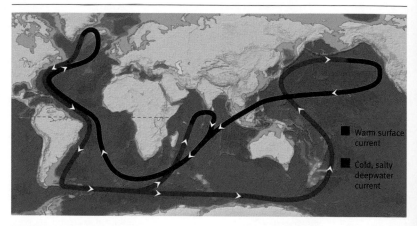

- ■ Warm surface current
- ■ Cold, salty deepwater current

THE TROPICAL BOILERHOUSE

Different parts of the Earth receive different amounts of incoming solar radiation. The amount an area is warmed by the Sun, called the net solar radiation, equals the total incoming radiation minus the radiation that is reflected back into space.

PERSISTENT FOG
San Francisco Bay often experiences foggy conditions, produced when mild, damp air flows over the cool California Current.

OCEANIC CONVEYOR BELT
The thermohaline circulation is a belt of moving water. Cold, salty water sinks in the North Atlantic Ocean and flows south to drive the conveyor.

Regions that are often cloud-free, such as the subtropical oceans of the southern hemisphere, reflect little and have a large net solar radiation. The highly reflective ice-sheets at the poles give them a small net solar radiation, even in summer. This distribution of energy produces a tropical

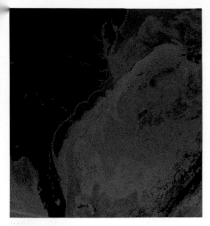

THE GULF STREAM
Warm water (in orange and yellow) flows from the Gulf of Mexico along the coast of the US before crossing the Atlantic toward Northern Europe.

"boilerhouse" that exports heat by convection toward higher latitudes. Wind-driven surface ocean currents, such as the Gulf Stream, move warm water toward the poles, while cool water, such as the Canaries Current, moves in the opposite direction. Deeper water follows a different pattern, known as the thermohaline circulation, which is driven by variations in temperature and salinity of the water. It carries water from the bottom of the North Atlantic Ocean south into the Southern Ocean and on into the Indian and Pacific Oceans, where it wells up to the surface to return to the Atlantic. It may take tens of thousands of years for water to complete one cycle.

Patterns in heat transportation can also be seen on a smaller scale. Warm ocean eddies have been identified using satellite images of the North Atlantic Drift. Eddies pump heat and water vapor into the atmosphere over an area of a few hundred miles.

WINDY WINTER

The difference in temperature between the tropics and polar regions is roughly double in winter what it is in summer, largely because of the contrast in temperature between polar day and polar night. As a consequence, wintertime winds over middle- and high-latitude oceans are stronger because the greater the temperature difference, the stronger the wind. This makes winter weather more changeable.

HEAT TRANSFER IN STORMS
Violent tropical storms are an important means of heat export. They carry vast amounts of warm, moist air from the tropics into higher latitudes.

Air masses

Large bodies of air with a particular temperature and humidity are known as air masses. They are created when air stagnates over warm or cold areas of land or sea, making the air hot or cold, and moist or dry. Air masses are largely responsible for determining an area's weather.

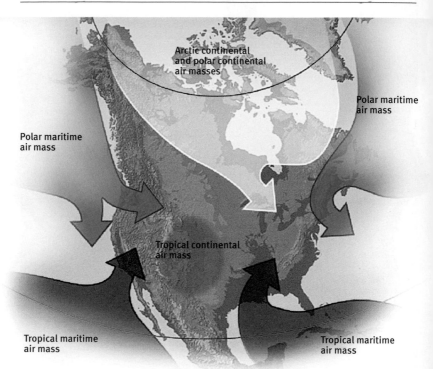

Arctic continental
and polar continental
air masses

Polar maritime
air mass

Polar maritime
air mass

Tropical continental
air mass

Tropical maritime
air mass

Tropical maritime
air mass

THE DYNAMICS OF AIR MASSES

Air masses are primarily defined by the area in which they originate. They are classified as continental or maritime—depending on whether they originate over land or sea—and arctic or antarctic, equatorial, tropical, or polar, depending on the particular region in which they are formed. Air masses are created when a large volume of air remains over a surface for a prolonged period and takes on the climatic qualities of that surface. This generally means that maritime air masses are more moist than continental ones—and often bring precipitation. Tropical or equatorial air masses are warmer than polar or arctic ones. Air masses extend far into the troposphere and may cover millions of square miles.

MULTIPLE AIR MASSES
Most regions are influenced by more than one air mass. The US, for example, is affected by five. Tropical continental air forms over the land, moist air arrives from tropical and northern oceans, and cold, dry air approaches from Northern Canada.

Air masses can be modified as they travel across the globe. As a maritime air mass passes over a mountain range, for example, much of its moisture will be lost as rain, creating a drier air mass. This creates a "rain shadow"—the side of the mountain that faces the oncoming, moist air mass is cooler and wetter, but the other side, over which the air mass passes once it has lost its moisture, is warmer and drier. As warm air masses pass over cold-water currents, water vapor contained within them can condense into fog, cloud, and rain.

POLAR CONTINENTAL

The extensive mid- to high-latitude high-pressure zones (see pp.66–67) over the huge continental land masses in the northern hemisphere are the sources of polar continental air mass. The air flowing out of these regions is very cold and dry, and produces clear winter days in places such as Tokyo (right).

ARCTIC MARITIME

Air becomes cold and dry after stagnating over the frozen Arctic ice cap. This can produce intensely cold conditions in Arctic Canada or Siberia. If such air spills south over the ocean, it is warmed by crossing the water, and may bring snow showers to areas such as northern Scotland (left).

POLAR MARITIME

In the northern hemisphere, polar maritime air may begin life over Greenland. In the southern hemisphere, it originates over the Southern Ocean. It starts cold but is warmed and moistened as it moves over water, producing damp days in mid-latitude locations such as Melbourne (right).

ANTARCTIC CONTINENTAL

Continental air over Antarctica is a dry, cold air mass that is only found on or very near the Antarctic continent. It quickly changes character when it crosses the surrounding Southern Ocean, reaching the southern parts of South America, Africa, and Australasia as polar maritime air.

TROPICAL MARITIME

These warm, moist air masses flow across the subtropical oceans toward the west coasts of Europe and the Americas. As they track across progressively colder ocean, they lose heat to the sea. This "stabilizes" the air, producing cloudy, humid weather in areas such as British Columbia (right).

TROPICAL CONTINENTAL

Air moving slowly over hot, dry land will become a hot, dry tropical continental air mass. These air masses are responsible for the dry seasons in regions near tropical deserts, such as the Sonoran Desert in Arizona (left). Tropical continental air masses can cause droughts.

EQUATORIAL

These humid air masses originate within 15 degrees of the equator. They bring cumulonimbus cloud to tropical rainforests and other humid low-latitude areas that experience frequent heavy downpours. The air from equatorial air masses converges at low levels to form a band of deep convection known as the Inter-Tropical Convergence Zone.

Weather fronts

Fronts are areas where two air masses of different temperatures and humidities meet. These moving boundaries bring cloud and precipitation with them, and many of the most heavily populated places in the world rely on the activity of fronts to provide rainfall.

WARM FRONTS

A warm front occurs at the leading edge of warm, moist tropical air that replaces cooler air as it moves. The warm air rises over the cool air, forming a boundary with a shallow slope. As it rises, the warm air cools and water vapor in it condenses to form cloud and rain. A few hundred miles ahead of the surface front, cirrus cloud is common. Moving toward the surface front, the clouds gradually thicken and lower. The sequence of clouds will typically be cirrostratus, altostratus, and finally nimbostratus just ahead of the surface front.

WARM FRONT CLOUDS
Approaching warm fronts are signaled by a belt of high, thin cloud. This is usually followed by lower, thicker clouds and steady rainfall.

Thick rain clouds

Surface front

Cold air mass

Warm air mass

Thin, high cloud

WARM FRONT
A rain-band ahead of the surface front may be a few hundred miles across. The front is followed by a "warm sector" with mild, humid air.

Shallow gradient

Rain cloud

MAPPING FRONTS

Fronts are represented on weather maps by curved lines with symbols that denote the particular type of front. These lines show the surface position of the front. The symbols on each front show the direction in which the front is moving. This map shows a warm front, a cold front, and an occluded front where the two have met over North America.

Warm front

Cold front   Occluded front

COLD FRONTS

The warm sector behind a warm front is followed by the leading edge of a sweep of much cooler and drier air. The cold air cuts under the warm air, forming a boundary with a steep slope. This is a cold front, which often brings a band of tall cumulus clouds, created when air from the warm sector is scooped up by the advancing cold air. These clouds produce brief, heavy showers, followed by clear blue skies and good visibility.

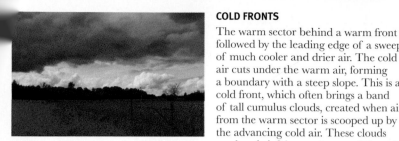

COLD FRONT CLOUDS
An advancing cold front can create turbulent cumulus clouds bringing heavy, sometimes thundery, showers.

Warm sector

Deep storm clouds often form above the cold front

Heavy rain on front

COLD FRONT
The heavy but short-lived rain produced by a passing cold front is followed by a drop in temperature and humidity as fresher air replaces the warm sector air.

Steep gradient

Pressure builds behind front

OCCLUDED FRONTS

Cold fronts travel faster than warm fronts. A cold front can catch up with a warm front and push underneath it, lifting the warm air off the ground. This is known as an occlusion. This process is continuous, so that after a few days, a system that started with a warm and cold front, joined at one point, becomes fully occluded, with no warmer air left at the surface. Occlusions tend to wrap around a low center, with a narrow band of thick cloud that can produce heavy rain.

OCCLUDED FRONT
The warmer air is forced upward by the cold air of the cold front. The rising warm air produces increased cloud and rain.

Warm air is lifted off the ground

Thick clouds form as the air rises and cools

Heavy rain often marks the occlusion

Cold air mass moves faster than warm air

Cold air pushes under warm air

Highs and lows

Highs and lows are pressure systems that affect day-to-day changes in the weather. A high-pressure zone occurs where a mass of air descends through the atmosphere, and a low-pressure zone where the air is rising. Air moving from highs to lows at low altitudes is the wind we feel.

HIGH PRESSURE

Highs (also known as anticyclones) are extensive regions, perhaps a few thousand miles across, in which there is a large mass of air in the "column" that stretches from the surface to the edge of the atmosphere. The air sinks slowly toward the surface, then moves outward as wind at low altitudes.

Pressure is measured in hectoPascals (hPa), also called millibars. "Standard" pressure at sea level is defined as 1013 hPa, but relative values determine highs and lows, so a pressure of 1015 hPa may be a high one day but not another.

LOW PRESSURE

Lows (also known as cyclones) tend to be more compact than highs and contain a smaller mass of air. They are characterized by the deep ascent of air, which cools as it rises, allowing water vapor to condense. This produces widespread cloud and precipitation.

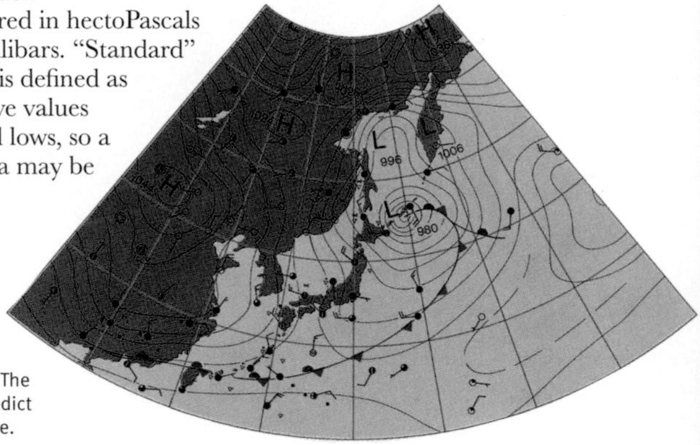

MAPPING PRESSURE
A synoptic chart shows a low near Japan and a complex of highs across eastern Russia and China. The chart helps forecasters predict how the weather will evolve.

AIR CIRCULATION IN HIGHS AND LOWS
In the northern hemisphere, air sinks in an anticyclone and spirals out in a clockwise direction at low altitudes. It flows toward centers of low pressure where it spirals upward in a counterclockwise direction at low altitudes. In the southern hemisphere, air sinks counterclockwise and rises clockwise.

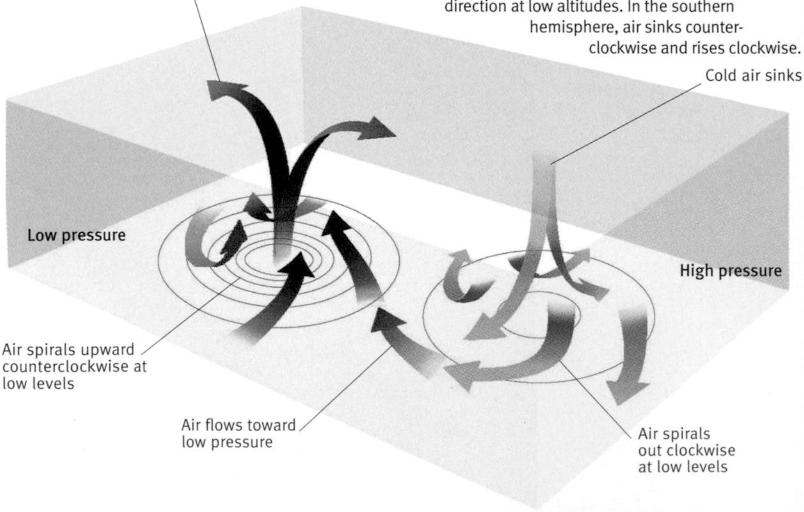

Rising warm air draws more air in

Cold air sinks

Low pressure

High pressure

Air spirals upward counterclockwise at low levels

Air flows toward low pressure

Air spirals out clockwise at low levels

HE PRESSURE GRADIENT

Air at the bottom of an area of high pressure will move toward a low as it is forced out by the weight of the column of air above it. How fast the air is shifted from high to low depends on the size of the pressure difference coupled with the distance between them. This determines the pressure gradient (how fast pressure changes horizontally). The steeper the gradient, the stronger the wind will be. The diagram below gives an abstract representation of how these factors interrelate.

Difference in pressure

Distance between high and low

Gentle wind
Small difference in pressure gives a shallow gradient

Strong wind
Big difference in pressure gives a steeper gradient

Strong wind over short distance
High and low close together gives a steeper gradient

The large-scale rising motion is fed by air that blows from adjacent anticyclones toward, and into, a low center.

To be defined as a low, it is the pressure relative to the surrounding area that is important. As with areas of high pressure, there is no single value that indicates a low, although a very low value, such as 940 hPa, would definitely be part of a deep low.

BAROMETER
An aneroid barometer indicates atmospheric pressure by the expansion and contraction of a small metal chamber.

MAPPING PRESSURE

The exact movements of weather systems, such as highs and lows, can be monitored by analyzing a sequence of synoptic pressure maps, which show mean sea-level pressure. The situation is often complex, and maps reveal a number of weather systems. Meteorologists need to predict how these systems will evolve in the future to produce forecasts.

POLLUTION UNDER PRESSURE
Areas of high pressure usually experience light winds, which means that the air does not circulate well. This can cause unpleasantly high levels of pollution in urban areas.

Convergence and divergence

Convergence is the process by which air comes together, and then either
warms and rises or cools and falls. Divergence occurs when air that has
risen or fallen moves away from an area. These processes enable the
vertical movement of air that is crucial in forming weather patterns.

CONVERGENCE

At low levels in the atmosphere,
convergence results in the slowing and
upward forcing of air and low pressure.
At high levels, it results in the slowing and
downward forcing, or subsidence, of air,
causing high pressure. This air movement
can be caused anywhere by the Sun or
radiant heat from the surface warming the
air, or on a larger scale when two air
masses meet each other. When large
volumes of air are forced to rise from low
levels, a piling up of cloud is the result.

The Inter-Tropical Convergence Zone
(ITCZ) around the equator is the largest
area of low-level convergence on the
Earth. Constant heat and humidity to
the north and south create a continuous
cycle of warm updrafts.
These create a band of
low pressure, leading to
thundery weather,
with a steady supply of
cumulonimbus clouds,
causing the extreme wet
and dry seasons found in
equatorial countries.

INTER-TROPICAL CONVERGENCE ZONE
A line of stormy convective cloud across
the northeast Pacific clearly identifies the
Inter-Tropical Convergence Zone.

Warm air converges and
rises from the surface

Sometimes a line of cumulus cloud marks the edge of the inland progression of a sea breeze, which is another example of convergence. This occurs where the denser, cooler, damper sea air forces the warmer land air over it. Convergence can be particularly strong in areas where cold and warm fronts meet each other. Thunderstorms may develop where a cold front undercuts a warm front.

DIVERGENCE

Divergent flow occurs at low levels when air sinks and spirals out from an anticyclone. In the subtropical Azores high, divergent flow creates the northeast trade winds on its southern flank and the mid-latitude westerlies on its northern side. On a local scale, a thunderstorm downdraft diverges when it flows away at the surface in all directions.

CHANGING PRESSURE

Convergence and divergence are responsible for the vertical movement of billions of tons of air through the troposphere. Convergence in the lowest 3,000 ft (1,000 m) supplies a cyclone with

SAND STORM
In arid and semi-arid regions, sand storms can occur at the leading edge of an area of convergence, where sand is sucked up with the rising air.

much of its energy, as air is forced upward to form towering cumulonimbus or spiraling rain-bands. This outflow of air is an important part of the development process if a cyclone is to intensify. It then circulates out, or diverges, from the top of the system in the upper troposphere. Conversely, upper tropospheric convergence occurs in subtropical highs, with air diverging at the surface. Any change in the strength of the divergence or convergence changes surface pressure, which is a measure of the mass of air pressing down on the Earth's surface.

THE DOLDRUMS
The ITCZ creates a calm maritime zone known as the doldrums, where sailboats can become trapped as winds cease for days.

Air cools and condenses, forming cloud, and diverges at high levels

CUMULONIMBUS CLOUD FORMATION
The cycle of convergence and divergence can create foreboding cumulonimbus clouds as the rising cloud "piles up."

The Coriolis effect

Warm air flows from the tropics toward the poles, while cold air flows back toward the equator. The motion of the air is also influenced by the rotation of the Earth, which appears to deflect winds to the right in the northern hemisphere and to the left in the southern.

THE SPINNING EARTH

It is because of the Earth's rotation that we experience an apparent force known as the Coriolis effect. The direction of the wind is deflected to the right in the northern hemisphere and to the left in the southern hemisphere. This is why the wind-flow around low- and high-pressure systems circulates in opposing directions in each hemisphere.

RELATIVE MOTION

Newton's First Law of Motion states that an object will continue in the same direction at the same speed unless a force acts upon it. This means that air moving across the Earth will maintain a constant speed even if the ground underneath it is changing speed, although friction with the ground will affect it slightly.

Air moving north from tropics deflected east

Air moving south toward equator deflected west

Earth rotates counter-clockwise, turning toward the east

Air moving south from tropics deflected east

Air moving north toward equator deflected west

DEFLECTED WINDS
As the Earth rotates counterclockwise, air moving across it is deflected to the right in the northern hemisphere and to the left in the southern.

GUSTAVE-GASPARD DE CORIOLIS

French physicist and mathematician Gustave-Gaspard de Coriolis (1792–1843) formalized the Coriolis effect in 1835. He formulated theories of fluid dynamics through studying waterwheels, and realized the same theories could be applied to the motion of fluids on the surface of the Earth.

The Earth rotates counterclockwise once a day around its axis. This means that a specific point on the surface travels faster the nearer to the equator its is. Conversely, the closer to the poles it is, the slower the surface travels.

At around 60°N and 60°S, the Earth's surface is moving at a speed of 519 mph (835 kph). At the equator, a greater distance is covered by the surface over the same period of time. Therefore, the speed at the equator is faster, at 1,038 mph (1,670 kph).

The deflection of the air can be illustrated by imagining that you throw a ball toward the equator from the North Pole. As the ball heads south the Earth, turning to the east, causes the ball to appear to deflect to the west, or right, as viewed by the observer at the North Pole. Alternatively, if the ball was thrown northward from the South Pole toward the equator, it would appear to deflect toward the west, or left, as viewed from the South Pole by the observer. This deflection is a major factor in explaining why winds blow counterclockwise around low pressure and clockwise around high pressure in the northern hemisphere and vice versa in the southern hemisphere.

PREVAILING WINDS

Global wind patterns are influenced by the Coriolis effect such that air that blows from the subtropical highs toward the low pressure in the northern and southern Atlantic does not blow due north or due south respectively.

TRADE WINDS
Sailors crossing the North Atlantic can exploit easterly winds to travel west in the tropics, and return east using westerlies further north.

These air currents are deflected by the Coriolis effect, resulting in south-westerlies in the northern hemisphere and north-westerlies in the southern hemisphere. These are the prevailing winds of the middle latitudes of their respective hemispheres.

Tropical oceanic winds in each hemisphere are similarly affected, and result in the north-easterly trade winds that dominate the tropical North Atlantic. These winds are consistent in both direction and strength, and have been well known to sailors for centuries.

BUYS-BALLOT'S LAW

Buys-Ballot's Law states that if you stand with your back to the wind (in an open area) in the northern hemisphere, pressure will be low on your left and high on your right (the reverse is true for the southern hemisphere). This is due to the balance between the pressure gradient and the Coriolis effect. The law is named after Dutch meteorologist CHD Buys-Ballot (1817–90), who provided empirical evidence of its validity in 1857.

Global circulation patterns

At any one time, the atmosphere contains many traveling weather systems with variable winds. When these winds are averaged over many years, both at the surface and at higher levels in the atmosphere, a well-defined pattern of large-scale "cells" of circulation appears.

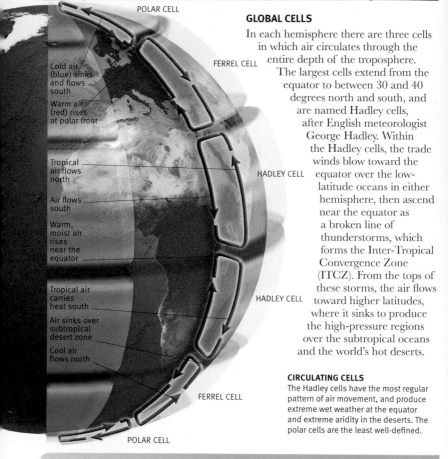

POLAR CELL

FERREL CELL

Cold air (blue) sinks and flows south

Warm air (red) rises at polar front

Tropical air flows north

HADLEY CELL

Air flows south

Warm, moist air rises near the equator

Tropical air carries heat south

HADLEY CELL

Air sinks over subtropical desert zone

Cool air flows north

FERREL CELL

POLAR CELL

GLOBAL CELLS

In each hemisphere there are three cells in which air circulates through the entire depth of the troposphere. The largest cells extend from the equator to between 30 and 40 degrees north and south, and are named Hadley cells, after English meteorologist George Hadley. Within the Hadley cells, the trade winds blow toward the equator over the low-latitude oceans in either hemisphere, then ascend near the equator as a broken line of thunderstorms, which forms the Inter-Tropical Convergence Zone (ITCZ). From the tops of these storms, the air flows toward higher latitudes, where it sinks to produce the high-pressure regions over the subtropical oceans and the world's hot deserts.

CIRCULATING CELLS
The Hadley cells have the most regular pattern of air movement, and produce extreme wet weather at the equator and extreme aridity in the deserts. The polar cells are the least well-defined.

WILLIAM FERREL

American teacher William Ferrel (1817–91) published two essays in the 1850s that were fundamental to understanding why winds blowing toward higher latitudes tend to be westerly, while those that blow toward the tropics tend to be easterly—a phenomenon known as the Coriolis effect. These essays built on the work of English meteorologist George Hadley (1685–1768), who had first proposed that wind patterns were determined by the rotation of the Earth. The overturning cells at middle latitudes are named after Ferrel.

CLIMATES AT THE CELL BOUNDARIES

At the boundaries between the global cells, air either rises, which is associated with areas of low pressure, or sinks, which is linked to highs. Over the world's hot deserts, at the boundaries between the Hadley and Ferrell cells, sinking air results in almost no rainfall, while at the boundary between the two Hadley cells, low pressure produces daily precipitation over the world's rain forests.

POLAR DESERT
Antarctica is the driest of all the continents. At the highest latitudes, the air typically sinks, producing stable and dry conditions.

TEMPERATE RAIN
At middle latitudes, locations such as Stockholm, Sweden, in Northern Europe experience frequent wet or snowy weather, which comes from traveling lows formed when moist air rises along the polar front.

EQUATORIAL RAIN
Near the equator, moist air ascends to form cumulonimbus clouds, which provide large amounts of precipitation to tropical rain forests.

In the middle cells, which are known as the Ferrel cells, air converges at low altitudes to ascend along the boundaries between cool polar air and the warm subtropical air that generally occurs between 60 and 70 degrees north and south. The circulation within this cell is completed by a return flow of air at high altitudes toward the tropics, where it joins the sinking air from the Hadley cell.

The smallest and weakest cells are the polar cells, which extend from between 60 and 70 degrees north and south to the poles. Air in these cells sinks over the highest latitudes and flows out toward lower latitudes at the surface.

WET AND DRY ZONES

Air converges horizontally at surface level in three regions of the Earth—the ITCZ (the boundary between the Hadley cells), and at the boundaries between the polar and Ferrel cells in each hemisphere. After flowing together, the air ascends, producing cloud. The wettest of the three areas is the ITCZ, where there is very moisture-rich air over the tropical ocean. The ITCZ provides the lifeblood rains of many regions within the tropics. In contrast, the sinking air of the Hadley cells causes the extreme aridity that characterizes the Sahara Desert and the Arabian Peninsula in the northern hemisphere, and the arid Australian interior in the southern hemisphere.

At the boundaries between the polar and Ferrel cells in the middle latitudes of either hemisphere, the flows of warm, moist air from the subtropics meet the cooler, drier currents spilling out from higher latitudes. The polar front forms the boundary between these two streams. The rainfall totals in these regions are generally smaller than those in the tropics because the air is less humid and the up-motions that produce the cloud and precipitation are weaker.

Upper circulation and jet streams

At low levels in the atmosphere, winds are slowed down by friction with the Earth's surface. Higher up, wind speeds can be much greater over a larger area, culminating in the mighty jet streams—fast-moving bands of air that blow around the globe at high altitude.

DISCOVERING THE JET STREAMS

In the 19th century, meteorologists tracking the movement of cirrus from the ground realized that the air flow at high altitudes must be very rapid. Between 1923 and 1925, Japanese scientist Wasaburo Oishi recorded unusually strong high-level winds around Mount Fuji, tracking balloons as they moved rapidly away once they reached the upper levels of the troposphere. Oishi had discovered a jet stream, but the news did not reach the wider world because, unusually, he published his findings in the Esperanto language.

The jet stream was rediscovered during World War II when US B29 bombers in a raid over Tokyo found that the planes' aiming sights were unable to lock onto their targets. They were flying at a speed of about 480 knots rather than their operational speed of 340 knots. A strong tailwind—the high-speed core of a jet stream—had caught them.

SUPERSPEED WINDS

There are four major jet streams—a polar-front jet stream and a subtropical jet stream in each hemisphere. They meander in wavelike paths around the world, which are constantly changing shape. Jet streams have a big influence on our weather, creating highs and lows, which they pull along with them. Large

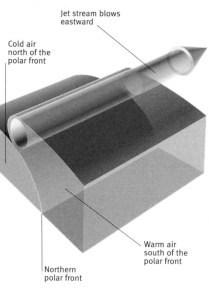

Jet stream blows eastward

Cold air north of the polar front

Warm air south of the polar front

Northern polar front

HOW A JET STREAM WORKS
Near the top of the troposphere, air pressure is higher on the warm side of a front than the cold side. Air flows toward the cold side, and the Coriolis effect (see p.70–71) causes this wind to swerve eastward.

wave movements in the jet streams can signal extreme weather conditions, such as droughts and floods. The air in jet streams reaches speeds of 280 mph (450 kph), but because they are more than 7 miles (11 km) up, jet stream clouds appear to move slowly.

Jet streams are produced when warm air meets and flows over much colder air in certain areas of the world. The greater

HIGH-LEVEL BOMBERS
High-flying B29 bombers were used by the US Air Force during World War II. They learned the effect of jet streams on flying speeds after planes started to overshoot their targets.

CARL-GUSTAF ROSSBY

Swedish scientist Carl-Gustaf Rossby (1898–1957) taught meteorology at the University of Chicago. In 1939, he identified the giant meanders in the jet streams now known as Rossby waves. He subsequently developed mathematical models to describe their motion.

ROSSBY WAVES

The jet stream pattern changes from zonal (top) to meridional (bottom) as warm air pushes north and cold air moves south.

Jet stream

Cold Arctic air

Warm subtropical air

the temperature difference, the faster the jet stream moves. This is why polar jet streams are more powerful than those in the subtropics. The US bombers in World War II encountered the polar-front jet stream, which today is avoided by passenger aircraft when flying east to west across the North Atlantic but used by them on their eastbound journey.

The polar-front jet streams snake around each hemisphere at the boundaries between the Ferrel and polar cells, where subtropical air and polar air meet. Sometimes the jets blow almost directly from west to east, which is called zonal flow. They often make large meanders north and south, called meridional flow. These meanders are called Rossby waves, and slowly move eastward.

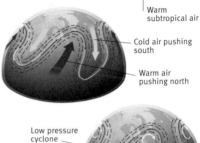

Cold air pushing south

Warm air pushing north

Low pressure cyclone

High pressure anti-cyclone

JET STREAM FROM SPACE

A jet stream is often invisible, but sometimes its position is revealed by a ribbon of icy cirrus clouds. This jet stream is passing over the Red Sea.

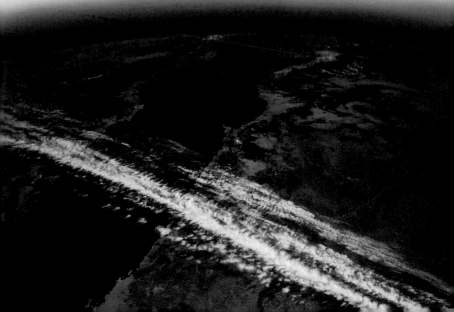

Evaporation and condensation

Water is the only substance that exists in solid, liquid, and gaseous states in the atmosphere. The processes of change from one state to another are of critical importance to our day-to-day weather and to the formation of life-giving rain in particular.

FROM LIQUID TO VAPOR

Evaporation is the process by which water changes from a liquid state to a gas, known as water vapor. The molecules in the water are constantly colliding, and each time this happens, energy is transferred from one to another. When the energy transfer is great enough, molecules fly off into the air, or evaporate. The ideal conditions for rapid evaporation are a breezy day with low humidity and strong sunshine.

Dry air speeds up the process by increasing the "humidity gradient" between a wet surface and the atmosphere. Water molecules also enter

GLOBAL WATER CYCLE
The water cycle is the process by which water moves around the planet, and is essential for all life on the Earth.

the water from the air, so the less water vapor there is in the air, the greater will be the net transfer of molecules to the atmosphere. Strong sunshine warms surfaces, giving energy to the water molecules and increasing evaporation.

FROM VAPOR TO WATER

Condensation is the process whereby water vapor changes into water droplets or ice crystals. The vapor always needs some sort of surface to condense upon —such as a blade of grass for dew, or a microscopic particle of sea-salt for a cloud droplet. To effect a change of state from water vapor to droplet, a degree of cooling of damp air is necessary. This can occur through, for example, the radiative cooling of the Earth's surface at night, or the expansion and cooling of

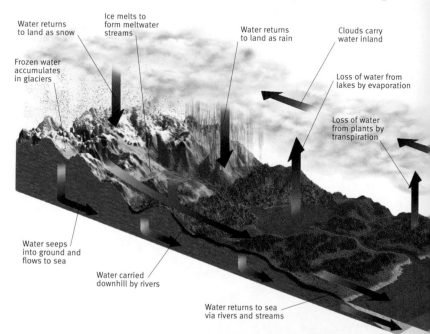

Water returns
to land as snow

Ice melts to
form meltwater
streams

Water returns
to land as rain

Clouds carry
water inland

Frozen water
accumulates
in glaciers

Loss of water from
lakes by evaporation

Loss of water
from plants by
transpiration

Water seeps
into ground and
flows to sea

Water carried
downhill by rivers

Water returns to sea
via rivers and streams

CONDENSATION UNDER DIFFERENT CONDITIONS

The temperature at which condensation occurs, called the dew point, depends on the humidity and pressure of the air. If this temperature is below 32°F (0°C), it is called the frost point, as the water vapor will condense into icy frost, not liquid dew. Calculating the exact value of the dew point and frost point is important to meteorologists when predicting frost or fog.

Jungle mist
With their frequent heavy rainfall and highly humid air, jungles can often experience misty conditions.

Dew on vegetation
Dew forms most easily on surfaces that do not conduct heat from the ground; grass is the most common example.

Fog over open land
To form, fog requires all the same conditions needed to create cloud. Fog is essentially cloud that is in contact with the ground.

Frost
When a surface is cooled to below the dewpoint of the surrounding air, the dew on it freezes to become frost.

an ascending layer or bubble of air. Condensation liberates heat so when water vapor condenses to make a cloud, warming occurs within it.

Dew is a common form of condensation, as is hoar frost in the colder seasons. Fog is another example, found in the lowest layer of the atmosphere when either radiative cooling has occurred inland or mild, damp air has flowed across a cooler sea. The technical difference between fog and mist relates to visibility; fog is defined as reducing visibility to less than 0.6 miles (1 km), while mist occurs with visibility of 0.6 miles (1 km) or more and humidity greater than 95 percent.

GLOBAL PATTERNS OF EVAPORATION

There is huge geographical variation in rates of evaporation, most of which takes place over the oceans. During the winter in the southern hemisphere, evaporation is greatest across the tropical trade-wind zone—the Sun and winds are strong there, and the air is warm. Latitudes between 40° and 50° south, known to sailors as the Roaring Forties because of their strong winds, have weaker evaporation because the water is cool, and the sunshine is both weaker and shorter in duration.

Water condenses and forms clouds

Loss of water from sea by evaporation

Water stored in seas and oceans

Global precipitation patterns

Precipitation is vitally important to all forms of life, but it is unevenly spread across the planet in location and frequency. Its distribution is strongly related to the pattern of highs and lows, and to seasonal change in the position of the Sun in the tropics.

2 (50)	
1.4 (35)	
1.1 (29)	
0.9 (23)	
0.7 (17)	
0.5 (13)	
0.4 (10)	
0.3 (8)	
0.2 (6)	
0.15 (4)	
0.08 (2)	
0.04 (1)	
0.008 (0.2)	

TROPICAL RAINFALL

The principal wet region of the tropics lies where the trade winds converge. This is known as the Inter-Tropical Convergence Zone (ITCZ). Over the low-latitude oceans, this feature stays north of the equator throughout the year. Across the tropical continents, it migrates north and south, following the seasonal change in the position of the

WORLD PRECIPITATION
Average daily precipitation (in inches and millimeters) is greatest over the equator and tropics, and least over the subtropical deserts and Antarctica.

Sun, to its northernmost extent in August and September, and its southernmost in January and February. This migration can be tracked most clearly over Africa. It is responsible for the contrast between the heavy summer

TROPICAL DOWNPOUR
The monsoon season in India occurs between June and September, and can bring up to 400 in (10,000 mm) of rain.

and weaker winter monsoons over southern Asia. Average annual rainfall is high in this region, fed by intense evaporation from the warm ocean and steaming jungle combined with rising air in the low pressure regions associated with the ITCZ.

EXTRATROPICAL RAINFALL

The wettest regions outside the tropics tend to be over the oceans, mirroring the tracks of frontal depressions. Within these depressions, extensive areas of deep cloud form as air rises across fronts and glides up above the low-level converging air. The wettest mid-latitude continental areas are the westward-facing coastal regions that lie in the path of frontal depressions. The drier areas are, broadly, the continental interiors away from the frequent depressions, which are dominated by anticyclones in the winter. Regions affected by frontal systems tend to see more precipitation in the fall and winter, when strong winds bring cloud and rain from the relatively warm oceans.

ARID AREAS

One-third of the Earth's surface is desert —an area with average annual precipitation of less than 10 in (250 mm)

DESERT DEW
It rarely rains in deserts, but there is precipitation at night in the form of dew. The darkling beetle in the Namib Desert stands still at dawn and collects dew on its body to drink.

—and some of the most arid regions are found around the poles. In Antarctica the temperatures are so low that the air hardly contains any water vapor. There is also an absence of weather systems or solar heating that would lift the air to produce cloud and precipitation.

COLD DESERT
At the South Pole, average annual snowfall is less than 4 in (100 mm), making Antarctica the driest continent. Despite this, 70 percent of the world's fresh water is found in the snow and ice of Antarctica, and heavy snow must once have fallen.

Weather phenomena

THE EARTH'S ATMOSPHERE EXHIBITS AN EXTRAORDINARY VARIETY OF WEATHER PHENOMENA. ON A LOCAL LEVEL, WE MAY FEEL A GUST OF WIND THAT LASTS JUST A FEW SECONDS. ON A GLOBAL SCALE, THE CIRCULATIONS OF HUGE TROPICAL HADLEY CELLS DETERMINE WHOLE REGIONAL CLIMATES AND WEATHER SYSTEMS.

The world's weather is perpetually on the move, pushed and shaped by air currents in the atmosphere. The way the atmosphere moves is extremely complex, driven by the very large inequality in temperature between the tropical boilerhouse and the two polar refrigerators. As heat moves from low to high latitudes, deep convective cloud may form into a thunderstorm as warm air is funneled up into a chilly atmosphere, releasing heavy rain or hailstones. Water vapor may rise high into the air and condense to form wispy clouds of ice crystals. If moist air cools at ground level, microscopic water droplets may fill the air to cause mist and fog. Pollution from industry may add other conditions of low visibility.

Our personal experience of weather from day to day is a tiny sample of the global weather system. The sweeping cloud and rain-laden frontal systems that affect so many parts of the world's middle latitudes

SNOWFLAKE
The ice crystals that form in high-level clouds can grow into six-sided flakes of snow, each with its own unique pattern.

are normally born thousands of miles away—the rain that falls on us may have evaporated from an ocean some hours or days before.

On shorter time-scales, some parts of the Earth suffer from tornadoes, which, like other types of extreme weather, need the components of an ideal "recipe" to come together. This does not happen everywhere in the world, but only in relatively limited regions. Often, the most intense and terrifying weather is the hardest to predict and protect against.

Many weather phenomena are interdependent. The occurrence of dew or frost, for example, often depends on whether a high-pressure system (anticyclone) is dominating the weather locally. The location and movement of this high is dependent on the global flow patterns that constantly evolve and shift. Rainbows occur only when the larger-scale conditions allow showers to develop with intermittent sunny spells.

Careful study of these phenomena, and how they are related to each other, has produced great advances in our understanding of the weather.

RAINBOW AND CLOUD FORMATION
Optical effects, such as rainbows, can appear when sunlight is refracted by water droplets, and can reveal a great deal about atmospheric conditions.

INTRODUCING CLOUDS

Clouds form when water vapor in moist, rising air condenses. They provide precipitation, and also help to regulate climate by reflecting solar radiation and absorbing outgoing terrestrial radiation. Without clouds, life on Earth could not exist.

UNDERSTANDING CLOUD SHAPES

The shape of a cloud reflects the way in which moist air has risen to allow it to develop. Some of the smallest clouds are fair-weather cumulus, a type of bulbous "cumuliform" cloud that is created by thermals that rise above the Earth's surface and cool the air to such a degree that condensation occurs. This happens on a horizontal scale of hundreds of feet. The cumulus cloud tops that we see are produced by the updrafts of air that rise inside the cloud.

On the largest scale, deep, precipitating layer clouds, also known as "stratiform" clouds, form within the extensive but gently rising air that is part of the circulation of frontal depressions. Many thousands of square miles of tropical-maritime air mass is forced to rise, which produces the distinctive circulations of these disturbances. Condensation is not only forced by upward motion within the atmosphere, but can often be produced as moist air flows over hills and mountains, causing orographic clouds to develop.

CLOUD OBSERVATION AND MODELING

The Earth's surface climate is tempered by clouds. Without them, the difference between day and night temperatures can be very large. Clouds play a critical role in determining the radiation balance of the Earth and its atmosphere. They can be a challenge to observers because it is difficult to assess accurately the proportion of the sky covered by clouds.

KEY TO CATALOGUE CODES, SYMBOLS, AND CLOUD TYPES

The system for classifying clouds uses four Latin terms: *stratus* (meaning "layer"), *cumulus* ("heap"), *nimbus* ("rain"), and *cirrus* ("curly" or "fibrous"). Some are combined, so that nimbostratus, for example, is a layer of raincloud. Clouds are also classified as high, middle, or low, according to the height of the cloud base above the surface. The set of clouds shown in the diagram here was finalized by international agreement in 1896. Since then, various sub-types have been added over the years.

CLOUD CODES AND SYMBOLS

Each cloud is represented by a two-letter code when making observations, such as "Cb" for cumulonimbus, and an internationally recognized cloud symbol, which is used on meteorological charts. This is the symbol for cumulonimbus.

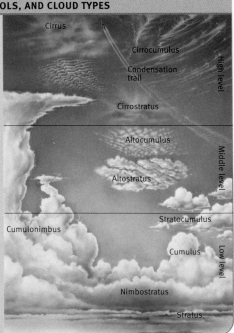

Cirrus

Cirrocumulus

Condensation trail

Cirrostratus

High level

Altocumulus

Altostratus

Middle level

Stratocumulus

Cumulonimbus

Cumulus

Low level

Nimbostratus

Stratus

Assessing the gradations of cloud between an overcast and a clear sky can be difficult, especially with the complication of perspective to distant horizons.

Representing clouds in weather and climate prediction models is a challenge too; they have to be "implied" from a combination of relative humidity and the calculated strength and location of rising air. Cloud climatologies, and their typical distribution, are deduced by grouping satellite observations to make seasonal and annual averages. Clouds are a sensitive part of the Earth-atmosphere-ocean system, and the large-scale view offered by satellites allows us to study the way cloud and distribution are changing in a way that might be consistent with climate change.

CLOUD DRAMA
Threatening cumulonimbus clouds gather over Havana, Cuba, at the start of the hurricane season. Soon, wind and heavy rain will lash the coast.

LUKE HOWARD

English pharmacist Luke Howard (1772–1864) formed the cloud classification scheme that is the basis of today's naming convention. His interest in clouds began with the dramatic sunsets produced by the two major volcanic eruptions in the summer of 1783. Howard proposed his cloud scheme to scientific colleagues in 1802 and later wrote a number of books, including *The Climate of London*, in which he noted that the city had an urban heat "island." He was also a keen observer, keeping a weather log for more than 30 years.

How clouds form

Clouds are created when damp air rises and cools, and water vapor in it condenses. A cloud's look shows how the air has risen to form it— from vast areas of stratus formed by the slow ascent of air into depressions, to individual cumulus clouds produced by strong, localized thermals.

SURFACE HEATING

When the surface of the Earth is heated by the Sun, air rises in thermals that may produce cloud. This surface heating tends to produce scattered convective cloud. If the air mass is cold, any thermals will be a lot warmer than their surroundings and will rise further through the atmosphere. They may ascend high enough to form a shower cloud. In mid-latitudes, showers produced by surface heating are common in spring, when sunshine is intensifying but the sea is cold. Clouds form over land, as the Sun warms the ground. Damp air is drawn in from the sea to replace the rising warm air, and in turn warms and rises.

CLOUD CAP
The condensation caused when air is forced upward by a mountain can create a persistent "cap" of orographic cloud, while surrounding areas are clear.

UNSTABLE AIR

As water vapor condenses in rising, cooling air, small amounts of heat are released. The heat warms the air mass a little and, if this makes it warmer than the surrounding air, it rises further. If there is water vapor left in the air, this too condenses and the cycle continues. This rising air is known as unstable air. If the air reaches a point where it has the same temperature as the surrounding air, it stops rising.

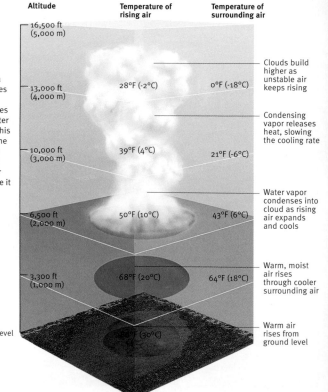

Altitude	Temperature of rising air	Temperature of surrounding air
16,500 ft (5,000 m)		
13,000 ft (4,000 m)	28°F (-2°C)	0°F (-18°C)
10,000 ft (3,000 m)	39°F (4°C)	21°F (-6°C)
6,500 ft (2,000 m)	50°F (10°C)	43°F (6°C)
3,300 ft (1,000 m)	68°F (20°C)	64°F (18°C)
Ground level	86°F (30°C)	

Clouds build higher as unstable air keeps rising

Condensing vapor releases heat, slowing the cooling rate

Water vapor condenses into cloud as rising air expands and cools

Warm, moist air rises through cooler surrounding air

Warm air rises from ground level

LOW-LEVEL CONVERGENCE

The air at low levels in the atmosphere may flow toward, or converge on, a line or center of circulation, where it rises to form clouds. The scale of this convergence varies from a large depression across hundreds of miles to an area just tens of miles in size. Low-level convergence can produce cumulus cloud and showery conditions, and when it causes a sharp uplift, it may lead to thunderstorms.

Clouds form where air expands and cools

Air is forced upward

CONVECTIVE CLOUDS
This cloud type usually forms from surface heating or air flow across high ground.

Converging air

FRONTAL UPLIFT

Air rises over large areas along fronts (the long boundaries that separate warm, moist subtropical air from much cooler, drier air from higher latitudes). Widespread and often deep layers of cloud are formed when the warmer, damper air is forced to ascend over a wedge of the drier, cooler undercutting air. Frontal clouds can stretch for more than a thousand miles.

Cold, dense air lies beneath the sloping warm front

Clouds form in cooling air above the front

FRONTAL CLOUDS
This cloud type appears where warm and cold air masses meet.

Warm air slides up over cold air at a warm front

OROGRAPHIC FORCING

Air is forced to rise over raised land, such as hills or mountains, and as it does so, it cools to form clouds. They may then dissipate in the wind or dissolve as they flow down the other side of the mountain as warmer, drier air. Because new cloud keeps forming on the upwind slope, however, it can have the appearance of a "cap" of cloud on top of the raised area. Conditions will generally be cloudy on the upwind side of the slope and less so on the downwind side.

Dry air descends on other side of ridge

Clouds form in cooling air

OROGRAPHIC CLOUDS
This cloud type is created when air rises over an elevated geographical feature.

Moist air is pushed up as it flows over a mountain ridge

Low-level clouds

Stratus clouds may occur as a continuous layer, or as ragged shreds of cloud just above the ground. Stratocumulus, cumulus, and cumulonimbus are also low-level clouds, with bases below about 6,500 feet (2,000 meters) above the surface of the Earth.

St

STRATUS

ALTITUDE Height of base 0–6,500 ft (0–2,000 m)

SHAPE Layered

PRECIPITATION Light

Most stratus clouds are featureless, low-altitude clouds that cover the sky in a blanket of gray or white. When people talk about "a cloudy day," they are usually referring to a sky filled with stratus clouds. The cloud layer can be thick enough to completely block out the Sun or Moon and may produce drizzle, snow, or snow grains, particularly over hills. If there are no other clouds above a thin stratus layer, the Sun or Moon may shine through it.

Stratus clouds develop in a number of different ways. Up-slope stratus clouds form when moist air is lifted by the wind as it blows against a cliff, hill, or mountain. Stratus clouds can also develop over the sea, when some moisture in the relatively warm air over the water condenses as it cools. During the summer, winds blowing from the sea may blow stratus clouds onto the coast, resulting in much lower air temperatures for these regions. Wherever stratus clouds touch the ground or meet the sea, they are classed as fog. This fog may later lift, due to an increase in the strength of the wind or a rise in temperature, and form stratus clouds again.

Although all stratus clouds are layered, there are various different types. These include stratus nebulosus, stratus fractus, and stratocumulus.

Stratus nebulosus —

ALTITUDE Height of base 0–1,500 ft
(0–450 m)
SHAPE Featureless cloud blanket
PRECIPITATION Light

Stratus nebulosus is the most common type of stratus cloud, usually bringing dull, gray weather. The clouds form a veil across the sky and have no distinct features. Usually, the only precipitation to fall from stratus nebulosus clouds is drizzle. As the sun heats the ground, stratus nebulosus clouds may rise and break. As the clouds rise, they may dissipate to become ragged stratus fractus clouds, or they may form layers of stratocumulus cloud.

Stratus fractus ---

ALTITUDE Height of base 0–1,500 ft
(0–450 m)
SHAPE Ragged and tufted
PRECIPITATION Light

These ragged shreds of low cloud normally appear in association with other clouds—especially with precipitation or soon after it has stopped—and often form beneath altostratus or nimbostratus. Stratus fractus clouds also occur beneath cumulonimbus and cumulus clouds, when they are known as stratus pannus. The stratus fractus clouds appear dark or gray against the lighter gray of the clouds above and move quickly across the sky, changing shape rapidly.

Stratocumulus ⌣

ALTITUDE Height of base 1,200–6,500 ft
(350–2,000 m)
SHAPE Cumuliform "lump" at base
PRECIPITATION Light

Stratocumulus clouds consist of large, rounded masses of stratus that form groups, lines, or waves. The clouds are gray or white and usually have darker shaded parts. Stratocumulus clouds can appear in many weather conditions. During dry, settled weather, the clouds may be dominant and persistent. Stratocumulus clouds are usually present near a warm, cold, or occluded front. Sometimes, they can be thick enough to produce light rain or snow.

CUMULUS

ALTITUDE Height of base 1,200–6,500 ft
(400–2,000 m)
SHAPE Cauliflower or fluffy
PRECIPITATION Occasional rain or snow showers

All cumulus clouds develop because of convection. As air heated at the surface is lifted, it cools, and water vapor condenses to produce the cloud. Near coasts, cumulus may form over the land by day as a sea breeze brings in moist air, which is then warmed by the land, and over the sea during the night as a breeze blows off the land over the sea, which is now warmer than the land. These clouds, particularly the cauliflower-shaped cumulus congestus, are often very striking.

Cumulus congestus clouds (below) generally develop from cumulus mediocris, which in turn have developed from cumulus humulis, but the cloud will not yet have reached the size of a cumulonimbus cloud. When it develops into cumulus congestus, cumulus cloud is typical of showery conditions and may

SUMMER THERMALS

Hang-gliders exploit thermals—columns of rapidly rising warm air—to stay in the sky. Thermals occur most often on summer days as strong sunshine warms the ground, which then warms the air close to the ground. This air lifts into the atmosphere, cooling as it rises. When it has cooled sufficiently, water vapor in the air will condense to form cumulus cloud.

even produce thunderstorms. Cumulus, stratocumulus, or stratus clouds may be present in the sky at the same time.

At a distance, rain, snow, or hail can sometimes be seen falling from these clouds, which can often be an impressive sight.

Cu hum

Cumulus humulis

ALTITUDE 1,200–6,500 ft (400–2,000 m)
SHAPE Detached with ragged tops
PRECIPITATION None

On clear mornings, especially during the summer, this type of cloud may form as the Sun quickly warms the ground. Stratus may also lift in convection currents and develop into cumulus humulis. When completely formed, the clouds have clear-cut horizontal bases and flattened or slightly rounded tops. At this stage of development, they are known as fair-weather cumulus.

When cumulus congestus is at the last stages of dissipating, it can take on the appearance of cumulus humulis.

Cu med

Cumulus mediocris

ALTITUDE 1,200–6,500 ft (400–2,000 m)
SHAPE Individual and heaped
PRECIPITATION Occasional showers

Cumulus mediocris is a development from cumulus humulis. Their outline is usually much more defined, with horizontal bases and cauliflower-shaped tops, although in fresh or strong winds, some raggedness may occur. Sunlit parts of the cloud can appear brilliant white, while the bases can be relatively dark.

The clouds are sometimes arranged in lines, known as "cloud streets," parallel to the wind direction. They may also form tall towers that are tilted by the wind. When well developed, cumulus mediocris clouds sometimes produce showers.

Whatever their stage of development, over land, cumulus clouds usually disperse in the late afternoon or early evening. Over the oceans, maximum cumulus activity occurs in the late hours of the night. As there is little change in the temperature of the sea beneath them, the height of the base of cumulus in the ocean trade wind belts is very uniform at around 2,000 ft (600 m).

Cumulonimbus

ALTITUDE Height of base 1,000–6,500 ft (300–2,000m)
SHAPE Fibrous upper edges, anvil top
PRECIPITATION Heavy rain and thunderstorms

Cumulonimbus clouds usually form after the Sun has heated the sea or land for several hours, causing warm air to rise and cool, and some water vapor to condense. If the weather conditions are right, a mature cumulus congestus cloud will grow in height and become a cumulonimbus. As this happens, water droplets begin to freeze and the appearance of the upper cloud portion alters to become wispy.

New cloud development around it may temporarily give a cumulonimbus the appearance of a "towering" cumulus. When this happens, lightning, thunder, or hail are sometimes the only indication that the cloud is a cumulonimbus. This may also be the case when a cumulonimbus passes nearly or directly overhead and the characteristic top is lost to view. With only the base visible, it is easy to mistake the cloud for nimbostratus, but lightning, thunder, hail, or other precipitation show that it is a cumulonimbus cloud.

The characteristic shape of these enormous clouds can only be seen as a whole when viewed from a distance, where the tops reveal a fibrous or

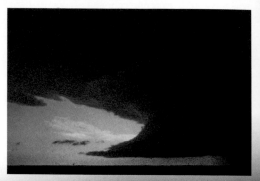

TOWERING WALLS
When seen close-up, the huge wall of a cumulonimbus cloud is an ominous sight, promising heavy rain and strong, gusty winds.

ANVIL TOP
A cumulonimbus cloud may develop an anvil top. This happens when the cloud reaches the tropopause, where the ice crystals within it are drawn out by strong winds.

striated structure in the shape of an anvil or plume. Cumulonimbus clouds may occur in isolation, surrounded by clear skies. When this happens, the top part of the cloud reflects sunlight, shining brilliantly, while toward the base, the cloud darkens. Rain or snow can often be seen falling from a cumulonimbus cloud, either at a distance or close-up.

Underneath the base, which will often be very dark, pannus (stratus) clouds frequently form. They may be only a few hundred feet above the ground and can merge to form a continuous layer of stratus. There may also be ragged cumulus clouds or a dense horizontal roll at the edge of a shower. A variety of other clouds, such as cirrus, altocumulus, altostratus, stratocumulus, cumulus, and stratus may be present at the same time as a cumulonimbus.

MAMMATUS CLOUDS

Turbulence within a cumulonimbus cloud may cause mammatus clouds to form, especially on the underside of the projecting anvil. These bumpy, multi-lobed features are most prominent when the Sun is low in the sky. Often, virga—streaks of precipitation that don't reach the ground—can be seen within the mammatus. The appearance of mammatus in a cumulonimbus may indicate that a storm will be particularly severe.

Medium-level clouds

Altocumulus, which often has layered or rippled elements, is the most distinctive of all the medium-level clouds, and is associated with various weather conditions. Featureless altostratus and nimbostratus often signal an approaching weather front bringing rain or snow.

Ac

Semi-transparent altocumulus　　ꞷ

ALTITUDE Height of base 7,000–18,000 ft (2,000–5,500 m)

SHAPE Bands or areas of individual cells

PRECIPITATION None on its own

This type of cloud produces a "mackerel sky," and is similar in form to stratocumulus, but has a higher base. Semi-transparent altocumulus appears at a single level, and is sufficiently transparent to reveal the position of the Sun or Moon (sometimes accompanied by a corona—a small halo effect around the Sun or Moon). These clouds are generally associated with settled weather.

The clouds usually appear white or gray with shading, although the dawn or dusk sunlight can produce a spectacular yellow or orange effect. The cloud can also be observed at more than one level, when the Sun or Moon may be totally masked. Altostratus and nimbostratus may also be present, which can signal an approaching weather front.

Ac cast

Altocumulus　　M
castellanus

ALTITUDE Height of base 7,000–18,000 ft (2,000–5,500 m)

SHAPE Turretlike features

PRECIPITATION Possible precursor to thunderstorm

Altocumulus castellanus—also called thundery altocumulus—is a sign of medium-level instability, and can be a precursor to thunderstorms. The clouds normally appear in the form of small individual "cells"—distinct closed circulations—with sproutings in the form of small towers. If conditions are cool and moist enough, they can develop into large cumulonimbus.

VIRGA

This phenomenon is precipitation that falls from a cloud but does not reach the ground or sea surface, as it evaporates into drier air beneath the cloud. Virga is usually produced by medium-level or high-level clouds. It can often be seen falling from high altostratus, which is a sign of an approaching warm front. As the front moves closer, the air at lower levels becomes more moist and the cloud lowers to become nimbostratus.

Ac

Altocumulus of a chaotic sky

ALTITUDE Height of base 7,000–18,000 ft (2,000–5,500 m)

SHAPE More than one layered band

PRECIPITATION Possible showers

A chaotic sky with many layers of different clouds is a sign of intense instability, when winds can blow from different directions. Altocumulus of a chaotic sky generally occurs at several levels with the different cloud bases ranging widely in height at any one time. More than one type of altocumulus can normally be observed at the same time. Clouds in a chaotic sky range from the relatively low, thick altocumulus to the relatively high, thin altostratus. The cloud sheets are often broken, with poorly defined cloud types. This is recognized by meteorologists as a specific type of cloud cover, and is associated with changeable weather.

As

Altostratus ╱

ALTITUDE Height of base 7,000–18,000 ft
(2,000–5,500 m)
SHAPE Layered and featureless
PRECIPITATION None

Altostratus evolves as a thin layer
from a gradually thickening veil of
cirrostratus. It may then thicken into
dense altostratus. Thin altostratus
normally has a higher base than the
dense variety, at 14,000–18,000 ft
(4,000–5,500 m). Thin altostratus is
usually gray or blue in colour, not white.

Important aspects to look out for when
identifying the cloud are shadows being
cast on the ground. Although it may still
be bright during the day, thin altostratus
will be thick enough to prevent shadows
appearing. Much of the cloud will be
translucent enough to see the Sun or the
Moon through it, as if looking through
ground glass, but halo phenomena are
never seen with thin altostratus.

Sometimes, mainly in the tropics,
altostratus may form when the
middle part of a cumulonimbus cloud
spreads out. Thin altostratus may
also be seen with small cumulus clouds,
and usually shreds of stratus will
also be present.

FRONTAL RAIN CLOUD

This false-color satellite image shows a deep and
vigorous area of low pressure moving eastward across
the Atlantic Ocean toward Europe. Typically, both
altostratus and nimbostratus will develop under
these conditions. The thickening altostratus continues
to lower until it becomes nimbostratus. At this stage,
some form of precipitation—either rain or snow—is
very likely. The frontal cloud within the area of
low pressure marks the boundary between
different air masses.

Ns

Nimbostratus

ALTITUDE Height of base 2,000–10,000 ft (600–3,000 m)
SHAPE Layered and featureless
PRECIPITATION Continuous rain or snow likely

Altostratus that continues to thicken is usually a good indicator that a weather front is nearing, and the chance of rain or snow is increasing. Eventually it can thicken into the rain-bearing nimbostratus cloud. Nimbostratus is a darker gray or more bluish gray than the thinner altostratus from which it often develops. The layer of cloud will cover much, if not all, of the sky, and the greater part of the cloud will be thick enough to completely hide the Sun or Moon. Where there is a dense covering of altostratus or nimbostratus, ragged shreds of stratus clouds are often present. Once precipitation begins to fall, it may last for several hours until the front finally passes over.

Mainly in the tropics and especially during any lulls in rainfall, nimbostratus cloud may break up into several different layers of cloud, which then rapidly merge again. When this happens, the cloud can show vivid variations in both color and brightness.

Ns

Thickening cloud

ALTITUDE Height of base 2,000–10,000 ft (600–3,000 m)
SHAPE Layered and featureless
PRECIPITATION Prolonged

As nimbostratus thickens further and the base lowers, rain or snow falls and the cloud's appearance becomes diffuse and unclear. Stratus pannus clouds move quickly beneath the nimbostratus base.

When the rain or snow becomes heavy, stratus clouds may disappear. The precipitation collects the water droplets that would have formed the stratus cloud as it falls to the ground.

High-level clouds

Because of their high altitude, cirrus, cirrostratus, and cirrocumulus clouds consist entirely of ice crystals. These wispy clouds drift magestically across the upper part of the troposphere, and can indicate local wind patterns.

Ci

CIRRUS

ALTITUDE Height of base 18,000–40,000 ft (5,500–12,000 m)
SHAPE Layered, tufted or patchy
PRECIPITATION None

All high-level clouds are types of cirrus, a common cloud that can be seen at any time of the year. They are made of ice crystals, so they are usually white, and form in a wide range of shapes and sizes. Cirrus can be a good indicator of the type of weather to expect in the coming hours. Cirrus cloud often forms, for instance, in advance of a warm front where the air masses meet at high levels.

Cirrus clouds may form dense shelves, which sometimes appear entangled with each other. They also form thick patches that may be dense enough to obscure the Sun, and are gray or silvery in color if viewed toward the Sun. Cirrus clouds in narrow bands or turrets are called cirrus castellanus. Those that form a more ragged shape are known as cirrus floccus. Dense cirrus clouds may develop from the upper portion of a cumulonimbus cloud that has detached from the rest of the cloud as it dissipates.

Ci

Mares' tails

ALTITUDE Height of base 20,000–40,000 ft (6,000–12,000 m)

SHAPE Hairlike tufts or hooks

PRECIPITATION None

Cirrus clouds that are shaped like commas and topped with a hook or a tuft are popularly called "mares' tails" and are one of the best-known cloud types. They get their name because they resemble white horses' tails flying through the air. Overall, these cirrus clouds may form a structure that looks like a fish skeleton, with a thick "spine" and filaments on either side. Mares' tails sometimes occur at the same time as other cirrus clouds, but on their own, they are usually seen during a spell of fine, settled weather. On warm days, especially during the summer, these clouds will not be thick enough to prevent strong surface heating, and cumulus clouds may develop.

CONTRAILS

An aircraft will sometimes leave behind a condensation trail, or contrail. These form when the air is cold and humid. Strong upper winds may spread the trails across the sky, giving them the appearance of cirrus or cirrostratus clouds. Contrails rarely form below 20,000 ft (6,000 m) in the winter and 28,000 ft (8,500 m) in the summer.

Cc

Cirrocumulus

ALTITUDE Height of base 20,000–40,000 ft (6,000–12,000 m)

SHAPE Layers or patches of cells

PRECIPITATION None

Cirrocumulus clouds are relatively rare. They never have any shading and often form ripples, which may resemble honeycombs. They can appear in waves that look like the skin of a mackerel and are known as a "mackerel sky" (some altocumulus clouds also appear in this pattern, and can be mistaken for cirrocumulus). Cirrocumulus clouds form when cirrus or cirrostratus are warmed from below, and subject to turbulent vertical air currents.

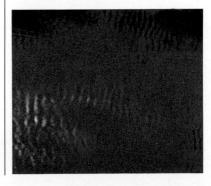

Cs

Cirrostratus

ALTITUDE Height of base 18,000–40,000 ft
(5,500–12,000 m)
SHAPE Layered
PRECIPITATION None

This thin, layered cloud is composed of ice crystals, and forms a veil that covers part or all of the sky. Cirrostratus cloud is often the forerunner to an approaching front. This means that the arrival of cirrostratus often heralds the imminent onset of unsettled, wet weather.

The relationship between cirrostratus and changes in the weather makes correctly identifying it very important. The best way to identify cirrostratus is to look for it slowly approaching over the horizon. Near the horizon, cirrostratus is often mistaken for altostratus, but the slow speed at which the cloud seems to move and change is a good indicator that it is cirrostratus. As it continues to invade the sky, cirrostratus usually grows thicker, although small cumulus clouds may develop at the same time. Where cirrostratus does not spread across the whole of the sky, the visible edges may be sharp and clean but are mostly irregular. Other types of cirrus clouds may be seen at the same time as cirrostratus.

It can be difficult to identify thin cirrostratus clouds, especially if the conditions for the observer are hazy or misty. A halo (see opposite) is sometimes the only indication that thin cirrostratus cloud is present.

Halo

ALTITUDE 20,000–40,000 ft (6,000–12,000 m)
SHAPE Full or part circle
PRECIPITATION None

The sight of a halo usually indicates that cirrostratus cloud is present, although, rarely, haloes may be seen with cirrus clouds. A halo is an optical phenomenon that centers on either the Sun (a solar halo) or the Moon (a lunar halo). Once a halo has appeared, it may last for more than an hour. If a weather front is approaching, the halo will remain visible until the cirrostratus cloud thickens and becomes altostratus.

Mock sun

ALTITUDE 20,000–40,000 ft (6,000–12,000 m)
SHAPE Part circular or lenticular
PRECIPITATION None

As the names implies, a "mock sun," also known as a sun dog or a parhelion, is a bright spot in the sky that resembles the Sun but is at a distance from the actual Sun. Mock suns occur when cirrus or cirrostratus clouds are thick enough to catch the light from the Sun and separate it into the individual colors of the spectrum. The higher the Sun is in the sky, the farther from the Sun the mock sun will be observed. This phenomenon is a sign that ice crystals are present in the clouds.

PILLARS

Optical phenomena known as pillars are seen occasionally at sunrise and sunset. They are formed by the reflection of sunlight from ice crystals in cirrostratus or cirrus clouds and make a vertical column of light above the Sun. They are usually blinding white in color. Sometimes these pillars appear simultaneously with mock suns. Seen here are a pillar (vertically above the Sun) and two mock suns.

Orographic and special clouds

Orographic cloud develops on a local scale because of the geographic features of an area, such as hills and mountains. Other rare cloud phenomena can form in regions of the atmosphere well above the height where the weather that affects us forms.

Kelvin-Helmholtz cloud

ALTITUDE Above 16,500 ft (5,000 m)
SHAPE Regular waves of cirrus cloud
PRECIPITATION None

The distinctive Kelvin-Helmholtz or "billow" clouds are a rare phenomenon. They occur when there is a strong vertical shear between two air-streams. The cloud pattern is produced when the wind blows faster at the upper level than at lower levels. The phenomenon is named after German Hermann von Helmholtz and Briton William Thomson Kelvin, scientists who studied the nature of turbulent air-flow.

Banner cloud

ALTITUDE Mountain-top
SHAPE Pennantlike
PRECIPITATION None

Banner cloud is a form of orographic cloud caused by the uplifting of the air. When the wind blows against a hill or mountain, it is forced to lift. Air cools as it rises, and the water vapor within condenses to form a cloud. Particular mountains, such as the Matterhorn in the European Alps (below) and Mount Everest in the Himalayas, have become famous for the frequent appearance of a banner cloud. As the name implies, these clouds form in a layer and then remain almost stationary, as the wind continuously blows from one direction. The prevailing wind determines the particular microclimates found around a hill or mountain. Areas to the leeward side of the hill can often experience shelter, with more sunshine, less rainfall, and higher temperatures than areas to the windward side, which is where banner cloud will develop.

Nacreous cloud

ALTITUDE 13–19 miles (21–30 km)
SHAPE Thin layer
PRECIPITATION None

Nacreous clouds have the appearance of pale cirrus or lenticular altocumulus, and show very marked coloring. The most brilliant colors appear when the Sun is just below the horizon and illuminates the clouds from below. The clouds can still be distinguished a couple of hours after sunset, when they look like thin gray clouds, and may remain visible by moonlight through the night. Nacreous clouds form below -109°F (-78°C), temperatures that occur in the lower stratosphere during the polar winter.

Noctilucent cloud

ALTITUDE 45–56 miles (72–90 km)
SHAPE Layered and tufted
PRECIPITATION None

It is still not known how these rare clouds form. Noctilucent clouds have mainly been observed during clear midsummer nights between the latitudes of 55–65 degrees, but only in the northern hemisphere. Although they resemble thin cirrus clouds in shape, noctilucent clouds are normally bluish or silvery in color. They can sometimes appear orange or red when they are close to the horizon. The clouds begin to appear at the same time as the brightest stars, but are more brilliant after midnight.

Lenticular cloud

ALTITUDE 6,500–16,500 ft (2,000–5,000 m)
SHAPE Lens-shaped
PRECIPITATION Possible light rain or snow

These orographic wave clouds form when, in stable air, the wind blows from the same or similar direction at many levels of the troposphere. As the wind blows across regions of hills and mountains, the air undulates in a downstream train of waves. If there is sufficient moisture in it, the air rising on the crest of a wave will condense into a cloud. These clouds can be seen over 60 miles (100 km) downwind of the hills or mountains that have triggered them.

INTRODUCING PRECIPITATION

Precipitation—whether it falls as rain, snow, or hail—is essential to life. The form it can take ranges from minute drops of drizzle within an extensive band of light rain, to enormous frozen hailstones in an intense, short-lived, and localized burst.

FORMING RAINDROPS

When water on the Earth is warmed by the Sun, it evaporates and turns into water vapor, which rises into the air. If the air cools sufficiently, the water vapor may condense around dust or other microscopic particles in the air, called condensation nuclei. Minute droplets of liquid water then become visible as a cloud. Droplets fall through the cloud and may coalesce into raindrops on their way down. As they fall, the drops create a downdraft. The raindrops fall to the ground once the downdraft they create is greater than the updrafts that created the cloud initially.

WARM AND COLD CLOUDS

"Warm" clouds, found most often in the tropics, are those with a temperature above freezing. They are produced by strong updrafts, so water droplets must grow large before they fall, resulting in large raindrops of warm, tropical rain. "Cold" clouds are those within which substantial portions are below 32°F (0°C).

PRECIPITATION IN A THUNDERCLOUD
The heaviest rain falls from huge cumulonimbus clouds, which may be over 9 miles (15 km) high. These clouds contain powerful air currents that cause strong local winds. Inside the clouds, these currents throw ice crystals up and down, and the ice crystals grow, becoming hailstones.

After rising many miles, the air reaches the tropopause and diverges to form an anvil-shaped thunderhead

Warm air cools as it rises, and water vapor condenses to form cloud. Condensation releases heat to warm air once more, and air continues to rise

Thunderstorm begins when parcels of warm air rise sharply

ALFRED WEGENER

German meteorologist Alfred Wegener (1880–1930) is best known for his theory of continental drift, the forerunner to modern plate tectonics. Wegener also studied polar air circulation and formulated an early theory of precipitation, setting out the importance of both ice crystals and supercooled droplets in the formation of snow.

FORMING FROZEN PRECIPITATION

Cloud droplets can remain liquid at temperatures well below freezing in a "supercooled" state, and all droplets become ice crystals only at or below about -40°F (-40°C). Snowflakes form when supercooled droplets freeze onto ice crystals in a process known as "accretion." Ice crystals stick to other crystals by "aggregation" to form larger

HAILSTORM
Hailstones can range from the size of peas to oranges, depending on the intensity of the storm cloud in which they were generated.

flakes. The snowflakes may melt as they fall and reach the ground as rain. If the air temperature is low enough, however, the snow will reach the ground. Hailstones are formed in storm clouds when ice crystals from high in the cloud fall to a lower level but are thrown up again by powerful updrafts, collecting layers of ice by aggregation.

SNOW DRIFT
Once snow has settled on the ground, it may be slow to melt because it forms a white layer that reflects sunlight.

Water droplets in the cloud grow into raindrops, and ice crystals grow into hailstones

Raindrops and hailstones become heavy enough to start falling, dragging down the air around them to create a downdraft

Some of the rain evaporates in the air beneath the cloud before reaching the ground then condenses back into the cloud as the air rises

Downdraft blows from the base of the cloud and moves quickly ahead of the storm as a "gust front"

Torrential rain and hail follow the gust front, rarely lasting more than an hour, and then the thundercloud moves away or decays

Rain

Liquid precipitation falls in raindrops that vary in size from tiny drizzle as small as $\frac{1}{50}$ in (0.5 mm) in diameter, to large raindrops up to $\frac{1}{5}$ in (6 mm) in diameter. Rain is classified according to how it is generated, such as by an approaching front, by convective cloud, or by a cyclone.

Frontal rain

CLOUD Thick stratiform
DURATION Up to six hours
INTENSITY Light to heavy

Frontal rain is precipitation from clouds that form when warm, moist air glides up and over fronts. At a cold front, cold air advances beneath the warm air, lifting it up and producing heavy cloud and intense rain. In the summer, cold fronts can cause severe thunderstorms. At a warm front, the warm air advances and rises over the cold air, producing layer cloud and light rain. The rising motion of air that produces layer cloud is gentler than at a cold front, so the rain is lighter. Frontal rain falls mostly in mid-latitude regions, where warm tropical air meets cold polar air. Areas of the world that are affected by frontal rain include western Europe, western North America, and western Australia.

Orographic rain

CLOUD Thick stratiform
DURATION Up to 12 hours
INTENSITY Light to heavy

As an air mass blows from the sea over hilly land, the damp air rises and condenses. Cloud produced in response to the topography of the land in this way is known as orographic cloud. Above the orographic cloud is a rain cloud that forms over the sea—called a "seeder" cloud. Rain from this cloud falls through the lower orographic cloud, or "feeder" cloud, and washes many of its tiny cloud droplets out. This means that hilly coastal land is wetter than lower coastal areas.

Convective rain

CLOUD Tall cumuliform
DURATION Showery—generally an hour or less
INTENSITY Light to intense

Convective rain falls from cumuliform clouds. The rain varies in intensity and duration depending on the size of cloud. Cumuliform cloud is created by strong updraughts, or convective currents, particularly in warm, humid regions. Raindrops can grow to their maximum size—about $^1/_5$ in (6 mm)—in these clouds.

Slow-moving, vigorous convective storms can produce huge amounts of rainfall. If the updraught is very strong, cumulonimbus clouds may be created, producing a thunderstorm. The heaviest rainfalls ever recorded are usually due to vigorous storms of this type that develop over a restricted region and move slowly.

Convective rain is "showery"—it is usually short-lived and relatively intense. Meteorologists define such falls as "slight" (up to $^1/_{12}$ in, or 2 mm, per hour), "moderate" ($^1/_{12}$–$^5/_{12}$ in, or 2–10 mm, per hour), "heavy" ($^5/_{12}$–2 in, or 10–50 mm, per hour), and "violent" (more than 2 in, or 50 mm, per hour).

Cyclonic rain

CLOUD Thick stratiform
DURATION Up to several days
INTENSITY Light to heavy

Cyclonic rain is precipitation that can occur on a very large scale. It is produced by moist air that converges within low-pressure areas. The air spirals gradually toward the area of lowest pressure, and, as it does so, ascends and cools, producing extensive cloud and rainfall.

Cyclonic and frontal conditions often produce prolonged periods of rain, but for some of that time at least, the precipitation may be very light and fall

in the form of drizzle. Drizzle is formed by the coalescence of minute water droplets in stratus clouds with low bases. These clouds are normally produced by gentle upcurrents of moist air. A thick drizzle will produce a fall of up to $^1/_{24}$ in (1 mm) per hour.

Snow, ice pellets, and hail

The three main types of solid precipitation are all made from frozen water. Snow and ice pellets are nearly always winter events, while hailstones are a common feature of thunderstorms so are at their biggest and most damaging in spring and summer.

Snow

CLOUD Cumulus and stratus
DURATION Brief showers to a few hours
INTENSITY Light to heavy

Snow forms when tiny ice crystals in clouds stick together to become snowflakes. Some become heavy enough to fall to the ground. Snowflakes that fall through wet air that is slightly warmer than 32°F (0°C) will melt around the edges and stick together to produce big flakes. Snowflakes that fall through cold, dry air produce powdery snow that does not stick together. Snowfalls on a large scale are defined as "slight" (up to ⅕ in, or 5 mm, per hour), "moderate" (⅕–1½ in, or 5–40 mm, per hour), and "heavy" (more than 1½ in, or 40 mm, per hour). When combined with strong winds, a snowfall can create blizzards and drifts.

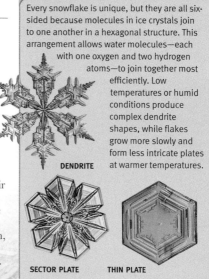

SNOWFLAKES

Every snowflake is unique, but they are all six-sided because molecules in ice crystals join to one another in a hexagonal structure. This arrangement allows water molecules—each with one oxygen and two hydrogen atoms—to join together most efficiently. Low temperatures or humid conditions produce complex dendrite shapes, while flakes grow more slowly and form less intricate plates at warmer temperatures.

DENDRITE

SECTOR PLATE   THIN PLATE

Ice pellets (sleet)

CLOUD Tall cumulus
DURATION Brief showers, occasionally prolonged
INTENSITY Light to heavy

Ice pellets form when snowflakes start to melt on their way down, then fall through sub-freezing air, where they refreeze into grainlike particles. Sometimes the snow may only partially melt, and will fall as snow pellets encased in a thin layer of solid ice.

Ice pellets are generally smaller than hailstones and bounce when they hit the ground. Showers of ice pellets are usually short-lived, but up to 2 in (50 mm) has been recorded in a single storm in eastern North America. Ice pellets can accumulate on the ground in a similar way to snow, but form a smaller, denser covering, which can be hard to clear away. In North America, a shower of ice pellets is called sleet, a term used for a mixture of melting snow and rain in the UK.

Hail

CLOUD Tall cumulus
DURATION Short-lived, tens of minutes
INTENSITY Light to heavy

Hail is a shower of round or irregularly shaped pieces of ice, known as hailstones, which are formed inside cumulonimbus clouds. They originate as small ice particles or frozen raindrops that are caught in the updraft of air inside a cumulonimbus cloud. As they ascend, they grow by gathering water on their surface. How big they grow depends on how strong and extensive the updraft is, and how much water is in the cloud. If they are in a very vigorous cloud, the hailstones may go up and down a number of times, adding a layer of ice each time. Eventually, they become so heavy that they can no longer be supported by the updraft, and fall to the ground. Most hailstones are smaller than 1 in (25 mm) in diameter, but they can grow up to 6 in (150 mm) in diameter— even a golf-ball sized hailstone may cause widespread damage to property and crops. Hailstones should not be confused with snow grains or pellets, which are smaller and fall from stratus clouds.

Dew and frost

The ground cools quickly on still, clear nights, which can allow the water vapor in the air to condense into water droplets or ice crystals. The temperature at which this happens is known as the dew or frost point, when water droplets or ice crystals form on the ground.

Dew

WEATHER Anticyclonic, light winds, clear sky, temperature above 32°F (0°C)

APPEARANCE Very small water droplets on, for example, blades of grass

Dew usually forms during the calm weather associated with high-pressure systems. The process of dew settling from the lower layers of the air is known as "dew-fall." Up to $^{1}/_{50}$ in (0.5 mm) of dew can form at night in some climates, averaged over the year. Although small, this amount is significant enough for dew to become an important source of moisture for some plants and animals in arid areas. Dew can be collected for human use from canopies erected above the surface. When conditions are right, many gallons of water can be obtained from a canopy measuring just 100 sq ft (10 sq m).

Hoar frost

WEATHER Anticyclonic, light winds, clear sky, temperature at or below 32°F (0°C)

APPEARANCE Small, feathery ice crystals on vegetation such as leaves and grass

Hoar frost is a type of ground frost formed by ice crystals shaped like needles and feathers. It forms when water vapor in the air condenses onto a surface with a temperature below 32°F (0°C). Ground frost is more common than "air" frost—when the air is at or below 32°F (0°C)—as the strongest cooling occurs at the surface. A few feet above this and the air will sometimes be above freezing, depending on the conditions.

Rime frost

WEATHER Windy at higher elevations, with supercooled water droplets present in fog or cloud

APPEARANCE Opaque, milky accretion upwind of, for example, fence posts and wire

This type of frost is different from hoar frost because it is formed from tiny fog or cloud droplets. These supercooled droplets freeze when they come into contact with cold surfaces, forming thick, white frost. Rime frost often occurs in exposed places, usually on higher ground. The fog droplets may freeze instantly on contact with an object, such as a wire fence or a tree branch, building up on the windward side as a thick layer of white ice that may be an inch or more deep. This process is known as "riming." Occasionally, rime can build up on the wings of an aircraft as it flies through clouds of supercooled droplets, and will affect its aerodynamic stability.

Frost hollow

WEATHER Anticyclonic, light winds, clear sky, temperature at or below 32°F (0°C)

APPEARANCE Sheltered area white with hoar frost

Hoar frost is a relatively common sight on open land during the colder months, and may form in particular areas, known as frost hollows, depending on local topography.

During nights when conditions are right for hoar frost to form, the air at ground level cools quickly. On sloping surfaces gravity pulls small but measurable flows of the denser, cold air down-slope. This current of cold air is known as a katabatic wind (see p.174). The wind can flow down valley networks, but may cease blowing in basin- or hollow-shaped landforms, or features such as manmade embankments. The temperature may be as much as 15°F (8°C) lower at the bottom of a hollow than land 600 ft (200 m) higher up. These hollows may be small local features or extend over many miles, and experience more frequent frost than surrounding higher ground.

Delicate plants and crops may be damaged by frequent frost. Removing obstacles to the air-flow, such as hedges, may ease hard frosts and protect crops.

LOW VISIBILITY

It is very important for forecasters to predict low visibility,
which varies seasonally and geographically, and has a wide
range of causes. Visibility can be reduced by fog or by
pollution, snow, sand, or dust whipped up by the wind.

Radiation fog

ORIGIN Humid air, light wind, clear sky
LOCATION Inland (fall and winter only)
VISIBILITY Less than 3,300 ft (1,000 m)

The definition of fog is water droplets
suspended in the lower atmosphere that
reduce horizontal visibility to less than
3,300 ft (1,000 m). As its name suggests,
the cooling required to produce
radiation fog is caused by the Earth
radiating heat at night. The weather
conditions that promote the formation
of radiation fog are clear skies (to boost
heat loss), and calm or near-calm wind
conditions. The layer of air near the
ground must be humid so that the
cooling will reduce the air temperature
to its dew point—the point at which
water vapor condenses into water.
These conditions are satisfied most
commonly in the fall and winter, inland.
Once cooling occurs in the evening,
the cold surface-air flows down slopes
and will often pool in valleys and
hollows, so fog tends to be more
common in such locations.

Other types of fog include up-slope
fog and hill fog. Up-slope fog is produced
by the cooling of humid air that ascends
the windward slope of a hill. Hill fog is
simply where a stratiform cloud base is
lower than the hilltops that it shrouds.
"Arctic sea smoke" is a relatively rare,
shallow form of fog, which is produced
by very cold air flowing over a warmer
water surface.

Advection fog

ORIGIN Swiftly moving, mild air over cool surface
LOCATION Over sea (spring, early summer) and snow
VISIBILITY Less than 3,300 ft (1,000 m)

Advection fog forms when relatively warm and damp air blows across a cooler surface, and requires fairly swiftly moving air to form. The air loses heat to the cooler underlying surface, which is usually sea or snow. Sea fog forms most commonly when the sea is cool during spring and early summer. Advection fog is also common when a warm front passes over snow.

Dust- and sand-storms

ORIGIN Dry cold-front or thunderstorm outflow
LOCATION Arid and semi-arid regions
VISIBILITY Less than 3,300 ft (1,000 m)

Dust- and sand-storms are whipped up in deserts by strong winds. Dust-storms reach great heights, while sand-storms are typically up to 130 ft (40 m) tall. They occur when downdrafts flowing away from desert thunderstorms pick up dust or sand. To be officially classed as a dust- or sand-storm, visibility must be less than 3,300 ft (1,000 m).

Blizzards

ORIGIN Strong winds, lifted snow
LOCATION Wintertime high-latitude continents
VISIBILITY Less than 650 ft (200 m)

Blizzards occur either when snow is falling in windy conditions or when it is lifted from the ground by strong winds (known as a ground blizzard). The precise definition of what constitutes a blizzard varies from country to country, but all feature very strong winds, low temperatures, and visibility reduced to at least 650 ft (200 m). Visibility can be much lower than this, sometimes dropping to a few feet.

A "whiteout" is an extreme form of blizzard in which downdrafts and heavy snowfall combine to create a situation in which it is impossible to tell the ground from the sky.

Industrial pollution

TYPICAL COMPONENTS Sulfur dioxide, nitrous oxides

DURATION Long-lived

Industry is a major source of air pollution, which may be borne on the wind to affect areas that are thousands of miles from the source. One notorious example was the nuclear accident at Chernobyl, Ukraine, on April 26, 1986, which led to the release of radioactive material that reached many parts of western and northern Europe.

Volcanoes

TYPICAL COMPONENTS Sulfur dioxide, hydrogen chloride, sulfate aerosol

DURATION Long-lived slow emission to brief, intense eruption

Volcanic eruptions blast vast amounts of ash and noxious gas into the atmosphere. Large eruptions can affect the weather around the world as the ash spreads through the atmosphere and partially obscures the Sun. The ash produced by the eruption of Mount Pinatubo in the Philippines in 1991 reduced the amount of sunlight reaching the Earth by approximately 10 percent. Average global temperatures fell by about 1°F (0.5°C) as a result.

The sulfur dioxide released by volcanoes reacts with sunlight, oxygen, dust particles, and water in the air to form a mixture of sulfate aerosols (tiny particles and droplets), sulfuric acid, and other oxidized sulfur compounds. This gas and aerosol mixture produces hazy atmospheric conditions known as volcanic smog, or "vog."

Urban pollution

TYPICAL COMPONENTS Carbon monoxide, small particulate matter, photochemical smog
DURATION Diurnal variation with traffic flow, intermittent smog, weather related

For the first time in history, over half of the world's population now lives in cities, where vehicle exhausts emit noxious gases. Where diesel fuel is used, harmful microscopic particulate matter is also emitted. The pollution is concentrated in calm anticyclonic conditions when there is little mixing of the air either vertically or horizontally. Pollutants such as sulfur dioxide and carbon monoxide promote the production of ozone and "volatile organic compounds" in the atmosphere, which can lead to eye irritation and breathing difficulties.

Urban pollution is particularly bad in summer, when high temperatures speed up chemical reactions. In cities built in "bowls" (low-lying areas surrounded by hills or mountains), such as Los Angeles (below) or Mexico City, pollution is often trapped to form photochemical smog.

THE GREAT SMOG

From December 5 to 9, 1952, a lethal smog choked much of London. The weather was anticyclonic and a stable inversion in the lower atmosphere trapped pollution. Some 4,000 people died as a direct consequence of the thick smog, which was caused by the huge amounts of particulate matter pumped into the stagnant air from domestic and industrial coal fires. The Great Smog led to the establishment of the Clean Air Acts of 1956 and 1968, which led to the adoption of smokeless fuel.

CYCLONES AND OTHER STORMS

Cyclones are large-scale circulations of rising air, cloud, and precipitation, which may feature thunderstorms or tornadoes. In the tropical summer, cyclones can be violent and destructive, while further from the equator, they often bring winter storms.

DEFINING A CYCLONE

"Cyclone" is a general term that covers a variety of weather phenomena associated with low atmospheric pressure and spiraling winds—from violent tropical cyclones to the more moderate, unsettled cyclonic conditions of the mid-latitudes. Powerful cyclones can cause widespread devastation due to destructively strong winds and persistent, heavy rain. They commonly travel some distance across oceans before making landfall. If they are intense, with low central pressure, they can bring devastating coastal inundations in the form of a storm surge.

The largest cyclones are typically over one thousand miles across in frontal systems outside the tropics, but are slightly

DARK SPIRAL
As air is sucked into the tornadic vortex, the dark column will throw up a debris cloud. The tornado may last from a few minutes to an hour or more.

smaller in the tropics, taking the form of powerful tropical cyclones or weaker monsoon depressions.

Cyclones are important components of the atmosphere's general circulation and, although they often bring cloudy and

TROPICAL DEVASTATION
Palms strain as a cyclone makes landfall in the Caribbean. The storm surge that follows in its wake may cause flooding for several miles.

TORNADO CHASERS
Trained scientists use hi-tech equipment to monitor the dynamics of severe storms. This group is tracking a severe storm in Oklahoma.

windy weather, provide a reasonably reliable supply of water to much of the world's population. Cyclones rotate counterclockwise in the northern hemisphere, and clockwise in the southern hemisphere.

MEDIUM-STRENGTH CYCLONES

The higher latitude oceans and adjacent land areas sometimes witness the passage of powerful polar lows that are over one hundred miles in diameter. These form over the polar ocean on the cold side of the polar front and must have winds of at least 10 mph (15 kph) to qualify in this more intense category of mesoscale (mid-range) vortices. Their relatively small scale and remoteness means that polar orbiting satellite imagery is invaluable in spotting and tracking them. Polar lows can produce strong winds with heavy snowfall.

TORNADOES

One of the most terrifying of all weather events is the dark, spinning column of rising air that forms a tornado. Violent tornadoes generate the fastest windspeeds ever recorded—stronger than a hurricane.

A tornado is essentially a "micro-scale" cyclone, but its development is orchestrated by a much larger-scale air-

flow. Just like the larger cyclones, a tornado's winds are governed by the magnitude of the horizontal pressure gradient around them (see p.67). In tornadoes this is massively stronger than the vortex of a large cyclone, but much more limited in area. Nevertheless, the devastation wreaked by tornadoes is often compounded by a whole group of them breaking out at once.

TRACKING THE CYCLONE

Most tropical cyclones are born over the tropical oceans, often thousands of miles away from their first landfall. Satellites locate a cyclone's center by mapping the position of the eye. This way, the cyclone's path can be compared to the forecast, to quantify any errors. Potential land targets are then alerted. The intensity of a cyclone can be predicted by studying its cloud features in satellite photographs.

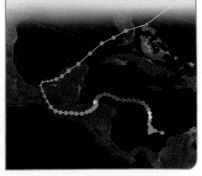

Tropical cyclones

The term "tropical cyclone" refers generally to a revolving storm that forms over tropical waters, where the sustained surface wind speed exceeds a certain strength. Such cyclones are about 300 to 500 miles (500 to 800 km) across and can cause widespread damage on landfall.

STORM TO CYCLONE

Tropical cyclones start their lives as tropical depressions with an average surface wind speed of 22–39 mph (37–63 kph), which strengthen to become tropical storms with winds from 40–73 mph (64–119 kph). This is when they are given a name, such as "Cyclone Nargis."

When a storm reaches an average surface wind speed of 74 mph (120 kph), it is known as a hurricane in the North Atlantic and northeast Pacific Oceans, a typhoon in the northwest Pacific Ocean, and a cyclone in the southwest Pacific and Indian Oceans.

Strongest winds spiral around the calm eye of the storm rotation

High-level winds swirl outward

Low-level winds swirl inward

Spiral rain-band

STORM CLOUDS

A cyclone is composed of cumulonimbus clouds that produce torrential rain. The tallest of these surround the eye, which is 20–35 miles (30–50 km) wide. Above them, a shield of cirrus circulates out in the opposite direction to the low-level winds.

SAFFIR-SIMPSON SCALE

In 1971, civil engineer Herbert Saffir and US National Hurricane Center meteorologist Bob Simpson formulated a five-point scale of hurricane intensity. The development of cyclones from one category to another can be seen clearly from space.

	WIND [MPH (KPH)]	SURGE [FT (M)]
Category 1	74–94 (120–152)	~5 (~1.5)
Category 2	95–109 (153–176)	6–8 (2–2.5)
Category 3	110–130 (177–210)	8–13 (2.5–4)
Category 4	131–155 (211–250)	13–18 (4–5.5)
Category 5	156+ (250+)	18+ (5.5+)

Category 1

Category 2

Category 3

Category 4

Category 5

at high altitudes, as a layer of cirrus cloud spirals away from the center.

STORM DAMAGE

The high winds of a cyclone can cause widespread destruction, but an equal threat to coastal areas is the risk of inundation from the tidal surge that accompanies the storm. Low pressure over the ocean causes the sea surface to dome up underneath the low. Over the open ocean, this surge is usually an extensive low bulge up to about 1½ ft (0.5 m) high. Once it runs onshore, however, it can reach up to 20 ft (6 m) or more in extreme cases and produce widespread, serious flooding, which is exacerbated if it coincides with a high tide. Rainfall is a third problem, especially if the tropical cyclone slows after it crosses a shoreline. Some 10 in (250 mm) or more of rain can fall in a day.

THE STRUCTURE OF A CYCLONE

At the center of a tropical cyclone is a calm, cloud-free "eye," in which air sinks through the entire troposphere. This is surrounded by a ring of thunderstorms known as "hot towers." It is here that the strongest surface winds blow, in a counterclockwise direction in the northern hemisphere and clockwise in the southern.

Across the ocean surface surrounding the eye, thunderstorms form in spiral rain-bands. The clouds are created and maintained by evaporation from the warm tropical oceans. Heat and moisture circulate out of the system

HIGH WAVES
Massive wind-driven waves, exaggerated by the storm surge, crash over the sea walls in Havana, Cuba, as Hurricane Wilma passes over the island on October 24, 2005.

Development of a tropical cyclone

Forecasters are constantly striving to improve their understanding of the evolution of tropical cyclones. Their predictions are aided by frequent monitoring of the track and intensity of these violent storms via satellite imagery. North Atlantic hurricanes are the most closely watched of all.

BREEDING GROUNDS

Tropical cyclones form over the tropical ocean, at least five degrees north or south of the equator, where the ocean temperature is at least 80°F (27°C). Any closer to the equator, and the Coriolis effect will be too weak to cause the cloud to rotate.

Tropical cyclones may develop from storms that occurred thousands of miles away. North Atlantic hurricanes typically start life as a thundery disturbance over land before running over the sea off the coast of West Africa, often near the Cape Verde Islands. Tall cumulus clouds gather into a cluster of thunderstorms that circulate around a low pressure center and move toward the west, carried along by the trade winds.

GROWTH OF A HURRICANE

As it runs toward the Caribbean, the low will intensify if the very warm, very damp air swirling toward its center at low levels is outweighed by the amount

ISABEL APPROACHES
Hurricane Isabel hit the east coast of the US in September 2003. This category 5 storm caused 16 deaths and $4bn-worth of damage.

A HURRICANE BORN OFF WEST AFRICA
In late summer, storms move from east to west into the Atlantic, where in certain conditions, they develop into hurricanes as they cross the tropical ocean.

STAGE ONE
Cumulonimbus clouds cluster off the coast, and are fed by rapid evaporation from the ocean. If wind speeds are uniform through the depth of the troposphere, the clouds do not disperse.

Strong offshore winds at high and low levels

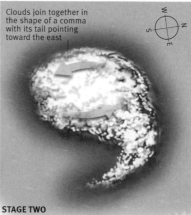

Clouds join together in the shape of a comma with its tail pointing toward the east

STAGE TWO
Due to the Coriolis effect, warm, moist air curves toward the middle of the cluster, transporting heat and moisture upward. Pressure falls at the surface, and evaporation increases.

of cooler air circulating out of the system at high altitudes. If more air leaves than is brought into the system, the surface pressure will fall and the winds will strengthen. A hurricane also needs certain other ingredients to grow, determined by the large current of air it is moving in. For the thunderstorms to reach great heights and to persist, the air in the mid-troposphere must be very humid—otherwise, the growing clouds will be suppressed by the dry air being drawn into their circulations.

The gradually strengthening winds over the sea evaporate more moisture into the hurricane, making the cumulonimbus clouds grow taller. Hurricanes may sometimes weaken and then strengthen again on their sea voyage, perhaps because of changes in the ocean surface temperature. They lose intensity once over land, as the supply of moisture from the warm sea or ocean is lost. Despite this, torrential rain can still fall a long way inland.

KATRINA'S EYE
A research aircraft monitors the calm eye of the storm as it passes over Hurricane Katrina on August 28, 2005. These aircraft are specially designed to withstand hurricane-force turbulence.

OBSERVING HURRICANES

The tropical cyclones that hit the Caribbean form and track over the tropical North Atlantic, where there are few opportunities for surface observations. Forecasters rely on satellite images to pinpoint the eye and therefore the track of any tropical cyclone. They also review the latest satellite images to monitor the accuracy of their track predictions.

Satellites offer a remote view of hurricanes. In addition, aircraft take detailed observations by flying a number of transects through approaching hurricanes. The planes provide high-quality data from onboard instruments and from dropsondes—devices dropped from planes that provide readings of temperature and pressure at different heights as they fall.

Calm eye of the storm

Spiral rain-bands circulate toward eye

STAGE THREE
As the storm moves west over warmer water, the winds blow in ever-tightening circles as more and more warm, moist air is transported upward, and pressure in the eye drops.

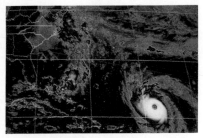

TRACKING STORMS
The National Hurricane Center in Miami, Florida, tracks the movement of hurricanes on computers. When a hurricane is still out over the Sargasso Sea, forecasters predict whether or not it will hit land.

Case study: Hurricane Katrina

In 2005 there were 26 named storms in the North Atlantic, three of which attained category 5 status—the first time this had happened for about 150 years. One of these, named Katrina, was probably the most destructive hurricane ever to have made landfall in the USA.

A STORM BREWS

Katrina developed on August 23, 2005 as a tropical depression 185 miles (300 km) south of the Bahamas. It had developed into a tropical storm when it reached the Bahamas the next day, and was named Katrina. On August 25, it made its first landfall near Miami, causing some flooding. By this time it had become a category 1 hurricane.

The storm deepened dramatically as it moved over the Gulf of Mexico and was declared a category 5 hurricane on August 28. Air pressure at the center fell by 32 hPa in 12 hours to 909 hPa, due in part to the unusually warm water in the Gulf. Winds of 175 mph (280 kph) roared around the center as the hurricane lay some 280 miles (450 km) south-south-east of the Mississippi Delta.

INTENSE RAINFALL
The rainfall for the last week of August 2005 can be seen on this radar map, with Katrina's path in green. In the wettest places, 16½ in (417 mm) fell in Perine, Florida, and 15 in (378 mm) in Big Branch, Louisiana.

WIND DAMAGE
By the time the hurricane had made landfall in Florida, mandatory evacuation orders had been issued in at-risk housing areas.

dikes constructed to protect the city, which is situated in the low-lying Mississippi Delta. Most of the city was flooded, including the entire downtown area.

Nearly 2,000 people died as a result of Hurricane Katrina. The poorest neighborhoods were the worst affected. Thousands were left stranded on the roofs of their homes for days before the emergency services could reach them. In all, an estimated $81 billion of damage was caused, and hundreds of thousands of people were forced to leave the city. In 2007, the population was still barely half its pre-Katrina size.

THE LEVEES BREAK

Katrina was unusually large and its hurricane-force winds extended 75 miles (120 km) from the eye. Even though the system had weakened to a category 3 when it reached the Louisiana coastline at around 7:00 a.m. on August 29, winds were still as high as 125 mph (200 kph), and had whipped up waves as high as 56 ft (17 m)—the highest ever recorded in the region.

The hurricane tracked slowly toward the city of New Orleans. A huge storm surge 28 ft (8.5 m) high caused 53 breaches in the levees—a system of

FLOOD DAMAGE
About 80 percent of the area of New Orleans flooded when the levees broke. Parts of the city were under 15 ft (4.5 m) of water.

Frontal depressions

Although the heat of the tropics generates powerful cyclones, the mid-latitudes get their share of storms from similarly spiraling areas of low pressure. Particularly in winter, these lows, or depressions, bring changeable temperatures, cloud, rain, and sometimes gale-force winds.

HOW DEPRESSIONS START

Cyclones form when warm, damp, subtropical air meets cooler, drier air in mid-latitude regions, such as the Eastern Seaboard of the United States, or the southwestern Pacific. These systems can often bring unsettled or even violent weather, but, crucially, they also bring rain to many densely populated regions of the world.

The development of cyclones is linked to the high-speed jet streams (see pp. 74–75) that snake around the world, marking the boundary of the warm and cold air masses that meet along the polar front. The buoyant warm air is forced above the denser polar air, causing a band of thick, "frontal" cloud to develop, while some of the subtropical moisture condenses along the boundary of the air masses.

ATLANTIC LOW
A broad Atlantic depression sweeps into northern Europe. Frontal cloud stretching for a few thousand miles will bring wind and rain.

The movement of air across the polar front reacts with the jet stream and can cause pressure to drop along part of the front, which creates the start of a cyclonic circulation. Once a low has formed, it moves with its attendant fronts in a "wave," with warm air following the warm front, and cool air flowing in behind the cold front. The waves tend to move northeastward in the northern hemisphere, and southeastward in the southern hemisphere.

INTENSE SYSTEMS

The intensity of the low will vary, but some can deepen significantly, producing more severe storms. Just

PREDICTING STORM SURGES

Prediction takes into account the shape of the coast and the angle at which the storm strikes. A shallow coastal area is more easily overwhelmed than a steep coast. The US Sea, Lake, and Overland Surges from Hurricanes (SLOSH) program predicts surge height around the United States.

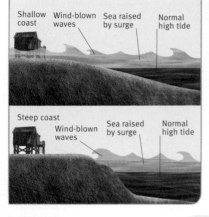

Shallow coast — **Wind-blown waves** — **Sea raised by surge** — **Normal high tide**

Steep coast — **Wind-blown waves** — **Sea raised by surge** — **Normal high tide**

PACIFIC FRONT
A long band of frontal clouds can be seen moving southwest across the Pacific in this meteosat image.

APPROACHING DEPRESSION
Areas on the southeastern coast of Australia are prone to frontal depressions sweeping eastward across the Pacific. Here, rain stops play at a tennis match in Melbourne.

seas, the dome of the surge rises, sometimes inundating low-lying coastal areas. A surge is at its most dangerous when it coincides with a very high tide. Flooding from storm surges is likely to become worse as global warming causes sea levels to rise.

FLOODS AND GALES

Frontal depressions are wind and rain makers. An active system might produce rainfalls of 1–2 in (20–50 mm) over a large area, so a season that brings an unusual run of these lows will also bring a high flood risk. In the winter, in the colder regions of mid- and high latitudes, frontal depressions bring snow or even blizzards if the cyclone is deep enough.

as with powerful tropical cyclones, deep depressions (those with a low central pressure) draw the sea surface up as they move across it. For each 1 hPa fall in atmospheric pressure, sea level increases by ½ in (1 cm). This "storm surge" moves in unison with the traveling frontal low as a broad, flattened dome of water in the open sea. However, if the track of the low moves across shallow

SURGE BARRIER
The Thames Barrier in London was built to protect the city from North Sea storm surges. Many English and Dutch coastal areas have experienced devastating inundations in the past.

Bombs

Frontal depressions in mid latitudes can bring far more severe weather than rain and gales. As the central pressure of a cyclone falls, so the wind strengthens. In rare circumstances the pressure falls at a very rapid rate, forcing violent winds from the system, known as "bombs."

RECIPE FOR A BOMB

Bombs are extremely rare events. Detailed analysis of satellite imagery and improving global and regional computer forecasts have increased scientists' understanding of bombs and their ability to predict them.

A bomb's cloud features are distinctly different from those associated with weaker depressions. They can be identified by the presence of a very large, curved "cloudhead" that descends into a hooklike narrow tip. An important ingredient in the extremely rapid "deepening" of winds and low pressure in the center of a storm, is the presence of a narrow plunge of dry air from the stratosphere into a cyclone's circulation. Scientists believe this dry air evaporates cloud droplets and ice crystals, causing increasing differences in temperature in the cyclone, and leading to dramatic falls of pressure that force a rapid intensification in the wind.

MOUNTAINOUS WAVES
Over the oceans, bombs cause extremely dangerous sea conditions, with massive, wind-driven waves and a longer-period swell.

STING IN THE TAIL

Detailed studies of a number of bombs have revealed the relatively localized nature of the most violent winds. The hook-shaped tip in the cloud pattern, known as the sting jet, is the location of the most extreme winds and tends to appear on the southern edge of

ANATOMY OF A BOMB

If the low pressure at the center of an extratropical cyclone falls by 24hPa or more in 24 hours, the system is classed as a bomb. This computer simulation of the bomb that struck the UK and northern France in October 1987 represents the small area of 30 miles (50 km) where the most violent winds occurred. The colored sting jet is shown descending from the cloudhead. The jet is about ½ mile (1 km) deep and descends from a height of about 3 miles (5 km) to the ground over 3–4 hours. Snow and rain falling into it evaporate and cool it as it descends, helping to accelerate it to speeds of more than 100 mph (160 kph).

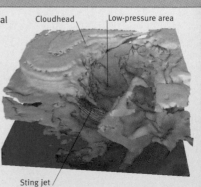

Cloudhead   Low-pressure area

Sting jet

FLATTENED FORESTS
The devastation wreaked by the 1987 bomb can be seen in aerial pictures of the French and English countryside, where millions of mature trees were knocked flat.

the cyclone. This localized feature is a few tens of miles across, descending from a height of about 3 miles (5 km) from the distinctive cloudhead—also a feature of rapidly deepening pressure and wind. The band of the sting jet's extreme winds typically occurs some 90 miles (150 km) from the storm center.

PERFECT STORM

On October 30, 1991 an explosive "deepener" off the eastern seaboard of the United States produced unbelievably high waves of 100 ft (30 m). The main satellite image below pinpoints the center of the bomb, which deepened by an amazing 60hPa in 24 hours. The event became known as "the Perfect Storm"

because of a rare confluence of factors. An extratropical cyclone that began over Nova Scotia moved back into the Gulf Stream, where it became a tropical storm and was absorbed into another hurricane. The huge waves caused by the storm sank a fishing boat, resulting in 12 deaths.

BOMB DAMAGE

Bombs also wreak havoc over land. In the UK and northern France, the "Great Storm" of October 1987 blew down some 15 million trees, and caused 18 deaths. Such events are better predicted today than a few decades ago. Bombs no longer catch weather services completely unawares because of better observations, particularly over the oceans, and better representation of all the factors leading to their growth in forecast models.

THE 1991 NOR'EASTER
The so-called Perfect Storm of 1991 can be seen developing in this satellite sequence, beginning as an oceanic "nor'easter" and ending up as a subtropical system.

Atlantic nor'easter

Subtropical storm

Thunder and lightning

When tall convective clouds develop into cumulonimbus, they can be charged with electricity, just like a battery. If the charge becomes great enough, giant sparks leap from the cloud to the ground. The intense heating from these explosive flashes of lightning generates thunder.

HOW LIGHTNING STRIKES

Lightning is a huge electrical discharge that flows between clouds, from a cloud to the ground, or from a cloud into the air. There is no consensus about how the discharge originates, but the leading theory is that it is related to hail and smaller particles falling through ice crystals and supercooled droplets. Heavier, negatively charged ice particles gather in the lower reaches of the cloud while lighter, positively charged crystals gather at the top, effectively forming the opposite poles of a battery.

The heavier, negative charge creates a potential difference between the bottom of the cloud and the positively charged ground directly beneath it. When the electrical charge within the cloud reaches a certain critical point, electrons flow between two areas of opposite charge to establish a channel to the ground. The bolt of lightning follows this channel, lasting for about one 10,000th of a second.

SUPERCELL
The most severe thunderstorms are known as "supercells." The electrical activity within a supercell may produce spectacular displays of lightning.

BUILDING A CHARGE

As ice particles and supercooled droplets collide in a cloud, they lose or gain electrons. The heavier, negatively charged particles sink to the bottom, and induce a positive charge below, at the surface. Air is a poor conductor, but if the potential difference is large enough, an electrical current can flow between the negatively charged cloud base and the positively charged ground.

Smaller, positively charged ice crystal is carried to top of cloud

Electron is transferred from one particle to another

Larger, negatively charged hail falls to bottom of cloud

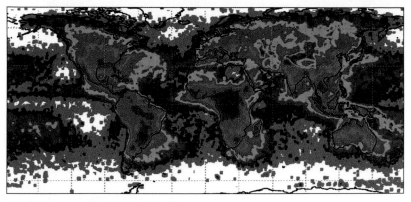

Lightning frequency *Flashes/ ½ sq mi (km²)/year*

0.1   0.4   0.8   2   6   10   30   60

WORLDWIDE LIGHTNING FREQUENCY
The areas with highest lightning activity are over land seen in the hot, humid tropical continents. Activity mainly drops off rapidly over water.

About one in five flashes are cloud-to-ground. Most other flashes travel from cloud to cloud. Lightning heats the surrounding air to some 54,000°F (30,000°C), making the air expand rapidly and sending a shock wave rippling away —we hear this as thunder.

WHERE IN THE WORLD?

Thunderstorms are most often created by intense surface heating, so they are common in areas where the weather is hot and humid. The land masses therefore witness

more lightning storms than the oceans, and tropical areas are more at risk than those in the higher latitudes. Regions of high activity include the Inter-Tropical Convergence Zone over the continents, and areas in the path of tropical cyclones. Closer to the poles, activity is higher over the continental interiors, particularly in spring and summer.

LIGHTNING DAMAGE
When lightning hits a tree, the massive heat of the strike causes the sap to boil and expand almost instantly, ripping the tree apart.

Lightning

All lightning is produced by the build up of electrical charges within clouds, but viewed from the ground, it can take on a variety of forms. The stroke may stretch between clouds or between cloud and the ground, or it may be hidden by clouds and cause the sky to light up.

Cloud to ground

FREQUENCY About 20 percent of global total
MOTION Vertical or near-vertical

Cloud-to-ground lightning starts within a cloud when the potential difference reaches 1 million volts per foot (3 million volts per meter). A rush of electrons flows out of the cloud toward the ground in a series of extremely short zigzagging steps known as a "stepped leader." When it nears the surface, a current moves up from an exposed object, such as a tree, to meet it. The leader is invisible; what we see is the flash of the "return stroke" that flows back up the path of the stepped leader as streak lightning. Forked lightning occurs when the stepped leader is one of a few strokes that makes contact with the surface. A typical lightning flash consists of a few leaders, each followed by a return stroke.

Cloud to cloud

FREQUENCY About 80 percent of global total
MOTION Horizontal or near-horizontal

Lightning can occur entirely inside clouds as electricity is discharged from one part of the cloud to another, or between neighboring clouds without contacting the ground. This is known as cloud-to-cloud lightning. It may light up a cloud from inside as sheet lighting, or appear as visible strokes of lightning flashing across the "anvil" bases of thunderclouds. These often generate multiple strokes, which can be seen as a thundercloud passes overhead or begins to break up, and are dramatic to witness.

Sheet lightning

FREQUENCY Dependent on cloud cover
MOTION Vertical or horizontal

Sheet lightning is the type most commonly observed from the ground, and is a general description of the appearance of a lightning strike, rather than a specific category. It occurs when a stroke is obscured by cloud so that the entire sky flashes white. The hidden flash may be streak, forked, cloud-to-ground, or cloud-to-cloud lightning. Cloud-to-cloud lightning is quite common, while cloud-to-air strokes, which may also be concealed within sheet lightning, are less so. These most often occur from cumulonimbus clouds into the adjacent atmosphere. About 90 percent of cloud-to-ground strokes are "negative," flowing from the negatively charged cloud base, but occasionally the base is positively charged, most often during severe thunderstorms. Such positively charged lightning has a stronger current and a longer-lasting flash, and can be extremely destructive.

Ball lightning

FREQUENCY Uncertain; few thousand reported
MOTION Horizontal

This highly unusual form of lightning has been seen only a few thousand times, but detailed descriptions have been given by scientists who have witnessed it. It takes the form of a brightly luminous "ball" of plasma about 8–12 in (20–30 cm) in diameter. Most sightings occur in thundery conditions, and the ball descends from the thunderclouds at the same time as the lightning stroke, appearing to "float" slowly through the air or to dart around. Unlike other types of lightning,

it may last for several minutes. Ball lightning has even been known to enter buildings. How it is formed is still not known for certain, as data is still scarce. Scientists have attempted to reproduce similar objects in the laboratory in an effort to discover their origin.

Optical effects

A range of beautiful optical phenomena can be produced when sunlight passes through water droplets or ice crystals in the atmosphere. Some of these effects are harbingers of a change in conditions, and form the basis of a number of weather sayings.

RAINBOWS

We sometimes see rainbows in showery weather. They appear when the Sun shines from behind the observer to illuminate a rain shower in the distance. Light travels more slowly through water than through air, which causes it to be refracted, or bent, as it passes from one to the other. As light passes through raindrops, each of its wavelengths—or colors—is refracted by the drops at a slightly different angle—from red at the lowest angle through to violet at the highest. Some of the light is reflected off the back of the drop, where the water's surface tension acts like a mirror, and this reverses the order of the spectrum. The red wavelength is reflected at a high angle and forms the top edge of the rainbow, while violet runs along the bottom.

Sometimes a weaker, secondary "rainbow hat" forms outside the brighter primary one. Its color sequence is the reverse of the primary rainbow because the light producing it has undergone two internal reflections within the raindrops.

CIRCLE OF LIGHT
A rainbow appears when the Sun is shining behind the observer and it is raining in front of them. The semicircle is centered around the observer's shadow.

REFLECTION AND REFRACTION

When a sunbeam hits a raindrop, it is refracted into the spectrum of colors. Most of the light passes straight through the drop, but a little is reflected back toward the observer off the internal surface at the back of the drop. It is this light that we see as a rainbow.

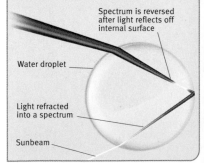

Spectrum is reversed after light reflects off internal surface

Water droplet

Light refracted into a spectrum

Sunbeam

CLOUD IRIDESCENCE
This spectacular display of pale greens, reds, and blues is most commonly seen in middle- to high-level cumulus clouds, which comprise water droplets of varying sizes.

HALOES

These circular optical phenomena are produced when either light from the Sun or sunlight reflected by the Moon passes through ice crystals in the atmosphere. The light is refracted by ice crystals in high-level cirriform cloud, creating the effect of a ring of light around the Sun or Moon.

CREPUSCULAR RAYS

Light from the rising or setting Sun may be scattered in hazy conditions—caused by dust, smoke and other dry particles in the atmosphere—to produce sunbeams known as crepuscular rays. Rays shining upward are often pale blue or whitish in color. At twilight, when the Sun is below the horizon and the rays are separated by hills and clouds below the horizon, the rays may be reddish. Downward-shining crepuscular rays can appear when the Sun shines through small holes in a layer of cloud, an effect known as a "Jacob's Ladder."

CORONAS AND IRIDESCENCE

Light is diffracted—meaning that its direction is deflected—when it passes around the edge of objects such as water droplets in a cloud. This produces a corona, which appears as a circle around the source of the light, such as the Moon, when the droplets are the same size. If the droplets vary in size, the complex pattern of diffraction produces a display of colors called iridescence.

BROCKEN SPECTER

This effect is produced when an observer stands above the upper surface of a cloud, or cloud layer, with the Sun behind them, viewing the shadow they have cast on the cloud top. The light is reflected back from uniformly sized cloud droplets in such a way that a circular "glory" appears around the point directly opposite the Sun.

CREPUSCULAR RAYS
Due to linear perspective, crepuscular rays appear to diverge as they shine away from a cloud, but they are in fact nearly parallel to each other.

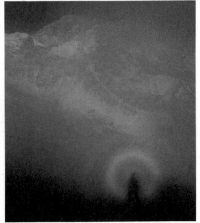

BROCKEN SPECTER
The optical phenomenon Brocken specter is so named because it was first noted on the Brocken, the highest peak in Germany's Harz upland.

Tornadoes

A tornado, or "twister," is a narrow column of air that spins very rapidly around an extremely localized but intense low-pressure center in contact with the ground. It is commonly marked by a funnel cloud but may be observed as debris is thrown up from the surface.

LIFE CYCLE OF A TORNADO

A tornado's development can be described by a sequence of phases. The first is the "dust-whirl stage," during which light debris twists upward from the ground. This is often accompanied by the development of a funnel cloud, which emerges from the cloud base of the thunderstorm. This is followed by the "organizing stage," during which the funnel cloud descends further and intensifies. The next, most damaging phase is called the "mature stage," when the funnel cloud is at its widest and is vertical or near-vertical. During the "shrinking stage," the funnel becomes tilted and diminishes, although conditions can still be dangerous. Finally, the "decay stage" sees the tornado weaken into a ropelike feature that breaks up as it dissipates.

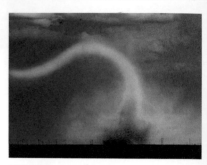

DUST-DEVIL
A dust-devil lasts only a few minutes because cool air is sucked into the base of the rising vortex, cooling the ground and cutting off its heat supply.

TRAIL OF DESTRUCTION

Tornadoes are usually about 300 ft (100 m) wide, so the swathe of damage they cause is relatively thin—but can be extremely severe. The narrowness of the

HOW TORNADOES ARE FORMED
Calm days with morning sunshine can later give way to tornadic conditions. Within hours a violent storm may be sweeping across the land, leaving in its wake a trail of devastation.

Warm air rises, forming cumulus and eventually cumulonimbus

STAGE ONE
Sunshine heats the ground, creating thermals. Shallow cumulus clouds are trapped under a layer of warm, dry air. As the day warms up, some clouds develop through this layer.

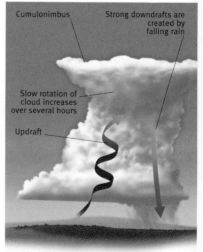

Cumulonimbus

Strong downdrafts are created by falling rain

Slow rotation of cloud increases over several hours

Updraft

STAGE TWO
Conditions are such that winds rotate with height. Once thunderstorms develop, usually late in the afternoon, the entire cloud begins to rotate, forming a supercell, or mesocyclone.

WATERSPOUT
A spinning column of rising air can develop over the sea. A waterspout is usually less violent than a tornado but it can it can capsize boats or destroy them if it collapses, dumping tons of water.

THE FUJITA SCALE

Created by University of Chicago storm researcher Tetsuya Theodore Fujita, the Fujita scale classifies the severity of tornadoes according to their windspeed, based on the amount of damage they cause.

F0: 40–72 mph (64–116 kph). Light damage—tree branches broken, signboards damaged.

F1: 73–112 mph (117–180 kph). Moderate damage—trees snapped, windows broken.

F2: 113–157 mph (181–252 kph). Considerable damage—trees uprooted, trains derailed.

F3: 158–206 mph (253–330 kph). Severe damage—cars overturned, roofs torn off.

F4: 207–260 mph (331–417 kph). Devastating damage—brick houses destroyed.

F5: 261–318 mph (418–512 kph). Incredible damage—steel-reinforced structures damaged.

funnel cloud means that there may be total destruction in one place next to an area left virtually untouched.

OTHER TYPES OF TWISTER

Much weaker and smaller tornadolike spinning vortices, known as dust-devils or dust whirls, can occur when strong convection takes place. They may form anywhere if the surface of the ground is heated enough, especially in hot and dry deserts. Vortices that form over the ocean are known as waterspouts, which develop from cumulonimbus clouds. Winds in waterspouts draw water up through the funnel and the sea spray can make the funnel look wider at its base. They do not usually exceed F0 on the Fujita scale.

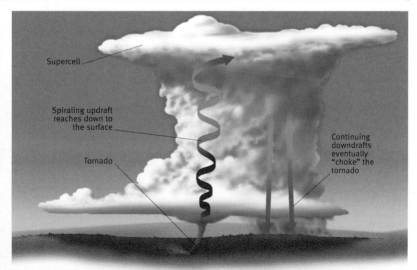

Supercell

Spiraling updraft reaches down to the surface

Tornado

Continuing downdrafts eventually "choke" the tornado

STAGE THREE
Updrafts and downdrafts within the cloud are very strong. The updraft narrows, rotating more quickly as it does so, just as a spinning ice skater tucks in their arms to spin more quickly. This rotation extends toward the surface as a funnel cloud, and becomes a tornado once it reaches the ground.

Case study: Oklahoma

On May 3, 1999, more than 70 tornadoes were recorded in Oklahoma. A mobile Doppler radar, capable of monitoring the velocity of particles caught up in the funnel cloud, measured a world-record speed of 302 mph (486 kph) near Oklahoma City.

TORNADO ALLEY

The highest concentration of tornadoes in the world occurs along "tornado alley," an area stretching north from Texas across the Great Plains to Iowa. Particularly in spring, dry continental air overruns lower-level warm, humid air from the Gulf of Mexico—providing the perfect recipe for a tornado. The highest risk of all lies across central Oklahoma where, on average, an F2 or stronger tornado strikes every other year.

Cold dry air

Warm dry air

Oklahoma City

Warm moist air

HIGH-RISK AREA
Tornado Alley is a corridor of land where a warm air mass from the south meets a dry air mass from the east, and a cold air mass from the north.

TROUBLE BREWS

During the afternoon of May 3, 1999, meteorologists kept a close eye on an area of deep convection that had developed over the southwestern part of the state. At 4:47 a.m., they issued a tornado warning as the first "twister"

RURAL DAMAGE
Most of the 70 tornadoes that formed in southwest Oklahoma on May 3, 1999 missed the towns in this largely rural state.

touched down some 50 miles (80 km) southwest of Oklahoma City. Oklahoma is a very rural state, so the chances of an urban region being hit are slim. Nevertheless, by the end, 40 people had been killed, and 2,300 homes destroyed.

Fifty more tornado warnings were issued that evening, finishing with the standard advice: "Move to an interior room or hall on the lowest floor. Stay away from windows." Much worse was to follow. As the evening unfolded, a

THE AFTERMATH
Houses in the path of the F5 tornado were completely destroyed. In all, over $1 billion-worth of damage was caused.

disastrously violent tornado reached F5 intensity twice as it approached Oklahoma City from the southwest.

URBAN AREAS ARE STRUCK

The first urban area to suffer was the community of Bridge Creek, where the world-record wind speed was recorded. The second area hit was Moore, a suburb of Oklahoma City. The winds were so strong that it was even suggested that the Fujita scale should be modified to include a category 6. Buildings along the tornado's path were totally destroyed.

At 7:00 p.m., the National Weather Service in Norman released the following statement: "At 6:57 p.m. a large tornado was moving along Interstate 44 west of Newcastle. On its present path… it will enter southwest sections of the Oklahoma City between 7:15 p.m. and 7:30 p.m. If you are in its path, take cover immediately. Doppler radar

TRAIL OF DEVASTATION
The F5 tornado ripped through Del City in the Oklahoma metropolitan area. The trail of devastation was narrow but complete.

indicated this storm may contain destructive hail to the size of baseballs… or larger."

This was not the only destructive tornado. Most of the town of Mulhall, north of Oklahoma City, was destroyed by an F4 tornado that even overturned the town's water tower. The last tornado struck a little before 2:00 a.m. on May 4.

Flash floods

In low-lying areas, narrow river valleys, and urban areas, localized, intense flooding can occur. Short-lived flash floods are often the result of slow-moving thunderstorms over high ground, which saturate the ground, leading to large quantities of runoff flowing rapidly downhill.

LOCALIZED FLOODING

Some areas are particularly vulnerable to flash flooding because of the local topography. Persistent rain in surrounding high ground can lead to runoff water inundating narrow valleys and the towns built in them.

This sequence of events occurred in 2004 in Cornwall, UK, where a number of narrow valleys drained from high moorland. On the afternoon of August 16, the village of Boscastle was overrun by a torrent of 140 tons of water per second, which swept away buildings. About 8 in (200 mm) of rain had fallen on the high ground surrounding the village, but just 9 miles (14 km) away, only 0.05 in (1.5 mm) fell, making this a very localized flood.

FLOOD CHANNEL
Towns in narrow valleys are particularly vulnerable to flash floods if there is persistent heavy rain in the hills surrounding the valley.

FLOODING FROM DISTANT RAINFALL

Sometimes, flash floods can inundate narrow valleys with water that has fallen as rain many miles away. On July 31, 1976, Big Thompson Canyon in Colorado was hit by a flash flood caused by persistent heavy rain in the Rocky Mountains about 20 miles

MOUNTAIN RUNOFF
Parts of the Yucatán Peninsula, Mexico, were devastated by mountain runoff from the torrential rain brought by Hurricane Dean in August 2007.

SLOT CANYON
The downpours that accompany thunderstorms can turn narrow, dry slot canyons into raging torrents in a matter of hours.

(50 km away). Up to 12 in (300 mm) of rain fell in just three hours, sending a torrent cascading down the canyon at a flow of 900 tons per second. Day trippers had no idea what was about to happen, and 145 people drowned.

URBAN FLOODING

Vulnerability to floods is much greater if the local soil is impermeable clay rather than more porous, sandy soils, which allow rainwater to drain away. Cities are particularly at risk of flash floods, as impervious, manmade surfaces, such as asphalt and concrete, cause up to six times more runoff than natural surfaces. Storm drains are built to carry the water safely away, but occasionally they fail to cope.

SUBMERGED CITY
Flash floods can engulf cities such as São Paulo, Brazil, so rapidly that people are caught in their vehicles. Flooding may take days to subside, leaving vehicles stranded.

On May 25, 2005, 5 ½ in (140 mm) of rain fell in São Paulo, Brazil—double the average for the entire month—and the city's flood defenses failed. The Pinheiros River burst its banks, flooding main roads and overwhelming drivers. In the sprawling favelas, or shanty towns, that surround the city, houses were destroyed by fatal mudslides. Like many cities around the world, São Paulo has grown rapidly in recent years, and its flood defenses have failed to keep pace.

DESERT FLOODING

The hard surface of the ground in hot deserts, known as desert pavement, absorbs very little water, so deserts are prone to flash floods when thunderstorms flow over them. Flooding in deserts may start as soon as an hour after the storm. Few people live in the world's deserts, but many American cities have been built in arid areas. In July 1999 several districts of Las Vegas, Nevada, were hit by flooding that caused millions of dollars' worth of damage.

FLOODED DESERT
It rarely rains in the arid hot deserts, but when it does, the parched ground absorbs little water. Wadis (dry river beds), like these in Israel, quickly flood. Many plants and animals take advantage of the brief floods to reproduce.

World climates

ALTHOUGH THE WEATHER CHANGES ON A DAILY BASIS, A REGION CAN BE SAID TO FOLLOW A BROAD PATTERN OF TEMPERATURE AND PRECIPITATION, WHICH IS KNOWN AS ITS CLIMATE. THE EARTH HAS A WIDE RANGE OF CLIMATES, FROM THE ARID, FROZEN WASTES OF ANTARCTICA, TO THE DENSE, EXOTIC JUNGLES OF THE EQUATORIAL REGIONS.

The distribution of climates across the Earth is dependent on such factors as latitude, elevation, distance from the ocean, and, for those regions at or near the coast, ocean currents. Traditionally, the patterns seen in an area over a 30-year period were considered to define its climate, taking into account its annual temperature range and monthly temperature and precipitation values. This method was used to divide the Earth into clearly defined climate zones. Nowadays, however, we are all too aware that climates are not stable —annual mean temperature has increased over the last few decades, and the seasonal distribution of precipitation has also shifted in certain areas.

Today, scientists see climate as a dynamic concept, based upon the large-scale circulation and interaction of the atmosphere and oceans. The traditional climatic divisions of the world are still referred to but are

MEDITERRANEAN FRUIT
Viticulture characterizes the Mediterranean climate, which features hot, dry summers and mild, wet winters.

defined by the distribution of characteristic plant communities, such as taiga forest, that go hand-in-hand with the precipitation and temperature of a region.

Climate scientists have become aware of large-scale fluctuations in pressure patterns across some parts of the Earth. These oscillations, such as those produced by El Niño, can cause significant seasonal weather anomalies worldwide.

On a smaller scale, the growth of cities has given rise to distinct urban climates—so-called "heat islands" that sometimes generate enhanced convective precipitation. Human society has also altered the land surface through deforestation and other land-use changes, affecting the local climate through changes in surface heating and soil moisture. Regional variability also occurs due to local winds, which are key to climate.

Although maps display well-defined boundaries between climate types, it is not the case that one climate type fits all. Each region has important local variations within a broadly similar climate regime.

FROZEN WASTES
The poles are among the Earth's most arid areas, with temperatures so low that the air cannot contain enough water vapor to produce snow.

CLIMATE ZONES

Climate is traditionally defined by the distribution of vegetation. Vegetation is an expression of the seasonal amount of precipitation and warmth received in a particular area. Non-vegetated areas, such as the poles, are also classified into zones, using seasonal precipitation and temperature criteria.

DEFINING CLIMATE

Climate zones were first identified in the 19th century, when for the first time, data from monthly and annual weather summaries became available to share worldwide. Knowledge of the distribution of vegetation was also increasing. These advances were first exploited by the Russian climatologist Wladimir Köppen, who recognized the crucial link between climate and vegetation and used it to set the boundaries of climate zones.

Köppen also considered long-term monthly temperature and precipitation values to formulate a definition of climate that allowed for seasonal changes. He took into account the annual range of temperature (the difference between the warmest and coldest months) and threshold values, such as all monthly mean temperatures above 64°F (18°C)—the temperature at which significant biological activity takes place. His final classification scheme was published in 1936, and is still used, with some modifications, today.

CLIMATE DISTRIBUTION

The colored areas of the map denote the climate zones classified by Köppen using his letter division scheme. Some climatologists have argued that the scheme contains groups, such as group C (temperate), that are too broad and should be further subdivided.

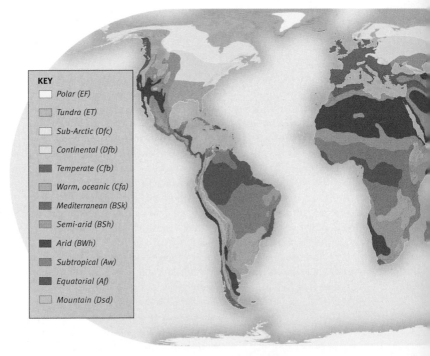

KEY

- Polar (EF)
- Tundra (ET)
- Sub-Arctic (Dfc)
- Continental (Dfb)
- Temperate (Cfb)
- Warm, oceanic (Cfa)
- Mediterranean (BSk)
- Semi-arid (BSh)
- Arid (BWh)
- Subtropical (Aw)
- Equatorial (Af)
- Mountain (Dsd)

monsoon, "w" for areas with a dry winter), or temperature ("a" for places with a hot summer, "b" for those with long, cool summers, "c" for those with a cool, brief summer, and "d" for brief summers and severe winters).

THE CLASSIFICATION SCHEME

Köppen's scheme divides the continents into five regimes of A, B, C, D, and E that are broadly classified according to the distribution of vegetation types. Group A covers tropical climates; group E, polar climates.

He used a second letter to subdivide these regimes into deserts (W), dry, semi-arid steppe (S), permanently ice-covered (F), and tundra (T). A further letter refers to precipitation ("f" for places with a more-or-less even annual spread, "m" for

EVOLVING CLIMATES

Köppen's work resulted in a world map of vegetation-related climate zones. In recent times, the dynamic nature of climates—both in how their distribution is determined by the circulations of the atmosphere and oceans, and in how they are changing relatively rapidly—has been increasingly understood. This means that there will be shifts in Köppen's climate zones if temperature and precipitation patterns continue to change over the coming decades.

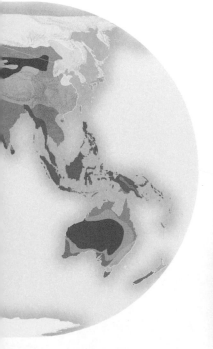

WLADIMIR KÖPPEN

Russian-German climatologist Wladimir Köppen (1846–1940) was born in St. Petersburg, Russia. His doctorate at the University of Leipzig studied the influence of temperature on plant growth. Köppen first formulated his famed classification of climates in about 1900, basing it on the principle that the distribution of vegetation is a reflection of the climates that permit their growth.

Humid, tropical climates

Humid, tropical climates are those with high annual rainfall and an average monthly temperature of at least 64°F (18°C). Areas with this climate stretch from Amazonia, across equatorial Africa to Malaysia and Indonesia, and consist mainly of tropical rain forest.

RAIN FOREST

The combination of persistent warmth and plentiful, year-round rainfall encourages the development of dense rain forest in many tropical regions. The high rainfall found in these areas is due to extensive cumulonimbus clouds that form in the belt of low pressure known as the Inter-Tropical Convergence Zone (ITCZ). The north-south seasonal migration of the ITCZ means that the rainfall is not spread evenly from month to month but peaks twice a year in many areas. These peaks are produced when the ITCZ moves to its

TROPICAL FRUIT
The banana plant thrives in hot, humid conditions, and it is cultivated throughout the tropics.

northernmost location in August, and its southernmost position in February. When rain falls, it is most common during the early to mid-afternoon as the shower clouds build.

Annual rainfall generally exceeds 5 ft (1.5 m) in rainforest areas, although in mountainous locations, orographic uplift can increase that total to as much as 13 ft (4 m). The low latitude of these climate regions means that there is only a small variation in the length of the day and the height of the Sun throughout the year. The annual range of temperature is small, typically 6°F (3°C) or less, making for a stable climate. Although this climate lies along or close to the equator, the maximum daytime temperature is moderated by

JUNGLE MIST

Misty conditions are common in the humid, calm interior of the jungle. Just a slight overnight fall in temperature can produce mist or fog.

SAMPLE CLIMATE—IQUITOS, PERU

Iquitos is a city that lies in the upper Amazon rain forest on the banks of the Amazon River. The climate is hot, and the annual temperature range is small—only about 4°F (2°C). The very slightly lower monthly temperatures occur during the middle of the year, from June to October. Rainfall is plentiful, with the highest values during the marginally warmer months from November to May. The total annual rainfall is about 6 ft (2 m).

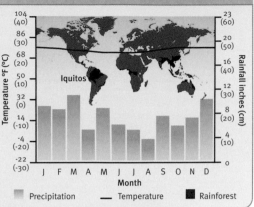

Precipitation — Temperature ■ Rainforest

BIODIVERSITY
More than half the world's species of flora and fauna are found in tropical climates, which are typically covered by a dense tree canopy.

FOREST FIRES
There can be times of drought in rain forests. Large fires can break out, as happened in Borneo in 2004.

humidity and cloud. During the night, cooling of the very humid atmosphere occasionally leads to misty conditions and sometimes even fog in rain forest areas.

MONSOON RAINS

The word "monsoon" comes from the Arabic word *mausim*, meaning "season." This climate type is characterized by a seasonal change in wind direction, accompanied by a marked change in rainfall. There is usually an annual rainfall of more than 5 ft (1.5 m). In southwest India, the southwesterly monsoon winds blow across the Indian Ocean, bringing heavy rains in the summer. In contrast, the winter is dry, due to the influence of northeasterly winds from northern India and the Himalayas. The elevated plateau of Tibet is thought to play a critical role in the evolution of this monsoon. By acting as a heat source at high altitude, it influences atmospheric circulation significantly, particularly

during the build-up of the summer monsoon. The southern coast of West Africa, overlooking the Gulf of Guinea, is another monsoon region where summertime southwesterlies blow in. They are relatively cool, after flowing across the equator from the southern-hemisphere winter. During winter in the northern hemisphere, the dominant wind blows off the Sahara, producing the warm, dust-laden Harmattan wind (see p.177).

Case study: South America

When it comes to climate, South America almost has it all. Stretching from the subtropical latitudes of the Caribbean Sea in the north, to the storm-riddled Cape Horn at 55 degrees south, its landscape ranges from arid desert to the humid greenhouse of the Amazon jungle.

THE LUNGS OF THE WORLD

The Amazon rain forest covers 2.1 million sq miles (5.5 million sq km)—half of the planet's remaining rain forest—and is vital because vegetation plays an important role in the chemical make-up of the atmosphere. During photosynthesis, plants take carbon dioxide from the air and release oxygen into it, which is critical to regulating the concentration of these gases in the atmosphere. This gaseous exchange is at its height in regions where vegetation is very "active" —jungles where the rainfall and temperature create vigorous growth all year round.

About 20 percent of the Amazon rain forest has been destroyed since the 1970s, for timber and to create land for farming. A sharp rise in global commodity prices has stimulated deforestation so that the land can be farmed for crops, an

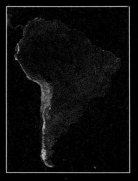

VARIED LAND
The Andes mountains stretch over 4,400 miles (7,000 km) from north to south, with the Atacama Desert lying to their west.

activity that is seriously detrimental to the local climate. Logging and burning also release carbon dioxide, contributing to global climate change.

THE ANDES

The thin longitudinal barrier of the Andes mountain range has its own climate but also plays a role in shaping climates some distance away. The chain stretches from Colombia and Venezuela in the north to the spectacular snow-capped peaks of southern Argentina and Chile. The Andes chain receives most of its precipitation on its western side, as winds blow ashore from the Pacific Ocean. This accounts for the dryness of areas to the east of the mountains, such as Patagonia and the southern Pampas lowlands, which cover parts of Argentina, Uruguay, and Brazil.

BRAZIL'S NORDESTE

Nordeste province is the most easterly region of Brazil. The area's short rainy season arrives when the Inter-Tropical Convergence Zone (ITCZ; see p.68),

PATAGONIA
Scrub grass covers tracts of Patagonia, which is starved of precipitation by the barrier of the Andes mountains.

SHRINKING RAIN FOREST
Current predictions are that a further
40 percent of the Amazon jungle will
be destroyed in the next 20 years.

in which constant heat and
humidity to the north and
south create a cycle of warm
updrafts and rain clouds,
migrates south during March
and April. Although the coast
of the region is humid, inland
the semi-arid "sertão" suffers
from severe drought when the
rainy season fails to arrive.
Research has shown that the periods
of drought are linked to unusual
surface temperature differences
between the two hemispheres in
the Atlantic Ocean, which cause a
shift in the ITCZ's location.

THE DRIEST PLACE ON EARTH

Sandwiched between the Andes and the
Pacific Ocean is one of the world's driest
places. The thin coastal strip of the
Atacama Desert holds the world record
for no, or very little, rainfall over many

SNOWY PEAKS
The peaks of the Andes Mountains have their own
extreme climate. There may be rain forests just
miles away from permanent snow and ice.

years—the evidence suggests that no
rain fell there between 1570 and 1971.
This desert region is dominated by the
persistent sinking air of the southeast
Pacific anticyclone, which prevents
warm, moist air from rising and forming
clouds. Added to this, the sea surface is
too cool to stimulate convective cloud
that could provide downpours.

Subtropical, arid climates

The world's hot deserts are mainly found across the subtropical continents, where the descending branch of the Hadley cells occurs. The subsiding air creates almost year-round clear skies. Narrow deserts also run along subtropical coastlines on the western sides of continents.

CONTINENTAL DESERTS

The world's hot deserts vary in size. By far the largest is the desert zone that links the Sahara in North Africa, the Arabian desert, and the Thar desert of Pakistan. In the northern hemisphere, hot arid regions exist in northern Mexico and the southwest US; in the southern hemisphere, they include the Kalahari and Australian deserts. Some arid areas are produced by rain shadows in the lee of extensive mountain ranges, such as Patagonia in Argentina and parts of the High Plains, east of the Rockies. Other deserts are a great distance from sources of water and not affected by precipitation-forming weather. The Gobi and Sinkiang deserts of China are the result of both of

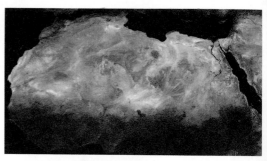

SAHARA FROM SPACE
The surface of the Sahara reflects about a third of the solar radiation falling upon the desert—otherwise temperatures would be even hotter.

these influences. Extreme aridity occurs in deserts affected by year-round atmospheric subsidence. Rarely, rain falls during the cooler season when, for example, a mid-latitude frontal system brings bands of rain into the subtropics. The intense surface heating in summer may occasionally spark a shower, but any rain is likely to evaporate before it reaches the surface.

LIFE IN THE DESERT
Tall saguaro cactuses in the Sonoran Desert of Arizona are specially adapted to living in the harsh arid environment.

DESERT DUNES

Some deserts contain extensive regions of sand, which are shaped by the wind into dunes. Large dune fields are known as "ergs."

The world's highest temperatures are found during the summer in subtropical continental deserts, where highs commonly exceed 110°F (45°C). During summer nights, temperatures can fall below 68°F (20°C). Winters are cooler, and temperatures can drop to below freezing during the starry desert nights.

COASTAL DESERTS

Very dry, coastal deserts are strongly related to the presence of cool ocean currents that flow toward the equator, adjacent to the coastline. These cool the air, which makes it much drier and results in cloud, but no rain. Coastal deserts are found in northern Chile, Peru, Namibia, Morocco, and Western Australia.

SAMPLE CLIMATE—LOVELOCK, NEVADA

Lovelock, a town in the Nevada Desert, is a good example of the climate of continental hot deserts. It has very low average annual rainfall, which occurs mainly during the winter. The large annual temperature range spans a monthly average of about 85°F (30°C) in the summer to about 32°F (0°C) during the "rainy" season. Most rain in Nevada falls on the lee side of the Sierra Nevada range.

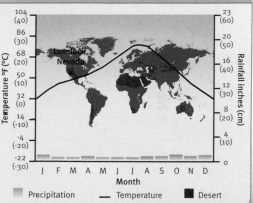

Precipitation — Temperature ■ Desert

Temperate climates

The temperate classification includes a range of climates, all of which have an average temperature in the coldest month of between 64°F (18°C) and 27°F (-3°C), and in the warmest month above 50°F (10°C). These climates have a wet summer or winter, or are wet all year.

MILD CLIMATES

There are four subdivisions of the temperate climate. Mediterranean climates occur on the western sides of continents between the latitudes of 30 degrees and 45 degrees. Summers are hot and dry, while winters are mild and wet. Humid subtropical climates usually occur in the interiors of continents, or on their east coasts, between the latitudes of 25 degrees and 45 degrees. They experience humid summers. Maritime temperate climates occur on the western sides of continents between the latitudes of 45 degrees and 55 degrees, and are dominated by changeable weather. Maritime subarctic climates occur poleward of maritime temperate climates, and form the edge of the temperate zone.

WET ALL YEAR ROUND

Temperate regions with no marked dry season principally cover mid-latitude and subtropical continental margins, and can be divided into areas with a cool, warm, or hot summer. The former is the case in Iceland, which experiences a maritime subarctic climate. The intermediate type is found across the British Isles, British Columbia, and New Zealand, which are maritime temperate regions. The warmest

TEMPERATE LANDSCAPE
Scotland typifies a maritime temperate climate, with high rainfall and a verdant landscape.

SAMPLE CLIMATE—GUANGZHOU, CHINA

Guangzhou, in southern China, experiences a humid subtropical climate. It has a mild winter and a hot summer, with a fairly large annual temperature range of around 27°F (15°C). The rainfall pattern shows a marked summer maximum and winter minimum. The wet, hot season is caused by the southwesterly and southerly flow of the summer monsoon, in contrast to the relatively cool and much drier days of the winter.

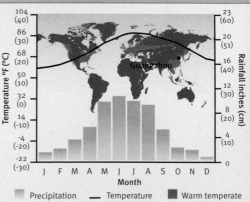

Precipitation   — Temperature   ■ Warm temperate

GREEN PASTURES
In England, which experiences a maritime temperate climate, the mild, damp weather is suitable for sheep and dairy farming.

climate with no prolonged dry season is found over the southeast US, southeast Brazil, and southeast China, which are classified as humid subtropical areas.

DRY SUMMER
Temperate regions with dry summers are sub-divided into those with warm or hot summers. Areas with warm summers are considered to have a Mediterranean climate (see pp.156–57). Regions with hot summers are found in limited areas such

SEASONAL CHANGE
Temperate regions have four distinct seasons, with cooler temperatures in the winter, but can experience unpredictable weather throughout the year.

as southwestern Australia, California's Central Valley, and the central Mediterranean, including Sicily and Malta. Vegetation commonly consists of mixed forest of short trees and shrubs.

DRY WINTER
Temperate regions with a dry winter tend to be 20 degrees to 30 degrees either side of the equator. Areas that experience a hot summer include a belt stretching from northern India, through northern Burma into northern Vietnam, and an area running from Zimbabwe to Tanzania. Regions with a warm summer include the higher regions of eastern South Africa and Ethiopia.

DECIDUOUS FOREST
New England is famous for its temperate deciduous forest, which is characterized by trees that shed their leaves and lie dormant during the cold winters.

Mediterranean climates

Named after the distinct climate region in southern Europe, Mediterranean climates also occur in other areas of the world where warm, dry summers are dominated by the poleward shift of the Hadley cell. Winters are wet due to frequent cyclonic disturbances.

THE ANNUAL ROUND

The low rainfall and prolonged sunshine of the Mediterranean region makes it a popular tourist destination. These large-scale stable conditions are caused by a persistent area of high pressure. From June to August, the region is dominated by the subsiding air of the subtropical anticyclone, marking the poleward limit of the Hadley cell's northward migration.

The vast Sahara Desert lies not far to the south, and sometimes the whole of the Mediterranean Sea and the land just to the north of it are engulfed by dangerously hot weather originating from North Africa. In recent years, extreme heat has claimed a large number of lives, particularly among the elderly. In July 2000, temperatures rose to 113°F (45°C) in parts of Greece, leading to power failures in Athens and forest fires caused by the parched conditions.

OLIVE GROVES
The Mediterranean region of Europe is famed for its rich agriculture, including the widespread cultivation of olives.

TUSCAN VARIATIONS
In the hills of Tuscany in Italy, the weather is slightly cooler and wetter than the typical coastal Mediterranean climate.

Similarly devastating heatwaves occurred in 2003, 2005, and 2007 in regions stretching from Portugal to in the west to Cyprus in the east.

The Mediterranean has unsettled weather during the winter. A significant number of rain-bearing cyclones form to the south of France and in the eastern Mediterranean Sea. These systems move eastward to produce poor weather in the central and eastern parts of the region.

SAMPLE CLIMATE—CAPE TOWN, SOUTH AFRICA

Cape Town's dry season lasts from November to March. On average, there are 10 hours of sunshine per day during summer, but the region does not suffer the deadly heatwaves of the Mediterranean, with average maximums of about 77°F (25°C). On hot summer days, a strong southeasterly wind, known locally as the Cape Doctor, often blows in off the ocean, relieving the worst of the heat. Average annual rainfall is 20 in (50 cm).

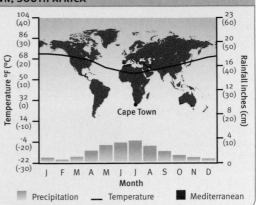

Cape Town

Month

Precipitation   — Temperature   ■ Mediterranean

MEDITERRANEAN VITICULTURE
All Mediterranean-type climates, including southern Europe, South Africa, and southern Australia, are ideal for growing vines for wine production.

This means that Iberia generally sees more dry winter days than Italy or Crete. Temperatures are mostly moderate, varying from chilly nights in central Spain to mild evenings on the coast of Malta.

SOUTHERN CLIMES

There are a few relatively small coastal areas of South Africa and Australia whose climate patterns mimic the seasonal variation of the Mediterranean climate. They fall under the influence of the southern hemisphere Hadley cell's southward migration to produce dry and sunny conditions. In the winter, these regions lie in the path of traveling frontal depressions that are brought from the Southern Ocean by westerly winds. Both these southern hemisphere regions are, like their northern hemisphere counterpart, famed for their wine production.

COASTAL IDYLL
The hot Mediterranean summer makes places such as the French Riviera popular with vacationers.

Cold, continental interior climates

In the higher northern latitudes, vast stretches of the continents experience a dry climate with a long, severe winter, a short summer, and rapid temperature change during spring and fall. These regions are characterized by the extensive forest known as the taiga.

TAIGA REGIONS

The climate type found in taiga (or softwood forest) areas is classified on the basis of the warmest month of the year having an average temperature of at least 50°F (10°C), and the coldest being below 27°F (-3°C). Large annual temperature ranges typify the region, which is covered by millions of square miles of taiga, comprising mainly fir and spruce. Covering most of inland Alaska, Canada, Sweden, Finland, Norway, and Russia, as well as parts of the northern continental United States and Japan, the taiga is the world's largest terrestrial ecosystem.

PERMAFROST
Permanently frozen ground, known as permafrost, stretches across vast tracts of the northern continents where mean annual temperature is less than 32°F (0°C).

The combination of temperature, low rainfall, and the short summer means that the growing season is limited across the taiga. The long-lived and intense cold results in frozen ground that may, in a few places, thaw out for the summer

EDGE OF THE TAIGA
Taiga forest gives way to tundra to the north of its range. In tundra regions, tree growth is hindered by low temperatures and short growing seasons.

SIBERIAN TAIGA
The trees of the northern Siberian taiga stand among an understory of dwarf shrubs. A carpet of mosses and lichens covers the ground.

FROZEN LAKE, CANADA
Lakes and other water courses freeze for much of the year. Melting ice dams can lead to flooding in the spring.

months. A temperature of 50°F (10°C) or more in the warmest month is necessary for the forest's survival. To the north of the region, on the cold side of the 50°F (10°C) isotherm (a contour linking points of equal temperature), tundra dominates. To the south lie the steppes. The southern hemisphere has no taiga because of the markedly different shape of the smaller, narrower continents found there.

WINTER CHILL

The temperature decreases rapidly in the fall, which lasts from August to September. The winter is long and severe across the taiga—the period over which the monthly mean temperature is near or below 32°F (0°C) typically lasts from October to April. Precipitation is low in winter because the season is dominated by persistent anticyclones—areas of high pressure and clear skies—across Eurasia and North America.

BRIEF SUMMER

Rapid warming takes place from April to June. The brief warm season experiences about the same proportion of annual precipitation as the much longer winter, with summer rain falling as frontal depressions pass over a region.

SAMPLE CLIMATE—ARCHANGEL, RUSSIA

The city of Archangel, or Arkhangelsk, lies on the Dvina River near the White Sea in the far north of European Russia. It experiences a large annual temperature range, with a mean temperature of 9°F (-13°C) in January and February, rising to 61°F (16°C) in July. Temperature change is swift in the fall and spring, while the winter is long. Frosts can hit in late August, and ice may begin to form on lakes during September.

Precipitation   — Temperature   Cool continental

Polar climates

The two polar regions experience slightly different climates, due to geological differences. The Arctic is mostly a frozen ocean, while Antarctica is a continent covered in thick glacial ice. What both have in common is a lack of warm summers, with temperatures rarely exceeding 50°F (10°C).

THE ARCTIC CLIMATE

Atmospheric circulation in the Arctic means that precipitation and thermal patterns vary a great deal across the region. The seas of northern Norway and northwest Russia are kept free of ice by heat transported by the ocean. West of this relatively mild and wet area are Greenland and Arctic Canada, which experience much colder conditions. The floating sea ice that extends across much of the Arctic basin in winter is just several feet thick, and the ocean circulates underneath it throughout the year.

Summers are cloudy and less cold, as large areas of stratiform cloud linger above the open water and partly melted sea ice. The long hours of daylight warm the Arctic in summer, although heating from the low Sun is fairly weak, particularly across the highly reflective surfaces of the snow and ice.

THE ANTARCTIC CLIMATE

The land in the interior of Antarctica is more than 2½ miles (4.5 km) high in places, and the ice is more than 2 miles (3 km) thick in many areas. The high elevation combined with the high latitude means that temperatures are very cold during the long, polar night. The interior is arid because the temperature is so low that the air cannot contain enough water vapor to produce snow.

ARCTIC MOSS
Only tiny plants can survive the harsh Arctic winter. Tundra moss lives in the frozen soil thanks to its very shallow roots.

SAMPLE CLIMATE—POINT BARROW, ALASKA

Point Barrow is not the coldest place on Earth, but it illustrates the dry nature of the world's highest latitudes. Its annual snowfall of 5 in (13 cm) is similar to the Sahara's rainfall. Its annual temperature range is about 63°F (35°C), a result of the continental character of the region while the Arctic Ocean is frozen. Only from June to September is the average daily temperature above 32°F (0°C).

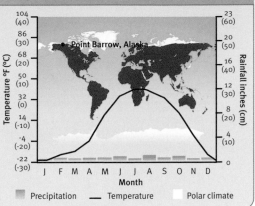

Precipitation — Temperature — Polar climate

Also, it is far removed from the snow-producing weather systems around the coast, where most snowfall occurs.

OZONE DEPLETION

Ozone is continually created and destroyed in the stratosphere. It is produced principally in the tropics, where the solar radiation is strongest, and is then transported to higher latitudes by the flow of air through the stratosphere.

ANTARCTIC OZONE HOLE
The hole in the ozone layer is largest in September, at the end of the harsh Antarctic winter. In this image, ozone-rich air is marked in green, yellow, and red; purple shows low levels of ozone.

In the winter, the circulation at stratospheric levels above Antarctica is like a spinning "well" of air. The strong westerlies at the edge confine the air "inside" so it gets colder and colder during the polar night. Temperatures can plummet to below -110°F (-80°C), creating icy stratospheric clouds, which provide the conditions necessary for manmade CFC gases to destroy the ozone. This process eats away at the ozone so that its concentration falls to dangerously low levels. In the spring, the ozone recovers to near-previous levels, resulting in gradual but continuous depletion.

ANTARCTIC MOUNTAINS
Much of Antarctica consists of mountain ranges or high plateaux. The continent's average elevation is 8,200 ft (2,500 m).

"THEN CAME THE WILD WEATHER,
COME SLEET OR SNOW, WE WILL
STAND BY EACH OTHER,
HOWEVER IT BLOW."

Simon Dach

LOCAL CLIMATES

Climate zones can be classified into categories with broad
weather characteristics in common. However, on a more local
level there is a natural variability within these zones due to
surface features and geographic location. Urban growth also
causes significant changes to the local climate.

PRESSURE SEESAWS

On a regional level, climate can be
affected by a phenomenon known as a
"pressure seesaw." These are changes
in the strength of the flow of air mass
between highs and lows in extensive
areas where there is a regular pattern of
pressure systems. One seesaw takes place
across the Pacific Ocean, where the
difference in pressure between the
southeast Pacific high and the Indonesian
low fluctuates, changing the strength of
the trade winds and the location of warm
water across the equatorial Pacific. This
is known as the El Niño Southern
Oscillation, often simplified to El Niño (see
pp.166–67), and it can cause catastrophic
regional weather disturbances.

The characteristic winds that are
produced by pressure seesaws can be
familiar to a local population as they
often signify a particular change in the
weather. These local winds may be given
names, such as the Harmattan, which
blows off the Sahara Desert.

MONITORING EL NIÑO

For most of the 20th century, El Niño was
thought of as a largely local phenomenon,
but the major El Niño event of 1982–83 led
to an upsurge of interest within the
scientific community.
Today, wind speeds and
ocean temperatures
are measured across
the equatorial
Pacific Ocean in
order to monitor
the evolution of an
El Niño event.

SYDNEY'S MICROCLIMATES
The Sydney area experiences seven different
microclimates, dependent on proximity to the
sea, urbanization, and height above sea level.

DESERT WIND
From November to March, the sandy Harmattan wind blows south from the Sahara into the Gulf of Guinea due to a regional pressure seesaw.

EFFECT OF ALTITUDE

Within climatic regions, most areas at the same height above sea level will experience a roughly similar temperature. The same cannot be said of areas at different heights: vertical changes in temperature are so strong that any climate regime can be markedly modified by the presence of a mountain chain. This is even true near the equator, for places such as the snow-capped peak of Kilimanjaro in Tanzania, Africa. The lower temperature in mountainous areas causes dramatic changes in the nature of the vegetation.

MOUNT EVEREST
Above the tree line, all mountainous regions experience a mountain climate, with cold temperatures and low precipitation year-round.

LOCAL MICROCLIMATES

Within a single region, local factors such as aspect, exposure, and soil type can produce significant microclimates—climates that occur on a very local level of perhaps just a few miles square. Some sites on sandy soil, for example, suffer lower minimum temperatures because the soil is dry. South-facing or north-facing slopes, in the northern and southern hemispheres respectively, are likely to see more convective cloud and possibly showers than the more shady slopes, as the greater exposure to sunlight results in higher evaporation. Microclimates also exist where bodies of water cool the local atmosphere, or in heavily urban areas where brick, concrete, and asphalt absorb the Sun's energy, heat up, and re-radiate that heat to the ambient air during the night.

El Niño

A phenomenon known as the El Niño Southern Oscillation causes massive change in the sea-surface temperature across the Pacific Ocean. This leads to dramatic variations in global weather, including floods and droughts, which follow a repeating but somewhat irregular cycle.

PRESSURE SENSITIVE

The normal distribution of atmospheric pressure over the Pacific Ocean is high pressure over the southeastern region and low pressure over the western equatorial area. The pressure gradient between these two centers creates latitudinal air circulation known as a Walker cell. Southeast trade winds blow at low levels within the Walker cell, driving warm water toward the western equatorial Pacific. This means that there is usually very warm water over the western equatorial ocean—around Indonesia, for example—and much cooler water along the west coast of equatorial South America. Every few years, the high-pressure area slowly weakens. The pressure difference between the centers lessens and then trade winds weaken and may even reverse to become weak westerlies. This change is known as the El Niño Southern Oscillation (ENSO). At other times, the high pressure

WATER TEMPERATURE IN A NORMAL YEAR
The warmer water of the Pacific is shown in red in this satellite image. It was taken during a normal year, so the warm area of water is in the west.

strengthens, and a zone of cooler water spreads across the central and eastern Pacific; this is known as La Niña.

Warm seas are a prime area for heavy rain and thunderstorms to form

Descending air brings dry conditions and high pressure

Accumulation of warm water

NORMAL YEAR
In normal years, the southeast trade winds cause warm water to accumulate in the western Pacific. Cooler water rises to the surface in the eastern Pacific.

South equatorial current

Southeast trade winds

Upwelling of cold, nutrient-rich waters

SHIFTING WARM WATER

The ENSO, usually known simply as El Niño (Spanish for "the boy"), can cause disastrous flooding in parts of South America. During El Niño, which may last for many months, the weakening trade winds, along with currents in the ocean, allow the warm water in the western equatorial Pacific to migrate slowly eastward over the course of a few months. Rising, showery air follows the large area of warm water, and the mainly dry islands in the central Pacific experience torrential downpours as the warm water slowly moves across them. When it arrives at the coasts of Peru and Ecuador, the rain may lead to flooding and mudslides. Conversely, the western Pacific may experience drought conditions.

La Niña (meaning "the girl") is the opposite to El Niño and often follows it, especially if El Niño was particularly strong. La Niña occurs when the trade winds strengthen and the warm water moves farther west than usual, with an upwelling of deeper, cooler water to the ocean surface in the eastern Pacific. The resulting heavy rainfall may bring flooding to the western Pacific, including Australia and Southeast Asia.

CALIFORNIAN STORMS
California is normally dry and sunny, but during El Niño years, the unusually heavy rainfall can cause flooding and mudslides.

AUSTRALIAN DROUGHT
El Niño brings warm, dry weather over the western Pacific. The lack of rainfall may cause severe drought in parts of Australia.

Southeast trade winds reversed or weakened

Descending air and high pressure brings warm, dry weather

Warm water increases the chance of heavy rain

EL NIÑO YEAR
During El Niño years, weaker trade winds mean that the warm water spreads eastward, replacing the usually cooler waters along the coast of South America.

Upwelling blocked by warm water

Warm water flows east, accumulating off South America

Case study: El Niño effects

El Niño and La Niña events markedly influence the weather within the Pacific Basin, most notably across the equatorial and tropical region. But they also affect the climate outside these areas, creating unusual weather conditions across the globe.

PACIFIC INFLUENCE

When an El Niño evolves, the Walker cell of air circulating latitudinally across the Pacific at the equator shifts eastward. Where the air in the cell is sinking, some regions suffer unusually dry seasons. For example, eastern Australia and Borneo are more susceptible to wildfires during an El Niño year, because vegetation becomes tinder-dry in the drought conditions. Other regions, where rising air creates deep clouds and thunderstorms, have unusually wet weather. For example, in Peru, torrential rains caused severe flooding in 1997 and 1998.

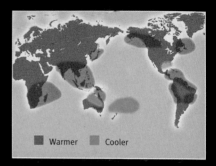

Warmer **Cooler**

TEMPERATURE EFFECTS OF EL NIÑO
An El Niño year affects different regions very differently. It may cause drought or flooding, and warmer or cooler than normal temperatures.

WIDESPREAD EFFECTS

The impact of El Niño is felt around the globe as air circulation patterns are altered. Deep convection across the central part of the Pacific Ocean carries relatively warm air high up into the troposphere. This warm air causes a pronounced Rossby wave in the jet stream that flows off Japan. The path of this high-level air current is changed, in turn changing the weather around it. As a consequence, the northwest of North America may be drier and warmer than average during an El Niño year, while the southeastern US may be cooler and wetter. A similar interaction with the jet stream occurs above the southern Pacific, leading to a risk of wetter than average summer weather across many parts of South America.

SUMMER RAIN IN BUENOS AIRES
People shelter from the heavy summer rain in Buenos Aires, Argentina. Northern Argentina may experience flooding during El Niño years.

FIRES IN INDONESIA
Wildfires increase in frequency and intensity during El Niño years. In Indonesia, in 1997 to 1998 and in 2006, the fires caused huge clouds of smoke that released more carbon dioxide into the atmosphere than would normally be released by the entire planet in one year.

When the warm water is in the central Pacific during an El Niño year, and the Walker cell shifts eastward, a mass of sinking air moves east to produce highs over the Caribbean Sea. Since cyclones normally form in areas of low pressure, this shift means that there are fewer tropical cyclones in the Caribbean than average during an El Niño event.

In East Africa, the seasonal rains may become exceptionally heavy during El Niño years. In 1997 and 1998,

DROUGHT IN AFRICA
West Africa may experience severe drought during El Niño years, when crops wither and livestock die.

torrential rain caused flooding that devastated crops in Sudan, and millions of people faced starvation. West Africa, by contrast, may experience drought.

ADVANCE WARNING
El Niño and La Niña events form and evolve slowly. Ocean surface temperature and other indicators are monitored every day via satellites to spot any anomalies. Areas likely to be affected receive warning of likely weather conditions months in advance, allowing them to prepare. Australia, for example, may be alerted to the increased risk of drought and bushfires.

North Atlantic Oscillation

The North Atlantic Oscillation (NAO), like the El Niño Southern Oscillation, is a large-scale pressure seesaw. The NAO is a significant cause of the year-to-year variability in winter weather across part of the northern hemisphere, from North America to western Russia.

HOW THE NAO WORKS

The NAO is a seesaw in pressure between the wintertime North Atlantic subtropical high—known as the Azores anticyclone—and the semi-permanent center of low atmospheric pressure between Iceland and Greenland—known as the Iceland low. This seesawing pressure governs the strength and direction of the prevailing westerly winds across the North Atlantic. When the pressure gradient is large—known as a "positive" phase—the strength of the westerly or southwesterly wind that blows from the subtropical to higher-latitude North Atlantic is strong. When there is a weaker pressure gradient, which is less common, it is known as a "negative" phase, and these winds are weaker. The NAO index, or indicator of the size of the effect, is based on monthly mean pressure in the Azores anticyclone and the Iceland low.

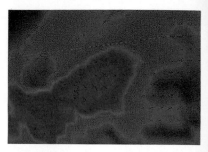

NAO INDEX
A positive NAO index (indicated by yellows and reds) causes the prevailing westerly North Atlantic winds to flow toward the northeast.

POSITIVE INDEX

A positive index occurs when the winter pressure gradient across the mid-latitude North Atlantic is larger than the long-term average. This brings a strong flow of mild, cloudy, and rain-laden air into northern Europe, carried by frontal depressions. Northern and central European winters tend to be wetter and milder than average. The larger difference also creates a stronger southwesterly circulation over the

POSITIVE NAO
A positive NAO index is linked to a strong flow of damp, mild air into northern Europe, resulting in wet and windy winters.

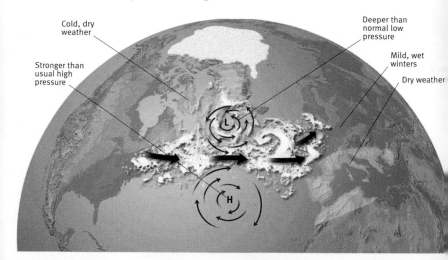

Cold, dry weather

Deeper than normal low pressure

Stronger than usual high pressure

Mild, wet winters

Dry weather

EFFECTS OF NEGATIVE AND POSITIVE NAO

Recent decades have seen a run of positive-index weather, which may be a cause of the raised winter temperatures seen in northern and central Europe. Such prolonged positive index weather has a detrimental effect on water resources in the Mediterranean. The region relies principally on wintertime frontal systems to provide rain, so in recent times the rarely seen negative-index seasons have been a welcome source of precipitation.

Positive index: dry winter in Sicily

Negative index: snow in Berlin

Positive index: wet and windy in Scotland

Negative index: rain in Rome

eastern half of the North American continent, which lessens the risk of Arctic air plunging southward. This produces warmer winters over the eastern United States.

NEGATIVE NAO

Weaker centers of low and high pressure in the North Atlantic Ocean result in a flow of cloudy, moist air into the Mediterranean during the winter.

NEGATIVE INDEX

The track of Atlantic depressions tends to run further south in a negative phase. Negative-index winters are characterized by cooler than average weather across northern and central Europe, and more disturbed, wet weather to the south, over much of the Mediterranean.

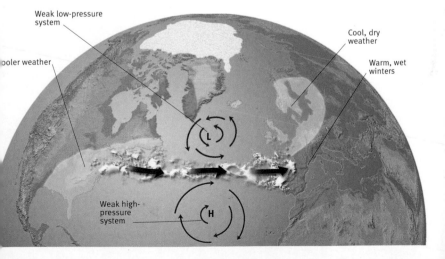

Weak low-pressure system

Cool, dry weather

Warm, wet winters

cooler weather

Weak high-pressure system

Urban microclimates

Large-scale migration into urban areas is leading to substantial growth in the size of cities. This means that urban microclimates, which may be just a few miles across, are likely to become more pronounced, as large cities exhibit signs of the "urban heat island" effect.

HEAT ISLANDS

An urban heat island is an area that is significantly warmer than its surroundings. The principal cause is that the materials from which buildings are made absorb sunshine during the day—into the fabric of the buildings— and then release it most strongly during the evening and night. The color of the materials used is also a factor. A black surface, such as an asphalt road, can heat up to be more than 70°F (40°C) warmer than a white surface.

A heat island is hottest under anticyclonic conditions when winds are very light and sunshine is prolonged. Heat-island effects are lessened under

HIGH AND LOW RISE
There may be more than one microclimate within a city—high-rise areas generate and radiate heat, while parks and bodies of water cool the surrounding area.

windy, unstable conditions because any heat is transported away by wind. Broadly speaking, the size of the heat island depends on the size of the city. The prediction is that, by 2015, there will be 21 megacities, each with a population of more than 10 million.

WETTER CITIES

When heat islands develop, the city's temperature can be several degrees higher than the surrounding countryside

ASIA BY NIGHT
The mass of well-lit urban areas in East Asia indicates the large number of locations that may experience the heat island effect.

CITY HEAT
False-color thermal images from satellites depict temperature change across land and sea, including the impact of large urban areas.

and suburban areas. This warmth can be great enough to create convective cloud, caused by rising warm air, which may result in showers falling over cities but not over the neighboring regions.

It is believed that a city's warmth can also enhance pre-existing showers that may drift across urban areas. Cities can be up to 10 percent wetter than the surrounding countryside during showery wet seasons, and they are thought to increase showery rain across a zone 30–45 miles (50–70 km) downwind of them.

URBAN AIR QUALITY

The health problem of smog in some cities has worsened due to rapidly increasing traffic volumes. Photochemical smog forms when sunlight hits pollutants in the air, such as nitrogen oxides from vehicle exhausts. The impact of smog depends on whether conditions are still or windy. Its dispersal also depends on street patterns and whether there are "canyons" between high-rise buildings to trap the pollution.

CITY STORM
Heat rising from a city can generate cumulonimbus clouds and a lightning storm, while the surrounding countryside may remain dry.

How local winds form

Winds can blow on a large, global scale or on a much smaller, local scale. Over land, features such as mountains can give rise to local winds. In coastal areas, winds flow between areas of high and low pressure that form when the land and the sea are heated by the Sun.

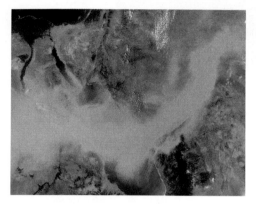

RED SEA WIND
A local wind called the Hababai blows from Arabia to Egypt, picking up sand on its way and creating sandstorms, such as this one over the Red Sea.

SEA AND LAND BREEZES

Many coastlines around the world experience sea and land breezes. Sea breezes occur when the prevailing weather conditions are favorable, and when the land is warmed sufficiently to heat the air above it and set the air in motion. The ideal weather is an anticyclone, producing just light breezes. If the day starts bright and sunny, the land will heat up much more quickly than the adjacent sea. After a few hours, this will lead to lower pressure forming inland, in contrast to slightly higher pressure over the sea. This pressure gradient drives the sea air inland. It moves as a kind of front, leading the cooler and moister sea breeze. At the leading edge of this air, the sea and land air converge and rise along a line that is more or less parallel to the coast. This convergence is sometimes marked by a line of cumulus clouds. Higher up, the air returns seaward and sinks over the water to complete a circuit. The sea air can penetrate more than 50 miles (80 km) inland if a strong sea breeze is established.

As the Sun goes down, the land cools more quickly than the sea, resulting in a seaward flow of cool air that is felt as a land breeze. This forms a circulation of air that is the reverse of the daytime one.

KATABATIC AND ANABATIC WINDS

Falling, or katabatic, winds are those that flow downslope under particular atmospheric conditions. They occur typically in mountainous or hilly areas when the sky is mainly clear and the winds are light or calm. These conditions

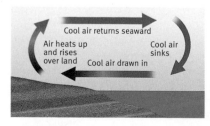

DAYTIME SEA BREEZE
During the day, the land heats up faster than the water. The air warms over the land and rises. Cooler air flows in to replace it, creating a sea breeze.

Cool air returns seaward
Air heats up and rises over land
Cool air sinks
Cool air drawn in

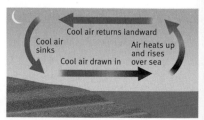

NIGHTTIME LAND BREEZE
At night, the land cools more quickly than the sea, and the airflow is reversed. Similar winds develop over large lakes, such as the Great Lakes.

Cool air returns landward
Cool air sinks
Air heats up and rises over sea
Cool air drawn in

UPSLOPE BREEZE
Anabatic, or rising, winds occur when the air in the sunlight at the top of a slope warms through convection. This creates a low-pressure area into which cooler air from the valley floor flows.

DOWNSLOPE BREEZE
In mountain areas, high ground loses heat rapidly at night. The air over the high ground cools and becomes denser, then flows downhill as a katabatic wind.

allow the air near the slopes to cool and become denser at night, before gently flowing downslope. Katabatic winds are usually light. However, in some places they can develop into strong gales. In Antarctica, air flows downslope from the icy interior towards the ocean, via valleys and gullies in the surface. The dense, chilled air is driven by gravity to form katabatic winds

OCEANIC WINDS
Winds are stronger over the ocean than over land because there is less friction between air and water than between air and land. There is no land in the Southern Ocean, so winds there regularly reach near-tropical cyclone speeds.

that are often very strong. On the coast, they can last for days, reaching tropical cyclone force or more.

Anabatic (rising) winds typically occur on calm, sunny days. The sides of a valley often receive more sunlight than the valley floor, particularly in winter, so warm up more during the day, heating the air above them. The warm air rises, drawing cool air up the slope to replace it. This creates a light, upslope wind.

Local winds

There are many local winds that blow in different regions around the world, ranging from hot to cold, destructive to relieving, and seasonal to all-year-round. The examples that follow illustrate the rich diversity in the winds themselves and their effect on surrounding areas.

Mistral

LOCATION Mediterranean

WEATHER Cold or cool, clear skies

SEASON Any, but strongest in winter and spring

RISKS Possible damage, strong gusts

The Mistral funnels down the Rhône Valley in southern France and shoots out across the Gulf of Lyon into the Mediterranean Sea as a narrow, powerful stream of cold mountain air. The wind develops in two ways. When a low to the east and a high to the west sit further north across France, Buys-Ballot's Law (see p.71) states that the wind will be a northerly. A low developing in the Gulf of Lyon also creates the atmospheric conditions for a northerly wind to blow down the Rhône Valley. The Mistral is squeezed down the narrow valley, and gains strength from katabatic air flow from the adjacent massifs—areas of high plateaux and mountains in central France. The resultant wind may reach 60 mph (90 kph), and it has been known to topple trains in the southern sector of

the Rhône Valley. The Mistral may occur during any month, but it is usually strongest from December to April, and is weaker, and least likely to produce strong flow, from June to November.

MEDITERRANEAN WINDS

Many winds blow around the Mediterranean Sea. In summer, dusty southerlies, such as the Sirocco and the Leveche, blow up from the Sahara, bringing hot air that causes heat waves and forest fires. Cold, katabatic winds, such as the Mistral and the Bora, blow down from Europe during winter. By contrast, warm föhn winds blow down the lee of the Alps away from the sea, warming central Europe.

Mistral · Föhn · Bora · Leveche · Sirocco · Sirocco

Harmattan

LOCATION North Africa
WEATHER Cool, hazy
SEASON Winter
RISKS Very poor visibility in thick haze

In winter, North Africa is dominated by a subtropical anticyclone that extends over it from the North Atlantic. Occasionally, dry air flows down from the north in the form of a cold front marked by a thick haze that can last several days. This is the Harmattan, and it collects dust as it passes over the Sahara Desert. Sometimes the dust generated in a strong Harmattan blows into the North Atlantic, occasionally stretching all the way to the Caribbean.

Santa Ana

LOCATION Western North America
WEATHER Warm, clear skies, dry
SEASON Fall to spring
RISKS Wild fires encroaching on urban areas

The Santa Ana is a dry, hot wind named after the Santa Ana canyon in southern California. It begins when an anticyclone develops over the high-altitude Great Basin, between the Sierra Nevada and the Rocky Mountains, in the western part of North America. These conditions generate a northeasterly katabatic wind that flows across southern California and out into the Pacific Ocean. The wind becomes warm and dry as air rushes down the Californian canyons. It generally coincides with clear skies, and the combination of windy, sunny, and parched conditions dries out vegetation to provide tinder for forest fires in the region.

The Santa Ana can create chaos, particularly across the Los Angeles basin, where homes have been built in forested areas that are at risk of wildfires. Once the fires have started, the gusty winds fan the flames furiously, spreading the fire at a dangerous pace.

Mountain climates

The height of land influences the climate, and the cold at higher levels is often exacerbated by the strong winds found in the middle and upper troposphere. High mountains can also affect the climate some distance away by producing dry rain-shadow regions.

TEMPERATURE FALL

High-altitude regions are generally much colder than lower parts of the Earth's surface. Air pressure decreases with altitude since there is a smaller mass of atmosphere above, and as the pressure decreases, air expands and cools. This happens at quite a rapid rate when the air is "dry." As the air is forced up and over high ground, it will cool by 17.6°F (9.8°C) for every 3,300 ft (1,000 m) of ascent. For example, cloud-free, sea-level air with a temperature of 68°F (20°C) will cool to about 14°F (-10°C) at the crest of a 10,000 ft (3,000 m) mountain or ridge. If the air is cloudy, it will still cool as it ascends, but at a slower rate, depending on how much water vapor there is to condense. When air sinks to the lee of high ground, the gradual increase in pressure compresses and warms it at the same rate as it cools when ascending.

WIND INCREASE

Wind speeds increase with height because higher in the atmosphere, the air is less affected by friction with the Earth's surface. This strengthening of winds high in the atmosphere can produce jet streams in the upper troposphere. Many mountain peaks rise up into the middle and even upper troposphere, where strong winds are more common than at lower altitudes.

PRECIPITATION AT HIGH ALTITUDES

Some of the world's snowiest regions are over mountains on the western regions of mid-latitude continents, where frontal depressions sweep in from the oceans. As the clouds rise over the mountains, they produce precipitation in the

THIN AIR

Oxygen is in short supply on high mountains, such as Everest. At its summit, air pressure is just 300 hPa—less than one third the pressure at sea level.

VOLCANOES

The subtropical oceans, which are dominated by dry, anticyclonic conditions, have a scattering of islands with tall volcanic peaks. For example, Mount Teide on Tenerife in the Canary Islands reaches just over 12,100 ft (3,700 m). On such islands, the lower levels have cloudy, wet weather, and lush vegetation grows on the exposed coasts. Higher up the islands, the conditions are drier and there is less vegetation.

form of snow. The Rockies in the west of North America, for example, receive some of the highest snowfall totals in the world. The combination of high winds, precipitation, and low temperatures often results in blizzard conditions on mountains.

At very high altitudes, the air is so cold that it cannot hold enough water vapor to produce substantial snowfall. This is particularly true of mountains that are far from major seas, oceans, and storm tracks.

Mountains also affect climate by creating rain

TEMPERATURE DECLINE
The foot of a mountain may have rich vegetation, while the peak is covered in ice. The point above which the environment is unable to sustain large vegetation or trees is known as the treeline.

shadows. Air blowing from the leeward side of mountains can become warm and dry. This lack of rainfall on the far side of a mountain range can produce very dry regions, such as the Atacama Desert in Chile, South America.

KILIMANJARO
Although it is close to the equator, Kilimanjaro in Tanzania, at 19,340 ft (5,895 m), is high enough to have a snow-topped peak. This glacial ice is now retreating, possibly due to global warming.

Climate extremes

The weather within any given climate zone can vary greatly from one region to another. Some places experience extreme weather conditions, such as torrential rainfall or severe drought, on a regular basis, and a few of these have produced astonishing weather records.

TEMPERATURE EXTREMES

The highest temperature ever recorded was 135.9°F (57.7°C) at Al' Aziziyah, just south of Tripoli in Libya on September 13, 1922. This reading was exceptional for the area, which rarely experiences extreme heat. The place with the highest annual average temperature is Dallol in the Danakil Depression of Ethiopia, with a yearly mean of 94°F (34.4°C). The lowest temperature on record is -128.5°F (-89.2°C) at Vostock in Antarctica on July 21, 1983, taken during the depth of the polar night.

DEATH VALLEY
The second highest temperature ever recorded was 134°F (56.7°C) in Death Valley, a desert in the Southwest.

RECORD RAINFALL

Surrounded by a warm tropical ocean, the Hawaiian islands receive large amounts of rainfall. The highest long-term annual rainfall is 38 ft (11.68 m) at

ATACAMA DESERT
The Atacama Desert in northern Chile is kept dry in part by the cold Humboldt Current in the Pacific Ocean. Some parts of the desert receive virtually no rain.

Mount Wai'ale'ale on the Hawaiian island of Kaua'i. The record for an individual year occurred at Cherrapunji in India, where 86.8 ft (26.46 m) fell from August 1, 1860 to July 31, 1861. The same location, which is in India's tea-growing district, holds the records for the most rain to fall in a month— 30.5 ft

CHERRAPUNJI
The wettest place on Earth, Cherrapunji in India, receives rain from both the winter and summer monsoons, but rain is heaviest in the summer.

(9.3 m)—and the most to fall in a day— 6 ft (1.84 m). The driest recorded place in the world is Quillagua in Chile, in the Atacama Desert. Between 1964 and 2001, the average annual rainfall was just 0.02 in (0.5 mm). The longest dry period

ANTARCTIC BLIZZARDS
Strong winds blow across Antarctica, making the temperature feel even lower, and creating blizzards. Penguins huddle together to survive.

ever recorded was the 142 months from October 1903 at Arica in Chile. This coastal strip of northern Chile is affected by high pressure from the South Pacific anticyclone and by a cool ocean current.

HAIL AND SNOW
The heaviest hailstone ever recorded weighed 2.2 lb (1 kg). It fell at Gopalganj in Bangladesh on April 14, 1986. The largest was recorded at Aurora, Nebraska, on June 22, 2003. It had an average diameter of 7 in (17.8 cm). Both fell during the spring or early summer, when cumulonimbus clouds are at their most powerful.

In the Northwest, frontal depressions sweep in from the north Pacific and drop huge amounts of snow as they rise over the Rockies. The largest snowfall in one day was at Silver Lake, Colorado, when 6.33 ft (1.93 m) of snow fell on April 14, 1921. The largest snowfall over a year was 102 ft (31.1 m) at Mount Rainier, Washington, between February 19, 1971 and February 18, 1972.

STRONGEST WINDS

The strongest near-surface winds ever recorded were measured by a mobile radar at a speed of 301 mph (484 kph), at a height of 105 ft (32 m) within an F5 tornado at Bridge Creek, Oklahoma, on May 3, 1999. The highest speed monitored at the standard anemometer height of 32 ft (10 m) was 233 mph (375 kph) on top of Mount Washington (right), in New Hampshire, on April 12, 1934. The winds at Bridge Creek were produced by a small-scale weather feature, but the Mount Washington winds were from a deep low pressure.

Weather forecasting

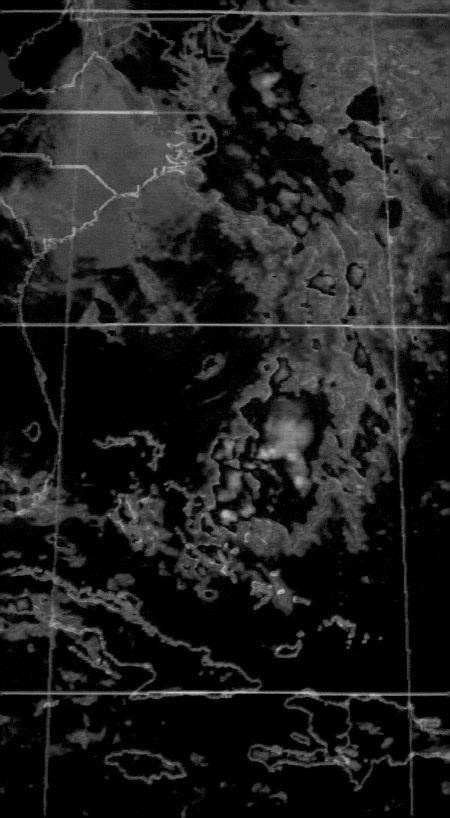

ATHER FORECASTING HAS ADVANCED AS IENTIFIC UNDERSTANDING AND METHODS OF DATA COLLECTION HAVE IMPROVED. TECHNOLOGY HAS INCREASED THE QUALITY AND QUANTITY OF OBSERVATIONS, THANKS TO THE MANY WEATHER SATELLITES THAT NOW ORBIT THE EARTH AND THE COMPUTERS THAT PROCESS THE DATA.

A weather forecast is the culmination of a highly sophisticated process involving a great deal of international scientific collaboration. Uniquely for scientific study, meteorological results are exposed to public scrutiny every day, right across the globe. Forecast quality has improved greatly in recent decades, partly due to a better understanding of the ways in which the atmosphere, continents, and oceans interact with each other over the short and long term, and on local and global scales. These advances have been achieved by highly organized national and international research programs.

The range and sophistication of the measurements that can now be taken play a critical role in forecasting, from traditional surface observations to measurements taken by modern radar and an ever-increasing number of weather satellites. Running hand in hand

COLLECTING DATA AT SEA
A network of moored and drifting buoys collect data in the oceans, and are vital to tracking the development of weather systems.

with the burgeoning data streams is the non-stop development of supercomputers, the power of which would have been hard to imagine even a couple of decades ago. Using their enhanced processing capability, computers can generate forecast models with ever-finer resolution.

Modern weather services now offer tailored forecasts to a diverse range of customers, from television channels to airlines. Computer programs can now model the whole globe, and many weather services can provide worldwide advice. Weather centers are becoming increasingly geared toward these commercial activities, which provide a major source of income.

Nevertheless, among all this high-powered technology and science there is, happily, still a place for the non-professional to take an active interest in both observing and forecasting the day-to-day weather. In fact, technological advances have made it easier than ever to own a sophisticated range of measuring instruments and set up a weather station at home.

SATELLITE IMAGES
Weather satellite imagery can be color-enhanced to highlight areas at risk of rain, seen here in red and pink, and help trace the development of storms.

THE SCIENCE OF FORECASTING

Modern weather forecasting requires supercomputers, which process weather observations from around the world. Supercomputers use mathematical representations of the physical processes at work in the atmosphere. Within a few hours, they can provide weather forecasts for several days ahead.

GATHERING DATA

To reach a scientific prediction of the future state of the atmosphere, accurate knowledge of current weather conditions is required. Observations from weather satellites, along with those from the surface of the Earth and through the atmosphere, pour into supercomputers. Global weather-prediction models use temperature, air pressure, humidity, and wind speed and direction data.

SUPERCOMPUTER PREDICTIONS

Supercomputers are the only way to quickly solve the complicated equations that govern how the atmosphere changes with time. Several million calculations are carried out every second, taking the computer less than two hours to produce a global forecast. The UK Met Office numerical weather prediction (NWP) model, for example, forecasts the weather in 6- or 12-hour increments up to 144 hours (6 days) ahead.

SUPERCOMPUTER

Immensely powerful computers with rapid computing speeds are essential for making the millions of calculations necessary for weather forecasts.

FACTORS AFFECTING FORECASTS

The factors taken into account by a supercomputer to generate weather forecasts are shown here. They include cloud cover, terrain, and atmospheric chemistry. Short-wave radiation is the energy received from the Sun, while long-wave radiation is the energy leaving the Earth. Short-wave and long-wave radiation are finely balanced, but are affected by cloud cover and greenhouse gases, which absorb and reflect radiation, impacting on temperature.

Longwave radiation leave the Earth

Shortwave radiation is reflected by the ocean

Deep convection causing tall clouds

Shallow convection causing low-level clouds

Wind-blown waves

GLOBAL GRID

Computer models divide the Earth's surface into a grid of squares, each of which has several "boxes" stacked above it. Programs use the latest weather data to assign values of temperature, wind speed, and air pressure to each gridpoint. The greater the number of vertical levels the model uses, the greater the accuracy of the projection.

The weather observations from around the world are mapped by computer onto a mesh of latitude and longitude intersections called "gridpoints." Digesting data from around the world, a numerical weather prediction model is then used, which is a computer simulation of the global atmosphere.

The computer produces a meteorological "analysis," which is a three-dimensional representation of the current global temperature, air pressure, humidity, wind, and cloud, involving around 15 million gridpoints. Supercomputers take the analysis as the starting point, and evolve the state of the atmosphere forward in time using an understanding of physics. Chaos theory, and its application to the way in which weather systems affect each other and evolve over time, also plays a major part.

MODELING THE WEATHER

Modern forecast models incorporate all the physical processes that play a role in determining the details of the weather. These include the temperature of the land and sea surfaces, their terrain and vegetation varieties, the impacts of hills and mountains on air flow (known as friction), the location and magnitude of evaporation, the latent and sensible heat flow from the Earth's surface, and the distribution and effect of clouds.

Shortwave radiation is reflected by clouds

Shortwave radiation is received from the Sun

Mountains and valleys cause friction in the flow of air

Sensible heat flux is caused by conduction, convection, and radiation

Turbulence diffuses temperature

Latent heat flux caused by evaporation

Gathering weather data

Accurate observations of weather conditions are taken from thousan of sites every day. Forecasters need to know conditions throughout the troposphere, so observations are taken at both ground level and high altitudes. Satellites provide images of weather systems from above.

SURFACE DATA

Many different observations are taken across the Earth's surface. These include the temperature; humidity; sea-level pressure and pressure "tendency" (the change over the previous three, six, or 24 hours); wind speed and direction; total cloud amount; cloud type, height, and cover; visibility; and current weather conditions. All the observations are converted into codes and transmitted to national forecast centers.

WEATHER STATIONS

Measuring instruments are kept at thousands of weather stations throughout the world, which meteorologists visit regularly to record data. Many stations send data automatically.

UPPER-AIR DATA

To forecast accurately, it is essential to measure what is happening in the atmosphere. Data should include details of how the temperature, humidity, and winds change with altitude at as many heights as possible. Weather balloons provide this information by carrying instruments that measure temperature, pressure, relative humidity, wind direction and speed.

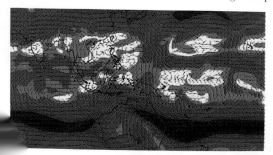

WEATHER CHARTS

Readings of temperature and wind speed in the upper atmosphere are taken by airplanes or balloons. Computers process this data to generate weather charts.

RADIOSONDE BALLOONS
Weather balloons are filled with hydrogen or helium and may travel up to 25 miles (40 km) into the atmosphere.

Thousands of balloons are launched around the world every day. They send data back to the ground via radio signals from a radiosonde. The balloons burst when they reach the lower stratosphere, which takes about an hour.

SATELLITE DATA

The first operational weather satellite was launched in 1960. TIROS I carried television cameras that took pictures of weather systems and transmitted them back to the Earth. The early satellites provided images of cloud patterns that helped forecasters spot the location of weather disturbances. Today, satellites transmit a wide range of data, including high-quality images of clouds and storms. Satellite images are used to track weather systems and are vital for giving early warnings and predicting the paths of destructive storms, such as tropical cyclones. Satellites also carry thermal and infrared instruments on board that can be used to measure cloud height and type, as well as to calculate land and sea temperatures.

AIRCRAFT DATA

Many commercial aircraft carry weather instruments. These automatically measure, log, and transmit data such as pressure, temperature, wind direction and speed, humidity, and even ozone concentrations. Observations are also transmitted frequently throughout the flight from the flight deck by the crew. On flights over oceans, for instance, flight deck observations are usually relayed at intervals of 10 degrees longitude.

BUOYS
Information about the weather at sea is collected by buoys, which also collect data on ocean currents, wave heights, and sea temperatures.

Anemometers measure wind speed and direction

Fin ensures that the buoy points into the wind

Remote sensing

Since the first operational weather satellite was launched in 1960, the capacity of technology to monitor weather remotely has greatly improved Remote sensing differs from direct measurement—using a rain gauge for example—by detecting emitted or reflected radiation, such as from clouds.

THE WEATHER FROM SPACE

With the launch of the US TIROS I in April 1960, only 30 months after Sputnik (the first satellite to be successfully launched), meteorology became the first serious application of satellite technology. Weather satellites today are either polar orbiting, spinning around the Earth at an elevation of about 530 miles (850 km), or geostationary, keeping pace with the Earth's 24-hour rotation at an elevation of 22,000 miles (36,000 km). Geostationary satellites "image" the same area of the planet at regular intervals.

Weather satellites produce high-resolution images of clouds and other objects in a range of wavebands, including the visible-light and thermal-

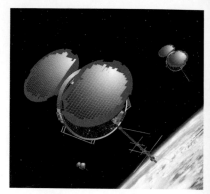

LASER SENSORS
Many satellites use lidar—similar to radar but using laser light rather than radio waves—to scan the atmosphere, sensing tiny particles such as aerosols.

infrared bands. Visible light detectors express the changing fraction of solar radiation reflected back to the satellite by clouds, and are limited to daylight hours. Thermal infrared detectors image the varying strength of long-wave radiation emitted to space by clouds and the cloud-free land and ocean surfaces. The strength of the signal depends on the temperature of the surface being imaged, so can be used around the clock, offering nighttime cloud maps.

Satellites are also used to produce huge numbers of vertical temperature

WORLD VIEW
The geostationary satellite Meteosat generates thermal infrared images of cloud and temperature patterns that can be viewed online daily.

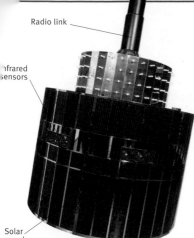

Radio link

Infrared sensors

Solar panels

ALL-SEEING SATELLITE
Weather satellites can see much more than clouds and surface temperatures. They also monitor forest fires, the extent of pollution, dust- and sand-storms, snow cover, ice-shelf melt, ocean currents, and wave heights.

Doppler radars scan an area in a similar way but have the added advantage of being able to sense whether moving atmospheric particles, such as rain, are moving toward the radar or away from it. This movement enables the meteorologist to create a map of low-level convergence and divergence lines (see p.68)—the former being areas where new thunderstorms are most likely to develop.

PRECIPITATION RADAR

Modern precipitation radars have a range of about 150 miles (250 km). They provide data that is mapped frequently to provide forecasters with up-to-date information. This data can be animated to highlight the progression and evolution of rain regions.

profiles down through the atmosphere. These are valuable in areas where surface readings are sparse, and can be used to forecast weather for a limited region. In addition, the thousands of pictures generated every day by geostationary satellites are used to create animations, identifying cloud features as they move from frame to frame. Both kinds of data are used in computer prediction models and have greatly contributed to forecasting accuracy.

Weather satellites play a vital role in monitoring climate change by imaging retreating polar ice and the changing temperature of the sea surface.

WEATHER RADAR
Radar was originally developed for military purposes before World War II, but was adopted by meteorologists to map the location and intensity of rain. Weather radars emit radiation in a series of shallow, conical, circular scans. The waves scatter back when they hit an object. This "backscatter" can be converted to a rainfall rate, while the travel time of the pulse from transmission to return marks the location of the rainfall.

SENSING A STORM
A precipitation radar captures a severe storm over the Red Sea in 2006. The sharp line marks the limit of the radar's sweep.

Weather instruments

A weather forecast can only be as good as the data it is based on. Measuring instruments need to be accurate and capable of taking frequent readings. Spread around the globe, they provide a picture of conditions across the surface and through the depth of the atmosphere.

Anemometer

MEASURES Wind speed and direction
LOCATION Mounted 33 ft (10 m) above ground level
SCALE Feet/meters per second or knots

Wind speed is measured with an anemometer, which counts how fast three hemispherical cups rotate around a vertical axis. The speed is an average over a few minutes that may be displayed on a dial or on a device called a logger. Wind direction is sensed by a wind vane that is designed to point into the flow. Direction is plotted on surface weather maps to the nearest 10 degrees (for example, 360 degrees is northerly, 180 degrees is southerly, 090 degrees is easterly, and 315 degrees is northwesterly).

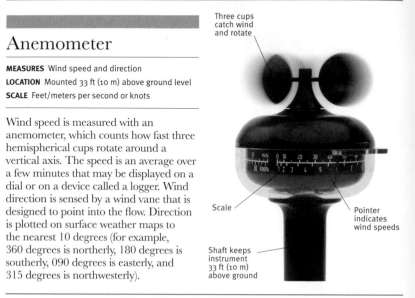

Three cups catch wind and rotate

Scale

Pointer indicates wind speeds

Shaft keeps instrument 33 ft (10 m) above ground

Hygrometer

MEASURES Air humidity
LOCATION Kept inside a Stevenson screen
SCALE Temperatures compared to give value of relative humidity by percentage

A hygrometer is a device for measuring humidity that consists of two thermometers. One has a dry bulb, while the bulb of the other is kept moist by being wrapped in wet fabric. The rate at which water evaporates from the wet bulb, which indicates the level of humidity in the air, is indicated by how fast the bulb cools. The level of relative humidity can then be determined by comparing the readings from the wet-bulb thermometer with those from the dry-bulb thermometer. The larger the difference between the two readings, the lower the relative humidity.

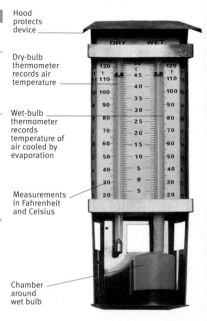

Hood protects device

Dry-bulb thermometer records air temperature

Wet-bulb thermometer records temperature of air cooled by evaporation

Measurements in Fahrenheit and Celsius

Chamber around wet bulb

Stevenson screen

MEASURES Contains instruments to measure temperature and relative humidity

LOCATION Exposed site, away from obstructions

SCALE Temperature in degrees Fahrenheit or Celsius, and relative humidity by percentage

The Stevenson screen provides the correct environment to accurately measure temperature and humidity. The screen is painted white to minimize any sunshine heating the air inside. The roof and floor of the screen have double layers to aid insulation of the interior, and the sides are composed of downward-angled slats to allow air flow through freely, while shading the interior. The temperature inside a Stevenson screen is the one used by meteorologists and quoted when reporting a day's "high," or when forecasting the overnight "low." It houses a hygrometer and one or two clockwork-driven weekly strip charts that log fluctuations in temperature and relative humidity.

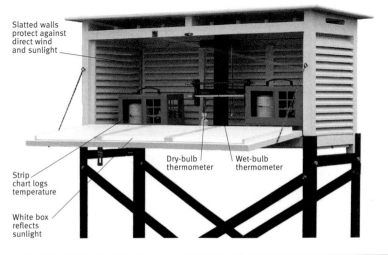

Slatted walls protect against direct wind and sunlight

Strip chart logs temperature

White box reflects sunlight

Dry-bulb thermometer

Wet-bulb thermometer

Barograph

MEASURES Atmospheric pressure

LOCATION In office, away from drafts

SCALE HectoPascals (hPa)/millibars

In addition to using a mercury barometer (see p.195), most busy weather stations will also record atmospheric pressure using a barograph. This senses the change in the height of a metal cylinder with a vacuum. As barometric pressure increases, the can is squashed a little and if the pressure decreases, it will "relax" a little. This changing distortion is drawn by a mechanically linked pen onto a chart wrapped around a rotating drum that is changed once a week.

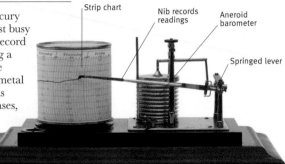

Strip chart

Nib records readings

Aneroid barometer

Springed lever

Weighted base

Rain gauge

MEASURES Precipitation (usually over a day)
LOCATION Open area away from any obstruction
SCALE Measured to nearest 0.004 in (0.1 mm)

Most rain gauges collect precipitation over a 24-hour period. The standard international gauge is a copper cylinder with a 5 in (12 cm) diameter removable funnel at the top. This directs precipitation into a collecting bottle through a small drainage hole that minimizes evaporation. The top of the gauge is usually 1 ft (30 cm) above ground level, with part of the gauge sunk into the ground to stabilize it. Rain, drizzle, or melted snow is decanted once a day into a tapered measuring cylinder.

Funnel

Copper drum

Reservoir for collecting water

Electric thermometer

MEASURES Air temperature
LOCATION Outdoors, in the shade
SCALE Measured to nearest 0.1 degree F or C

"Official" temperature readings and forecasts refer to the temperatures recorded inside the protection of weather screens using dry-bulb mercury thermometers. However, modern electronic probe thermometers have a use in field work. They measure air temperature by exposing a metal probe to the air and then display a reading of the temperature to the nearest tenth of a degree (Fahrenheit or Celsius). Electric thermometers are generally less accurate than mercury thermometers (an error rate for electric thermometers of less than 2°F (1°C) is unusual) but are useful in outdoor work because they are easy to use, and durable. Many versions have long electric cords, which allow readings to be taken at a distance. Some up-to-date models are capable of storing data that can be downloaded later.

Electric cord

Digital display

Thermometer

26.2

Case for battery

Probe measures air temperature

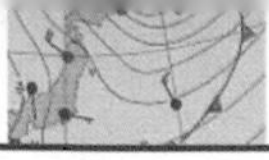

Wind vane

MEASURES Wind direction and speed
LOCATION Away from obstructions about 30 ft (10 m) above ground level
SCALE Degrees from north; mph or kph

The direction of the wind is measured by a wind vane—an aerodynamic plate that points into the wind. The wind direction is averaged over a period of a few minutes and reported to the nearest 10° from the north (0°) going clockwise. The standard height of the cups and vane at official weather stations around the world is 30 ft (10 m) above the ground level. The wind direction is where the wind originated, so, for example, a westerly wind is from the west. Wind vanes usually include an anemometer (see p.192), which records wind speed. The wind pushes on the cups and makes the instrument turn.

Wind vane   Anemometer

Barometer

MEASURES Atmospheric pressure
LOCATION Inside, away from drafts
SCALE Measured to nearest 0.1 hPa

Mercury barometers measure atmospheric pressure. The height of the mercury column fluctuates with changes in the mass of air above it. A lot of air in the column forces the mercury to rise, which registers high pressure. Low air pressure will lead to a drop in the height of the mercury. The instrument scale may be in inches or millimeters of mercury, but the pressure is quoted in hectoPascals (hPa) by meteorologists.

Height of mercury indicates atmospheric pressure

Wall attachment

Air pressure forces mercury up glass tube

Metal case

Computer forecasting

The ever-increasing number-crunching power of supercomputers means that the predictions made by forecasters are improving all the time. They can use models with a higher resolution and global scale to see important physical processes in ever greater detail.

EARLY DAYS

The forefather of modern-day computer forecasting was British mathematician Lewis Fry Richardson, who produced the first ever one-day weather forecast while working in an ambulance unit during World War I in northern France. He did this by carrying out a huge number of calculations by hand. Richardson published a ground-breaking book in 1922 laying the foundations of the methods used today, in which he explained how computers (in his time, human beings solving equations) could be organized around the globe to provide coordinated results.

The next major step occurred in the late 1940s and early 1950s, when John von Neumann and Jule Charney experimented with weather prediction using early digital electronic computers at Princeton University in New Jersey. Simple predictions of the upper-air over North America were shown to be better than the traditional subjective methods. Their work led to the first operational numerical prediction in 1955.

GOING GLOBAL

Early forecasting models could only predict the future state of the atmosphere over small geographical

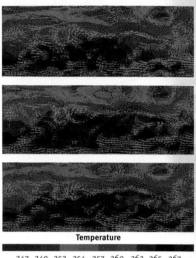

Temperature

247 249 252 254 257 260 262 265 267
(Kelvin)

COMPUTER SIMULATIONS
NASA's Earth System Modeling Framework software enables modeling of data such as temperature at 500 hPa (about 3 mi (5 km) up). These three simulations show temperature and wind direction.

areas. As Richardson had understood, an essential step was to represent the whole globe in the forecast because, for more than just a few days ahead, the weather is likely to be influenced by something happening thousands of miles away.

This has become possible over the last couple of decades. due to an increase in the resolution of the models (smaller spacing between the points at which the observations are assimilated), the

SUPERCOMPUTERS
The powerful supercomputers used by forecasters are composed of clusters of thousands of microprocessors operating in parallel.

SPOTTING PATTERNS
Meteorologists compare data from several different sources to spot patterns that can be used in a forecast.

larger volume and broader range of satellite data, and better representation of physical processes. These have been enabled by the continual increase in the speed of computers.

FUTURE DEVELOPMENTS

The most powerful computer processors, such those of the European Centre for Medium-Range Forecasts, are currently capable of a sustained performance of 4 teraflops, which means they can carry out 4 million million multiplications every second. Speed is increasing all the time, meaning that higher resolution models can be run, either globally or more locally, where one region will be modeled at a high resolution within the coarser-resolution global scheme. As satellites become ever more sophisticated, even more powerful computers will be needed to cope with the increasing quantity of data that comes on stream.

JOHN VON NEUMANN

Von Neumann (1903–57) was a brilliant Hungarian-born mathematician who worked on the design and development of early high-speed electronic digital computers. From 1930, he was based at Princeton, New Jersey, where, with Jule Charney, he put together the first computer-based weather predictions a few years after World War II.

Ensemble forecasting

The notion that natural systems are governed by dynamics that are random and chaotic has had a significant impact on gauging uncertainty in weather prediction. Supercomputers can quantify the uncertainty by running an "ensemble" of forecasts simultaneously.

NATURAL CHAOS

Chaos theory concerns the behavior of certain types of dynamic systems, including the atmosphere, that evolves over time. The systems develop from initial conditions that "set the scene" before they run forward in time. Chaotic systems are those that are sensitive to the initial conditions in such a way that any small perturbation (disturbance) in the initial stage can lead to quite different future states compared with a scenario in which the perturbation did not occur. The atmosphere is a "deterministic" system—its evolution depends on its initial state and the factors that govern its change over time. However, small perturbations that cannot be represented in the initial state can lead to very different predictions.

ENSEMBLE PREDICTION

The problem for meteorologists is that there are always small errors in the initial conditions every time a forecast is run. These errors can grow as the prediction evolves during a forecast cycle in such a way that the quality of the forecast over one, two, three, and more days will vary, depending on how chaotic the atmosphere is. This will vary from time to time so that the weather can be predicted better on some occasions than on others. The way in which the chaotic nature can be represented in the prediction is by running a number of forecasts at the same time, each of which will have a different contingent error that would be difficult to spot in the initial conditions of the global weather data that drives the model.

The European Centre for Medium-Range Weather Forecasting supplies ensemble predictions for organizations all over the world. It runs 50 such global forecasts every day at a resolution of 50 miles (80 km). The forecasts are then clustered into groups that show acceptably similar results over the forecast period. Sometimes, most of these 50 forecasts form one large cluster. When this is the case, the forecaster can be confident in the prediction. On other occasions there may be a number of different outcomes, so the forecaster is informed that he or she must be much

FORECASTING SEVEN DAYS AHEAD

Each colored line on these "spaghetti" charts represents an individual ensemble forecast. The red lines represent areas of warm air, green lines cooler air, and blue lines cold air. The charts show good agreement at day one, indicating a high degree of confidence in the forecast. On day three, detail has become less clear. By day seven, the individual ensemble forecasts reflect the chaotic nature of the atmosphere, leaving detailed forecasts less certain.

ONE DAY AHEAD

THREE DAYS AHEAD

SEVEN DAYS AHEAD

less confident in the prediction of the atmosphere's evolution over the period of days concerned. This modern method of gauging uncertainty is a very important addition in the resources of today's forecast centers.

Over the last few years, weather centers have begun to use ensemble prediction models to produce a range of forecasts. In the USA, the NOAA, for example, produces seasonal forecasts and predictions for the frequency and severity of tornadoes occurring in the Midwest (see pp.136–37). As the seasonal forecast covers a three-month period, it concentrates specifically on temperature and rainfall for the USA. These ensemble methods provide useful guidance for governments and businesses.

VORTEX
Turbulence is created at the tip of the vortex left in the wake of an airplane's wing. Study of the critical point beyond which a system creates turbulence was a key tenet in the development of chaos theory.

EDWARD LORENZ

US meteorologist Edward Lorenz (1917–2008) was the founder of chaos theory. In 1961 he discovered that marginally changing the initial conditions of a computer simulation of the atmosphere led to a significantly different prediction. A famous term of his—"the butterfly effect"—was introduced at the 1972 meeting of American Association for the Advancement of Science when he asked "does the flap of a butterfly's wings in Brazil set off a tornado in Texas?"

The short to medium term

Most people use weather forecasts to plan for the weather over the next 24 hours, while some will check the outlook for a few days ahead. Forecast centers can issue predictions for the whole globe, some out to 10 days ahead, which are critical to businesses and governments.

A FEW HOURS AHEAD

Short-term forecasts are the most commonly used of all forecast types— by almost everyone, from individuals to governments and industry. For example, short-term adverse weather conditions, such as a heavy shower, can have a high impact on the hour-to-hour operation of transportation systems, and can cause problems for a government's emergency planners. Intense rainfall can be dangerous for aircraft in and around airports. In some areas, heavy rain can also lead to landslides and flash floods.

Weather centers can predict the movement and change in the pattern and intensity of rainfall over the next few hours by processing the most recent sequence of rainfall radar-images. This is done automatically by computers tracking the past movement and evolution of "cells" of rain on radar images and forecasting their movement over a few hours into the future— a technique known as "nowcasting." This provides a useful warning system of short-term risks, particularly in relation to intense rainfall.

A DAY OR TWO AHEAD

Forecasts for a day or two ahead give users time to prepare for particular weather conditions. Food retailers, for example, can stock accordingly if a warm or cold spell is on the way (see p.219). Global forecasts cannot provide short-term predictions because their resolution (the distance between their data sources, such as weather stations and buoys) does not currently match that provided by the radar used for nowcasting. Instead, global forecasts provide detail of the worldwide weather several times a day. They normally generate 24-, 48-, 72-hour forecasts, and so on, although in exceptional

NOWCASTING

Two sequences of images for a coastal region of eastern Australia show rain-radar information mapped 30 minutes apart in the morning (top) and again in the afternoon (bottom). The information is very useful for planning for contingencies dependent on the presence, or lack of, rain. The data is available to everyone in real time on the internet.

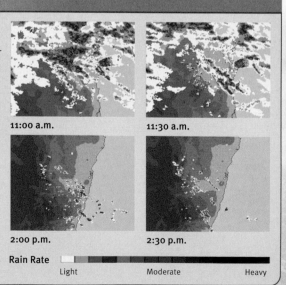

11:00 a.m.

11:30 a.m.

2:00 p.m.

2:30 p.m.

Rain Rate

Light   Moderate   Heavy

MEDIUM-RANGE PREDICTION

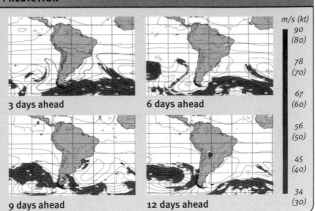

Mean sea-level pressure and wind speed at 850hPa (expressed in miles per second and knots) are shown in these medium-range predictions for South America. The data is used to calculate weather forecasts over land for up to 12 days.

3 days ahead

6 days ahead

9 days ahead

12 days ahead

| m/s (kt) |
| 90 (80) |
| 78 (70) |
| 67 (60) |
| 56 (50) |
| 45 (40) |
| 34 (30) |

circumstances, such as for a military operation, they can produce information for any time during the forecast period.

THREE TO TEN DAYS AHEAD

The medium term is normally taken to be the period from three days to about 10 days ahead, during which time the forecast of the weather is considered "deterministic" (see p.198). This means that the way in which the forecast evolves out to 10 days ahead is determined by how it starts out at "zero"—the time from which the model starts its forecast.

Modern weather centers run daily forecast models to 10 days or so into the future. The quality of the prediction will vary geographically and will deteriorate as the run progresses, because any errors in the initial data will have a larger and larger knock-on effect as time progresses.

Knowing the levels of uncertainty in a prediction over a period of days allows forecasters to pitch their summary accordingly. Such forecasts are used less intensively than 24-hour forecasts, but can allow preparation time, for example by a local authority expecting icy roads.

AUSTRIAN SNOW LINE

Subscribers to specialist forecasting services, such as the European Centre for Medium-Range Weather Forecasts, can obtain a specific short- to medium-range forecast. For example, the Austrian weather service may require a forecast for snowfall and the position of the snow line out to a week ahead.

The season ahead

Forecasting for an entire season is now possible thanks to increased computer power and a better understanding of the variables to be considered, such as ocean surface temperatures. Seasonal forecasting allows governments to prepare for drought, flood, or crop failure.

BEYOND THE DAY-TO-DAY

Forecasting for the season ahead is, by its nature, less precise than short-term forecasting. The weather over a period of days is dynamically related to its starting point on day one: it has what might be termed a "memory" of how things started. There comes a time, however, when the "memory" fades completely—this is the practical limit to detailed, day-to-day prediction. This means that numerical prediction models might be run out to 30 days, but the details of a particular day's weather later in the period would have little value. Predictions for the months ahead are made by taking account of the ever-changing oceans.

PREDICTING PROBABILITIES

Sea-surface temperature anomalies evolve slowly, over months, seasons, and years, and are known to be a factor in monthly and seasonal weather anomalies over many continental areas. The most obvious of these links is during an El Niño event (see pp.166–67), when substantial sea-surface thermal anomalies drive drier or wetter seasons

AUSTRALIAN FIREFIGHTING
Seasonal forecasts can indicate when particularly dry weather is likely, which is useful for areas prone to forest fires, such as the Australian bush.

over far-flung regions, mainly within the tropics or subtropics. Seasonal predictions must, therefore, represent the oceans and how they interact with the atmosphere.

SEASONAL TEMPERATURE FORECASTS

Probability maps can indicate whether a region's temperature is likely to be warmer (yellow to red shading) or cooler (navy to turquoise) than average. Calculations are based partly on changes in ocean temperature over time, which in turn affect the behavior of the atmosphere.

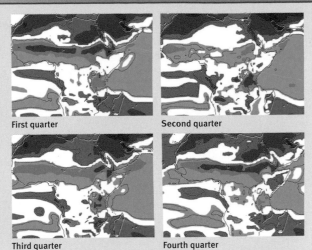

First quarter

Second quarter

Third quarter

Fourth quarter

Seasonal forecasting models can be run for six months into the future, for example, predicting the slow changes in the ocean's temperature. Any warm or cool anomalies in the ocean will feed into possible changes in the atmosphere's circulation, which may then impact on the original ocean thermal patterns.

A seasonal prediction of global surface temperature or precipitation anomalies will typically be produced by averaging a three-month period. This means that a map of the percentage probability of wetter or drier conditions than average, or cooler or warmer, can be created for any region. Using probability is the best way of expressing the results, to give a broad indication of the chance of any particular problem arising. Weather centers will run models a number of times as an ensemble, in order to see which outcome is the most likely over longer periods.

AFRICAN CROPS
Seasonal forecasting has made it possible to assess the chances that a growing season will be drier than average, allowing governments to plan for potential crop failures.

Broadcasting the weather

One of the main services weather forecasters provide is a broadcast of the latest prediction to the general public, by television or radio, via the web, or direct to cellphones. The way forecasts are presented has evolved in parallel with technology over the years.

EARLY BROADCASTS

The broadcasting of weather forecasts was pioneered in the UK, where a radio announcer read out the world's first broadcast, prepared by the Met Office, on November 14, 1922. The shipping forecast was added in 1924. An experimental television forecast was broadcast from Cincinnati, Ohio, in 1940, and the first regular broadcast began in Philadelphia in November 1947.

LIVE REPORTING
Occasionally the weather becomes the main news. Live satellite broadcasts from areas affected by severe weather, such as New Orleans (above) in 2005, beam real-time images around the world.

At first, TV forecasts took the form of a map with captions. The world's first on-screen presenter, George Cowling, presented the weather for the BBC using hand-drawn weather charts on an easel.

MODERN TECHNOLOGY

Weather services must ensure the information they present is not too technical, while showing enough detail

CHANGING TECHNOLOGY
In the first television forecasts, presenters drew weather fronts onto a chart. Nowadays, the presenter stands in front of a blank screen, and the weather map is added digitally to the broadcast.

for viewers to understand what the weather will be. Graphics need to be simple and attractive and easy to understand. Computer animations are now widely used to illustrate the movement and evolution of rain-bands and cloud patterns.

Increasingly sophisticated means of displaying the weather are available to broadcasters. However, trained meteorologists are usually required to prepare the forecast from the data available and accurately communicate it to the layperson.

WEATHER WARNINGS

Sometimes the rapid communication of an accurate forecast can be a matter of life or death. In "Tornado Alley" in the US (see pp.138–39), TV transmissions are immediately interrupted if it is judged that there is a significant risk of tornado damage. Up-to-date animated radar imagery is presented to illustrate the progress of severe weather, including the estimated time of arrival of the tornado at the various towns and cities at risk.

GETTING IT WRONG

On October 16, 1987, hurricane-force gusts hit the UK. The night before, TV weatherman Michael Fish referred to a viewer claiming that a hurricane was on its way. He assured viewers there was nothing to worry about, hours before the worst storm in 300 years. The damage was caused by a rare event known as a "bomb" (see pp.128–29), which at the time was poorly understood.

Effective communication and dissemination of information is more difficult in poorer parts of the world, due to factors such as the lie of the land and lack of infrastructure. Broadcasting to remote poor areas to provide weather warnings or other useful information is difficult, as many people in these areas may not have access to electricity. The recent development of clockwork radios could help to solve this problem.

QUIKSCAT
Forecast data used to be gathered by pen and paper. Now it is often sent directly to a computer. The QuikSCAT satellite monitors winds over the oceans and sends its observations to weather centers. The colors indicate wind speed (blue is low, yellow high), while the wind directions are indicated by the swirling white lines.

Weather in the news

News bulletins routinely end with a weather forecast for the day ahead. Sometimes the weather is the main news—a cyclone may batter tropical coasts or wildfires may bring a region to a standstill—since weather events can cause large-scale disruption, and even loss of life.

WINTER STORMS

Fall and winter are the seasons for storms in the mid latitudes. Blizzards may sweep across Japan, bringing traffic to a standstill. Meanwhile, deep Atlantic depressions can bring storm-force winds to northern Europe. Extremely cold and snowy conditions that disrupt everyday living are commonly reported in the news, followed by a forecast for how long the conditions will continue. The news media plays an important role, broadcasting severe weather warnings in time to allow people to take the necessary precautions to protect their homes from flooding, for example, or to decide against making non-essential trips.

Deep depressions can create storm surges that threaten low-lying coasts, such as those around much of the North Sea, leading to the risk of widespread inundation. These storm surges can cause widespread damage and hit the headlines, especially if they coincide with

BUSH FIRES
Heat waves in Australia can lead to rapidly spreading bush fires that threaten towns. News updates of developments, such as wind direction and speed, can save lives.

a spring high tide. Extremely thick fog or snowfall is also newsworthy if it threatens to cause traffic pile-ups or leave airline passengers stranded.

SPRING AND SUMMER TURMOIL

Springtime is the prime season for severe storms in some parts of the world. At this time of year, local and national news channels are on the alert for reports of tornadoes, such as those that strike parts of the Great Plains and the Midwest.

Summer is an even busier time of year than spring for weather problems. Although reports of excellent weather during public holidays are always well received, summer

HEATWAVES
In many parts of the world, summer Sun sends thousands to the beach. Weather reports provide the current Sun index to encourage people to protect their skin.

DISRUPTION TO TRANSPORTATION
Heavy snowfall can bring a whole region grinding to a halt, as happened in Hubei province in China in February 2008. News reports were crucial for those planning trips to Chinese New Year celebrations.

in either hemisphere brings the risk of tropical cyclones and the misery they can cause. News agencies will cover hurricanes that threaten the Caribbean and North America, typhoons that track across the Philippines and southeast Asia, and cyclones that bear down on Bangladesh, Madagascar, Mozambique, or north and west Australia.

Dangerously high temperatures are reported when they affect human health in regions of that are susceptible to the inflow of hot air from deserts, such as the Mediterranean and parts of Australia. Combined with a preceding dry spell, these conditions can lead to extremely dangerous bush and forest fires.

News coverage of potentially dangerous weather events raises public awareness of the areas at risk, and of what individuals could do to help, such as the international relief efforts in the wake of disasters such as Cyclone Nargis, which devastated the Irrawaddy Delta in Burma on May 2, 2008.

INTERNATIONAL NEWS

Disasters caused by extreme weather hit areas with a poorly developed infrastructure hardest. Swift relief efforts to help the victims of tropical cyclones in south Asia or the Caribbean, for example, benefit from the high profile afforded them by international news. Before the advent of high-speed news reporting, disasters were often not known about in the outside world until weeks later.

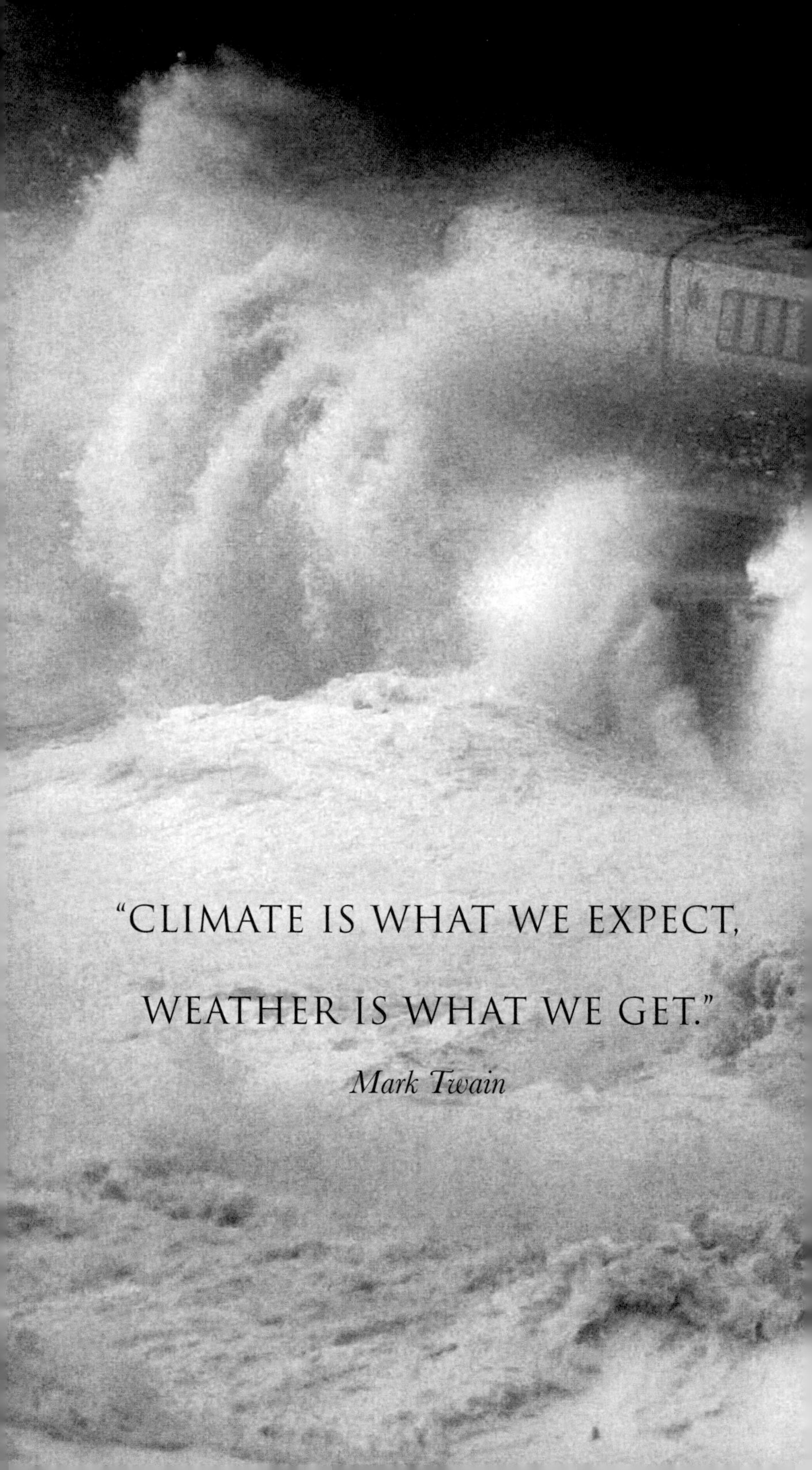

"CLIMATE IS WHAT WE EXPECT,

WEATHER IS WHAT WE GET."

Mark Twain

Forecasts for sailing

Accurate weather forecasting is essential for sailors. As well as providing warnings of gales, high seas, icing, and reduced visibility, specialist marine weather services can provide forecasts tailored to the oil industry or search and rescue teams.

WEATHER CENTERS

Sailing the world's oceans is a highly weather-sensitive operation. Saving time and avoiding damage to vessels and cargo is invaluable to shipping operators, so many maritime weather services offer a ship-routing scheme that is tailored to an individual vessel's handling at sea and the nature of its cargo. Ships taking cargo from Seoul to Sydney, for example, will be concerned with the risk of typhoons, so the ship-routing scheme will recommend the best time to depart and which course to take to minimize damage caused by high seas.

Maritime weather services also make predictions of ocean wave heights for a number of days ahead. This can include the location of potentially hazardous waves; waves of just 6 ft (2 m) can be a

FOG BANK
Even with the use of radar, near misses and collisions are common in fog, which is officially defined as visibility of less than 3,300 ft (1 km).

significant risk of capsizing to smaller vessels. Details of wave direction and period (the length of time between waves) are also supplied.

FORECASTING FOR ICY CONDITIONS

A dangerous natural phenomenon in high latitudes is the icing of ships. At below-freezing temperatures, precipitation and ocean spray freezes immediately upon contact with the exposed metal surfaces of a vessel. Up to 50 tons of ice can cover a boat

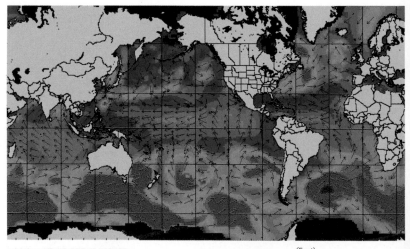

MEAN WAVE-HEIGHT FORECAST
Global forecast charts show wave height and direction. "Significant" wave height is the average height of the largest one-third of all waves.

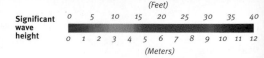

Significant wave height

				(Feet)				
0	5	10	15	20	25	30	35	40

0	1	2	3	4	5	6	7	8	9	10	11	12

(Meters)

ING FORECASTS
e of the world's first weather
rvices, the UK Met Office, was
stablished in 1854 to provide
orecasts to mariners and fishermen.

within hours. The vessel will lose
maneuverability and buoyancy, and
radio communication and navigational
devices may fail because of ice on the
antenna. The loss of stability can cause
sudden capsizing, with a high risk of
fatalities. Between 1963 and 1967,
19 Japanese vessels and 296 fishermen
were lost due to icing and overturning in
a single location—the Tatar Strait off
the coast of Russia. Forecasts can offer
early warning of dangerous conditions,
including where to shelter, and which
course to take to minimize icing.
Modern vessels are also armed with
anti-icing shields and devices that
vibrate to crack the ice.

FORECASTING FOR MARINE ACCIDENTS

Pin-point, detailed forecasts can be
made available for operations, such
as rescue and salvage, anywhere on
the world's oceans. A dedicated search
and rescue forecasting
package can determine the
search area for missing
people or vessels, suggest
the pattern the search
should take, and give the
likelihood of success.

Weather centers also
offer forecast models
tailored to accidents in
the oil industry that can
predict the direction an
oil spill will take. Such
models consider wind and

hydrodynamic data, whether the
spill was instantaneous or gradual,
and oil interactions with shoreline,
reed beds, and ice cover. Predictions
will indicate any coastlines at risk of
pollution, as well as whether the
prevailing sea conditions will help
to break up the slick.

ICE-BREAKING OFF NEWFOUNDLAND
Specialist weather centers offer forecasts of ice
cover, disintegration, and flow so that breakers
can be deployed to keep trade routes open.

CHECKING FORECASTS FOR SAILING

Various national weather centers support industries upon
which the marine environment has an impact, including
shipping, oil and gas, coastal construction, and marine law
and insurance. Information includes warnings, forecasts,
averages and trends, and detailed weather maps:

www.nws.noaa.gov/om/marine/home.htm
www.weatheroffice.gc.ca/marine
www.metoffice.gov.uk/marine
www.bom.gov.au/marine/index.shtml

Forecasts for aviation

Modern jet aircraft are increasingly able to operate in a range of weather conditions. Nonetheless, weather forecasts are of immense value to airlines, both to ensure safety, and to enable operations to run as smoothly and efficiently as possible.

SPECIALIZED SERVICES

The expansion in commercial and private aviation has led to an increasing demand for specialized aviation forecasts. These range from detailed information on conditions at the destination airport to weather that may evolve during a long-haul flight. There are two World Area Forecast Centers—based in Exeter, UK and Washington, USA—which offer a global service for commercial flights.

AVOIDING TURBULENCE
Pilots avoid turbulence in clear air by following forecast-based routes. They can also steer the aircraft round turbulent cumulonimbus clouds.

ON-THE-GROUND FORECASTS

Icing during a flight or on the ground changes the shape of the wings, which will dangerously compromise a plane's performance. Meteorological services forecast the likelihood of icing at departure airports so that operators can rearrange schedules if de-icing is necessary. The likelihood of icing depends on the temperature, cooling rates, and humidity. Airport authorities are also warned of the risk of snow.

KEEPING THE WINGS SMOOTH
If the wings of an aircraft ice up, they become too rough to allow a smooth flow of air over them, which greatly reduces lift. De-icing the wings before take-off is crucial in cold weather.

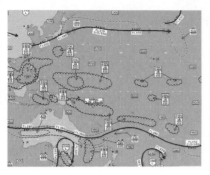

AVIATION WEATHER MAP
World Area Forecast Centers issue maps showing
weather of significance to aviators, including the
location of clear air turbulence and thunderstorms.

Weather conditions and forecasts for
the destination airport are provided as
a Terminal Aerodrome Forecast (TAF).
A typical forecast will include wind
direction and speed, visibility, and
weather for up to 24 hours ahead. It is
also important for pilots to know the air
pressure at the destination airport, which
reflects both the height of the airport
above sea level and weather conditions.
The pilot needs this information to set
the cockpit altimeter, which is in fact
a barometer that measures the weight
of atmosphere above the aircraft in
order to calculate its altitude.

IN-FLIGHT FORECASTS
For the flight itself, predictions are made
of the location and intensity of clear air
turbulence (CAT), in-cloud turbulence,
and cumulonimbus clouds, so that
the route can be planned to avoid
these potential hazards and maximize
passenger comfort and safety. CAT is
predicted automatically in forecast
models by quantifying the wind shear
at flight levels. This is the
rate at which wind speed
changes horizontally,
which occurs around
the core of a jet stream.
Large shear values make
the air choppy, resulting
in a bumpy ride. Flight-
level wind strength and
direction are also taken
into account when
planning the route, in
order to make maximum
use of tail winds. Other

warnings include the location of
any tropical cyclones or clouds
of volcanic ash. Ash can clog jet
engines and make them cut out.

FORECASTS FOR LIGHT AIRCRAFT
Light aircraft use a combination
of TAFs and weather reports for
their destination and any points
en route. The type of cloud and
the height of the cloud-base are
important information for light
aircraft. Pilots can become seriously
disoriented in thick, low cloud.

CHECKING FORECASTS FOR AVIATION

Weather centers provide specialist support for aviation, from
freely available information for light aircraft in the Australian
outback, to real-time observations fed directly to air traffic
controllers at major airports around the world.

http://aviationweather.gov
www.navcanada.ca
www.metoffice.gov.uk/aviation
www.bom.gov.au/reguser/by_prod/aviation
www.meteofrance.com/FR/aviation/index.jsp

Forecasts for sports

All outdoor sports depend, to some extent, on the weather. Some sports can only be played in certain conditions, while critical decisions in others may hinge on changes in the weather during the game. The result of a game or race may depend on the accuracy of a forecast.

FORECASTS FOR MOTOR SPORT

Every team in Formula 1 racing has a detailed tire strategy to cope with different weather conditions at the track. All teams have access to live rainfall radar imagery, which they use to predict the exact start and end of any rain during the race. This allows them to call drivers in to the pits to change to wet- or dry-weather tires at precisely the right moment—a decision that could win or lose the race, particularly on a drying track. Even in completely dry conditions, Formula 1 technicians keep a close eye on both the atmospheric and track-surface temperature to determine which of the various tire composites they need to use.

TIMING THE PIT STOP
Formula 1 teams watch the weather forecast closely, as tire choices are heavily dependent on track conditions at any given time.

WINTER SPORTS

Snow reports are widely available to skiers and snowboarders, including the depth and quality of the snow at different locations. If no snow is forecast, machines may be used to make artificial snow for important races and to augment snow for recreational skiing and boarding. Forecasters can also predict the risk of avalanche, which varies with different weather.

RAIN DELAYS
Many hours can be lost to the rain at tennis tournaments. Retractable roofs are used at some major stadiums to allow play to continue.

BAD LIGHT STOPS PLAY
Cricket matches need dry and reasonably bright weather to take place. Umpires carry hand-held meters to measure the light.

RAIN FORECASTS

Tennis tournaments that take place in temperate climates, such as Wimbledon and the French and US Opens, are prone to interruptions from rain. Forecasters use weather radar to monitor local conditions and advise the event organizers exactly when to draw the covers over the courts, ensuring that there can be a prompt resumption of play as soon as the rain stops. Other summer sports, such as cricket and baseball, also require dry conditions. If the forecast is bad, games may be canceled; if this happens, spectators at baseball matches are given a "rain check" that can be redeemed at another game.

HEAT HAZARDS

The best conditions for marathon runners are those that promote gentle heat loss from the body. Optimum conditions for most athletes are light breezes, mainly cloudy or overcast skies, and even some light rain.

COOL RUNNING
Marathon runners prefer cool conditions. In hot climates, races may take place in the evening or early morning to avoid the heat of the afternoon.

CHECKING FORECASTS FOR SPORT

Many specialist weather services provide information geared toward specific sports, allowing surfers to check the tides, skiers to assess snow conditions, and even golfers to choose a course for their weekend game.

www.snow-forecast.com
www.wunderground.com/ski/
www.surfline.com
www.weather.com/activities/recreation
www.ybw.com/weather/home.html

Forecasts for farming

Weather can make the difference between success and failure in agriculture. Providing timely warnings to farmers of short-term adverse conditions, or giving advice about the likely nature of a coming month or season, can prove to be economically vital.

PROTECTING CROPS AND LIVESTOCK

Many farming tasks must be carried out in specific weather conditions. At harvest time, weather centers offer advice on, for instance, the occurrence of a run of five days of dry weather. This allows farmers to plan haymaking or preparation of winter feed, which both require consistently dry conditions. If the forecast is for wet weather, they will know when to prepare silage or wet fodder, both of which require rain. Forecasts are also vital for crop spraying, which requires dry weather with little or no wind.

Short-term forecasts of extreme weather can enable farmers to take steps to prepare themselves. In the spring lambing season, protecting young

GRAPE HARVESTING
Viticulturists pick the optimum time to harvest grapes depending on how the summer's heat and rain have affected their alcohol content and skins.

CROP DUSTING
Crop-dusting aircraft fly at low altitudes in still, dry weather to prevent pesticides from evaporating or being dispersed by the wind.

animals from severe weather is essential. Paddy fields, a typical feature of rice-growing countries in east and south Asia, need water to thrive. However, fields can flood excessively in heavy rain, requiring the rapid deployment of pumps to preserve the crop.

Spring is a sensitive time for plant growth. Frost is a significant risk, so warnings are critically important. Some market gardeners guard against frost by growing their crop within plastic tunnels. Others, such as citrus-fruit growers, use heaters or wind generators to raise the temperature on chilly nights. This latter technique aims to keep air circulating to prevent frost.

WEATHER-BORNE DISEASE

Highly contagious diseases, such as foot-and-mouth, can be spread on the wind as well as by movement of livestock. Specialist weather forecasts can provide predictions of the trajectory and progression-speed of the viral infection as long as they are alerted quickly to the location and area of

1e outbreak. High-resolution forecast models are used to warn downwind areas that are under threat.

Some plant diseases can be more virulent in adverse weather conditions, as well as being spread on the wind. Blights that affect potato crops, for example, can thrive in a cool, damp growing season, and can be spread quickly by low-level winds. Meteorological advice on when to spray to counter blight is routinely available in commonly affected areas.

PEST CONTROL

Locusts can devastate farmers' crops in parts of Africa and Asia. Breeding grounds—usually where there are sudden blooms of vegetation after rain— can be mapped from satellites. Once identified, swarm movement can be predicted and monitored by radar. Swarms may be sprayed from aircraft or where they breed on the ground. The movement of types of fly or beetle that destroy crops can be monitored through diligent observation and reporting by farmers.

PREDICTING FOOT-AND-MOUTH
Predictions of atmospheric flow were used in South Korea to contain outbreaks of foot-and-mouth disease. Culling and quarantining were deployed in affected areas.

ASIAN SOYBEAN RUST

Soybean plants worldwide are susceptible to a fungus known as Asian soybean rust, which causes brown patches on leaves and destroys the crop. Epidemics spread in cool, wet weather during the growing season, and specialist weather centers commonly advise the best times for fungicide use.

CHECKING FORECASTS FOR FARMING

Specialist weather-forecast services for agriculture help farmers to decide when to harvest, prepare dry feed, plant crops, or spray pesticides. They may also advise on the movement of air-borne diseases, and the outlook for any severe weather.

http://www.nws.noaa.gov/
www.metoffice.gov.uk/agriculture
www.farmzone.com
www.awis.com/Ag/Ag_Weather.htm

Forecasts for industry

The operations of a wide range of industries are affected by the day-to-day variability in the weather. Modern forecast centers now offer services to commercial clients that are tailored to their particular needs, from local forecasts to advice on the climate of a region.

FORECASTS FOR CONSTRUCTION

When tendering for projects, construction companies need to estimate the likely downtime on a job to cost it correctly. They will take meteorological advice on the number of air frosts, days of rain, and the risk of winds over a certain speed. Certain activities, such as laying asphalt or pouring concrete, can only be done within a certain temperature range. These variables are also monitored continually during a project in order to schedule it efficiently.

FORECASTS FOR TRANSPORTATION

Warnings of freezing conditions or snowfall are issued to alert authorities to grit the roads or prepare snow plows.

STAYING SAFE

Working at the top of tall buildings is potentially very dangerous. Tall cranes cannot be used in high winds, and it is important to get workers down from the roof before a storm hits. Forecasts are used when deciding whether to wait for a storm to pass or abandon work for the day.

To improve accuracy, many weather centers now use automatic road-surface temperature sensors that offer real-time information on current temperatures.

Forecasts of high winds on exposed major roads or bridges are used by emergency services. High-wind warnings are also issued to rail companies, as is advice on the risk of lightning (which can damage rail signaling systems) and high temperatures (which can lead to rail buckling).

POWER SUPPLY AND DEMAND
Electricity planners watch the weather to anticipate supply and demand. Output from wind turbines and tidal power stations varies according to the weather.

FORECASTS FOR ENERGY SUPPLIERS

The energy industry needs to plan output in order to satisfy fluctuations in demand. Some fluctuations are seasonal, but changes over days or hours can lead to sudden increases in demand. Suppliers particularly need to know when there will be a run of cold or hot days, and when a change in air mass (with its attendant change in temperature) is likely to occur.

FORECASTS FOR RETAILERS

Many retailers use weather forecasts to maximize profits. A run of sunny, warm days from the spring to early fall may mean sudden demand for barbeque-related products. More subtly, demand for hot meals in summer decreases for every 2°F (1°C) above a particular temperature threshold.

STOCKING UP
Supermarkets plan their stock orders with the weather in mind. Demand for barbeques and salad vegetables goes up in hot weather, while the appetite for hot meals goes down.

KEEPING ROADS CLEAR
Snow plows and gritters are placed on stand-by by local authorities when heavy snow is forecast.

CHECKING FORECASTS FOR INDUSTRY

Weather services offer online forecasts to help with planning and allocation of resources, as well as historical weather reports to settle contractual claims. The detailed information offered on these sites, including predicted trends in rainfall and temperature, as well as ultraviolet indexes and satellite images, is also useful for the amateur forecaster:

www.nws.noaa.gov
www.bom.gov.au/watl/index.shtml
www.metoffice.gov.uk/construction

Weather and health

Health levels can be adversely affected by the weather. Problems may be caused directly, by extreme weather, or indirectly, by diseases or pollutants that are spread in certain weather conditions. Accurate forecasts allow people to prepare for such events.

HEATWAVES

Prolonged spells of unusually hot weather can lead to health problems for some, especially the elderly. Recent summers in the Mediterranean and continental Europe have seen severe heatwaves across parts of Portugal, Spain, France, and Greece. Persistently high temperatures can cause respiratory problems, strokes, and dehydration, all of which may be fatal. Similar problems have been experienced in major cities in the United States and China.

INSECT-BORNE DISEASES

Some tropical diseases are borne by insects. Research shows that insect carriers need particular combinations of temperature and humidity to breed and thrive. Monitoring weather conditions may be useful in predicting the spread of, for example, malaria, yellow fever, and Rift Valley fever, which are all spread by mosquitoes.

PREVENTING MALARIA
People in Malawi are given free mosquito nets as part of a government malaria-prevention scheme. Forecasts of wet, humid weather give warning of when such precautions will be most needed.

LETHAL SUN
Sports spectators in India protect themselves against the Sun's harmful UV rays by covering up. UV forecasts are given on a scale from 1 to 11. A reading over 3 means that skin should be covered.

AIRBORNE HEALTH RISKS

Poor-quality air in cities is a serious health issue. Pollutants in the air from cars, factories, and buildings can cause respiratory problems. High-pressure conditions result in still air that traps the pollutants in one place. On such days, people may be warned to stay indoors.

Pollen affects many millions of people each year. These microscopic grains can cause an allergic reaction known

POLLEN STORMS

Thunderclouds can suck in pollen grains, transport them over a large distance, and deposit them in shafts of rain in high concentrations.

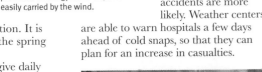

POLLEN GRAINS

Pollen is made up of microscopic grains. Very fine, powdery pollen causes most problems to allergy sufferers, since it is easily carried by the wind.

COLD SNAPS

Severely cold weather can lead to hypothermia, which is a particular risk for low-income communities unable to meet the cost of heating. Snow and ice also bring hazardous conditions in which accidents are more likely. Weather centers are able to warn hospitals a few days ahead of cold snaps, so that they can plan for an increase in casualties.

as hayfever, and even asthma attacks, in susceptible people. Pollen may be carried on the wind, so the weather can affect its location and concentration. It is mainly a problem during the spring and summer seasons.

Some weather services give daily forecasts of pollen concentration (known as the "pollen count") by comparing the location of the plant sources with wind direction and speed. Pollen concentration is also dependent on atmospheric pressure. If there are deep convective clouds, the pollen concentration will be relatively low because the grains will rise high inside the clouds. If, however, there are low-level layer clouds, or flattened cumulus clouds, the pollen grains will be trapped in a thick layer close to the ground.

HAZARDOUS CONDITIONS

Snowy or icy conditions often lead to accidents. Forecasting such weather helps cities prepare by gritting the roads and sidewalks.

AMATEUR FORECASTING

Forecasting the weather for a few hours or a day ahead is a matter of skill, dedication, and constant observation. The essence of prediction is to take a keen interest in the sky and its variations, to note any changes indicated by instruments to hand, and to keep a weather log on a regular basis.

PUBLIC INFORMATION

Although it is possible to attempt to forecast tomorrow's weather using only your local visual and instrumental observations, the task of prediction is made much easier by the mass of public information available from newspapers, television, radio, and the internet. Studying the patterns of highs and lows as they affect your region, and taking an organized view of how your local conditions are related to such changes, are an essential part of increasing your understanding of the weather.

CHECKING WIND DIRECTION
Use the eight points of a pocket compass to keep a regular record of the direction from which the wind is blowing.

WATCHING CLOUDS

It is important to observe changes of cloud type and cover, and to be able to compare these to the weather conditions predicted by public forecasts, such as an approaching warm or cold front. The form of cloud and how it evolves over a few hours or more is also an essential aid in predicting the short-term outlook.

MAKING REGULAR OBSERVATIONS
Keep a log book to note observations of cloud cover, wind, and air pressure. Ideally, these records should be taken at the same time each day.

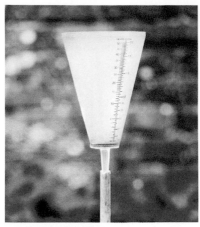

GAUGING PRECIPITATION
A simple rain gauge placed in the yard catches rain, enabling you to measure precipitation. This may be recorded in your weather log.

MEASURING PRESSURE

Having an aneroid barometer is useful for making forecasts. The pressure is indicated at the rim of the barometer's dial—in inches of mercury —by a moving pointer. A second pointer tells whether the pressure has fallen or risen. High pressure usually means dry conditions, while low pressure causes windy and often wet weather.

NOTING THE WIND

Using the eight points of the compass to note the wind direction and its variation with time is essential for understanding the movement and change in intensity of the highs and lows that move across the Earth. Wind direction can be assessed by eye from the motion of trees or smoke, and wind speed can be estimated visually by using the Beaufort scale (see pp.228–229). Through careful observation you can assess whether the wind changes direction with time, and whether it moves clockwise or counterclockwise. These changes can be associated with the approach and passage of weather fronts.

UNDERSTANDING AIR MASSES

A useful tool in amateur forecasting is to be able to appreciate what types of air mass are currently influencing your local weather, and whether it is likely to change over the coming hours. This skill will grow with your ability to accurately understand surface weather maps and to visualize the workings of the weather patterns associated with the approach and passage of a warm, cold, or occluded front (see pp.64–65).

Home weather station

The increasing affordability of sophisticated electronic instruments means that weather variables can be easily measured, processed, and stored by amateur forecasters. Homemade equipment is also still useful, and home stations can be as simple or complex as you wish.

Digital weather station

MEASURES Temperature, wind speed, air pressure, or more, depending on the package
LOCATION Console indoors, instruments outdoors
MOBILITY Instruments fixed

Digital weather stations offer a package of instruments and a console that provides readouts of the data being collected. Consoles may link to a personal computer where data can be displayed, stored, and uploaded to websites. Typical instruments include an anemometer, wind vane, thermometer, hygrometer, barometer, and rain gauge.

More sophisticated stations may also measure the ultraviolet index, solar radiation, leaf wetness, soil moisture, soil temperature, and water temperature.

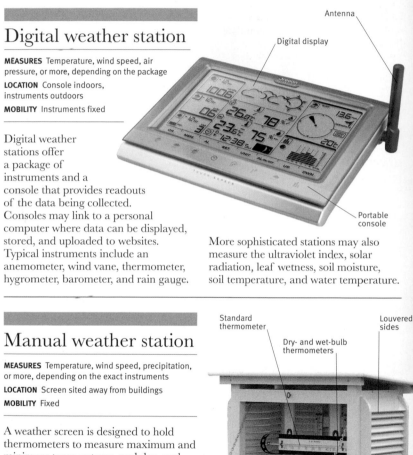

Antenna

Digital display

Portable console

Manual weather station

MEASURES Temperature, wind speed, precipitation, or more, depending on the exact instruments
LOCATION Screen sited away from buildings
MOBILITY Fixed

A weather screen is designed to hold thermometers to measure maximum and minimum temperatures, and dry- and wet-bulb thermometers to calculate relative humidity. Instruments for measuring wind, rain, and snowfall are sited outside the box. The screen should be positioned away from buildings to minimize their thermal impact on the thermometers. The door must open to the north in the northern hemisphere, south in the southern.

Standard thermometer

Dry- and wet-bulb thermometers

Louvered sides

Door oriented away from direct sunlight

Thermometer

MEASURES Maximum and minimum
daily temperatures
LOCATION Outdoors, in the shade
MOBILITY Can be repositioned as needed

A simpler and cheaper alternative to
a fully fledged weather station is a
basic maximum and minimum outdoor
thermometer, which has to be reset
each day. It should be sited in the
shade, preferably on a wall out of
direct sunlight, to partially simulate
the conditions inside
a weather screen. It is
useful to have more
than one thermometer
positioned around a
yard, to investigate
microclimatic variations.

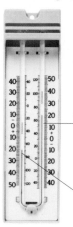

Highest
temperature

Lowest
temperature

Rain gauge

MEASURES Precipitation
LOCATION Well away from any obstruction such
as a building or tall tree
MOBILITY Moveable

A rain gauge can be made from a plastic
bottle, and must contain a permanent well
of water at a fixed depth in the base. Any
rain or melted snow will add to the water
to give an indication of how much has
fallen. However, to get an accurate
measure of inches or millimeters of
precipitation, you
will need to empty
the day's fall into
a calibrated
measuring
cylinder.

Bottle-top
acts as a
funnel

Markers
show base
level and
precipitation
fallen

Marbles
stabilize
the gauge

Hail pad

MEASURES Hailstone size and density of
hail showers
LOCATION Away from overhanging obstructions
MOBILITY Placed outdoors at first sign of hail

A hail pad can be constructed using a
styrofoam pad covered with aluminum
foil. When hail falls, it leaves dents in the
pad—the larger the dents, the bigger the
stones. After the storm, measure the size
of the largest, the smallest, and the most
common-sized hailstones. The density of
a shower can be measured by counting
the number of dents in a square foot or
square meter. Hail pads are useful in
areas that commonly experience hail,
such as the Midwest.

Foam pad covered
in aluminum foil

Hailstones leave
measurable dents

Weather sayings

Before reliable forecasting instruments were developed, people observed nature to make predictions about the weather. Much of this knowledge has been passed down in the form of sayings. Some old sayings come from the observations of sailors, for whom bad weather could cost lives.

USEFUL SAYINGS

"Red sky at night, shepherd's (or sailor's) delight, Red sky in the morning, shepherd (or sailor) take warning" is a fairly reliable piece of weather lore. A red sky forms at sunrise and sunset when dust and other particles—trapped in the atmosphere by high pressure—scatter blue light, leaving just red light. In the northern hemisphere, most weather systems travel from west to east. So, at sunset, a red sky indicates that high pressure is moving in from the west, and the next day will probably be fair. A red sky at sunrise means that the high pressure has moved east, and rainy weather may arrive from the west.

Another saying with some truth is "Mackerel sky and mare's tails make tall ships carry low sails." A "mackerel sky" is one with altocumulus clouds, and

HALO AROUND THE MOON
"A ring around the Sun or Moon means rain or snow coming soon" is usually accurate because the halo is caused by light refracting through ice crystals in high clouds. This may mean wet weather is on its way.

"mare's tails" is a common name for cirrus clouds. Both cloud types could develop before a storm with high winds, causing tall ships to lower their sails.

A familiar saying in New England is "A cow with its tail to the west makes weather the best; a cow with its tail to the east makes weather the least." Cows usually stand with their faces away from

RED SKY AT NIGHT
The idea that a red sunset brings fair weather first appeared in print in the Gospel of Matthew in the Bible. Like much folk wisdom, it may have been passed on orally long before it was written down.

MACKEREL SKY
A cloud pattern that looks like the scales of a fish may indicate that a warm front is approaching and the weather may turn wet.

DAWN RAIN
Many weather sayings, such as "rain before seven, fine before eleven" may be true for a particular place, but are unlikely to be true in other parts of the world. Most weather sayings relate to the middle latitudes, where weather is very variable.

the wind to feed. In this region, easterlies typically bring wet weather and westerlies often bring fair weather.

WEATHER SUPERSTITIONS

Weather predictions that have no basis in science are sometimes associated with religious festivals. It is said to rain for 40 days if it rains on the feast day of Saint Swithun on July 15 in the UK, and there is a similarly wet prediction in France and Hungary if it rains on the feast day of Saint Médard on June 8. In Russia, the weather on the Feast of the Protecting Veil, celebrated on October 1, is said to indicate the severity of the coming winter.

Groundhog Day takes place in Punxsutawney, Pennsylvania, on February 2 each year. A hibernating

groundhog is brought out, and it is said that if the rodent casts a shadow, winter will last six weeks more. If the weather is overcast, and there's no shadow, spring will come early. Again, this superstition is not supported by weather evidence.

Watching the wind

You can use visual indicators to estimate the strength of the wind in your vicinity by using the Beaufort scale, which was developed in 1805 by the British Admiral Sir Francis Beaufort (1774–1857) for use at sea. Adaptations of his scale are used by sailors and meteorologists today.

GAUGING THE WIND

The terms "gale force 8" and "storm force 10" are familiar to many of us, particularly from listening to radio broadcasts for shipping. The Beaufort scale is an internationally recognized scale that provides a good estimate of the average wind speed in knots at sea, and kph or mph over land.

The Beaufort scale was developed in the 19th century as a standard means by which to relate the wind strength to its effect on the sails of a man-of-war ship. In 1906, reflecting the growth of steam power, the British meteorologist George Simpson changed the observations to describe how the sea, not the sails, behaved. In the same year, he developed the system of land-based observations that are still used today. The scale was extended in 1946, when forces 13 to 17 were added to describe extreme cases, such as very strong tropical cyclones.

MAKING OBSERVATIONS

The land Beaufort scale is highly useful for the amateur forecaster, bearing in mind that the wind's impact will vary depending on local exposure. It may be that trees, for example, are susceptible to breezes from the south but not the northwest. Write your observations in a log book, recording the Beaufort number, and the direction to the nearest of the eight compass points.

MARITIME BEGINNINGS

The Beaufort scale was created to estimate wind speed at sea, which is always given in knots (kt), or nautical miles per hour. 1kt is equivalent to 1.2 mph.

THE BEAUFORT SCALE

The Beaufort scale allows the estimation of wind speed from the wind's effects, either on land or at sea. Force 12 is termed "hurricane force" because the speed is used to define when a tropical storm is upgraded to a hurricane. Certain countries, such as China and Taiwan, also use the extended scale up to force 17. Wave heights are for conditions in the open ocean.

BEAUFORT NUMBER	WIND DESCRIPTION	WIND SPEED MPH (KPH)	WIND EFFECT ON LAND AND AT SEA	
0	Calm	0 (0)	Smoke rises vertically Sea like a mirror	
1	Light air	1–2 (1–3)	Smoke drifts gently Ripples like scales	
2	Light breeze	3–7 (4–11)	Leaves rustle Small wavelets	
3	Gentle breeze	8–12 (12–19)	Twigs move Large wavelets with scattered whitecaps	
4	Moderate breeze	13–18 (20–29)	Small branches move Small waves with frequent whitecaps	
5	Fresh wind	19–24 (30–39)	Small trees sway Moderate waves with many whitecaps	
6	Strong wind	25–31 (40–50)	Umbrellas hard to use Large waves of 10 ft (3 m) with some spray	
7	Near gale	32–38 (51–61)	Whole trees sway Sea heaps up and foam is blown in streaks	
8	Gale	39–46 (62–74)	Difficulty in walking Moderately high waves of more than 18 ft (5 m)	
9	Severe gale	47–54 (75–87)	Roofs damaged High waves with toppling crests	
10	Storm	55–63 (88–101)	Trees blown down Sea surface has white appearance	
11	Severe storm	64–74 (102–119)	Houses damaged Waves of more than 38 ft (11 m)	
12	Hurricane	over 75 (over 120)	Buildings destroyed Waves of more than 46 ft (14 m)	

Cloud watching

An important skill for forecasting local weather is to understand the significance of different cloud patterns, and in particular, the way that they change over periods of a few hours or more. Watching the sky may enable you to predict the timing and intensity of rainfall.

PREDICTING SHOWERS

A good method of forecasting rain over a period of about an hour is to watch the development of cumulus clouds. If a day begins with little cloud but shallow cumulus soon appear, the heating of the Earth's surface must be sufficient, and the atmosphere unstable enough, to create convection. Unstable conditions occur when rising air is warmer than its environment—this is most likely in spring and summer over land.

With sufficient instability, the bubbles of air that produce the cumulus clouds will grow upward quite rapidly. The building up of the cloud tops, creating a "cauliflower" appearance, can be seen by watching them over one minute. The taller such clouds become, the more likely they are to produce a shower, so noting the direction that the clouds are moving, while monitoring the change in their depth, allows you to predict any showers and where they may fall.

PREDICTING FRONTAL RAIN

There is often a great deal of cloud in the warm air ahead of a cold front, which makes it hard to predict its approach from cloud patterns alone. However, a distinctive sequence of cloud types offers clues to the approach of a warm front, which brings widespread precipitation with it. Warm fronts are shallow, sloping features created when warm, moist air glides up and over heavier, cooler, drier air. An approaching warm front is usually marked by an increasing bank of high-level cloud, followed by lower, deeper clouds as the surface front arrives. This means that a recognizable sequence of clouds will herald a warm front and its attendant precipitation, wind shift, and temperature and humidity changes. The sequence typically begins with mare's tails cirrus, perhaps alongside cirrocumulus or cirrostratus. The cloud lowers and develops into altostratus, and may deepen to a lower base, from which precipitation falls. This is the leading edge of the warm front's rain-band falling from thick nimbostratus.

How far in advance you can forecast the onset of frontal rain depends on the front's slope (the steeper, the sooner) and how fast it is traveling. Typically, the first cirrus clouds occur 500–600 miles (800–1,000 km) ahead of the surface front, and since warm fronts usually travel at 20–35 mph (30–55 kph), rain will follow some 12 to 30 hours later.

CUMULUS BUILD-UP
It is possible to watch cumulus clouds develop extensively over an hour. As bubbles of warm air rise into the cooler atmosphere, the cloud tops take on a distinctive cauliflower appearance. The clouds may grow tall enough to produce showers.

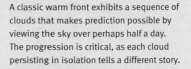

SPOTTING AN APPROACHING WARM FRONT

The arrival of a warm front will bring widespread rain alongside temperature and humidity changes. Being able to recognize the signs of an approaching warm front is an essential skill for the amateur forecaster.

A classic warm front exhibits a sequence of clouds that makes prediction possible by viewing the sky over perhaps half a day. The progression is critical, as each cloud persisting in isolation tells a different story.

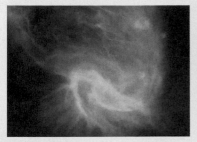

STAGE 1: CIRRUS
These clouds are a common sign of ice crystals condensing in the high-level warm air hundreds of miles ahead of the surface front.

STAGE 2: CIRROSTRATUS HALO
After the cirrus clouds, it may be possible to see cirrostratus, which announce their presence with optical effects such as a sun halo.

STAGE 3: ALTOSTRATUS
Closer to the surface front, altostratus appear several hours after the cirrlform cloud. The Sun may shine hazily through this cloud.

STAGE 4: NIMBOSTRATUS WITH FALLING RAIN
Immediately ahead of the surface front is thick layer cloud, bringing precipitation over a rain-band a few hundred miles wide.

Atmospheric stability

A key aspect of weather observation is understanding the effect of atmospheric stability on the development of clouds, and the corresponding effect on precipitation. If cumulus clouds grow upward, the atmosphere is unstable, and precipitation may follow.

MEASURING AIR STABILITY

Atmospheric stability is the consistency of temperature and humidity of air in the atmosphere, which are quantified by "lapse rates." Most of the time, the air temperature decreases with height. Meteorologists use radiosonde measurements to create a vertical profile of the air temperature around the world at different heights, known as the Environmental Lapse Rate (ELR). In some places the ELR may show a cooling with height, whereas other places may show a warming (this is known as an inversion). The ELR helps forecasters determine whether the atmosphere is "stable" or "unstable."

EFFECTS OF UNSTABLE AIR

On a sunny, cloudless morning, the heating of the land may be strong enough to produce "hot spots" of air above it. These areas of rapidly rising air are called thermals. Bubbles of dry air

UNSTABLE CLOUDS
On an unstable day, the anvil top of a deep cumulus cloud may flatten when it reaches an inversion at the tropopause (the boundary between the troposphere and the stratosphere).

cool at a fixed rate as they rise. They expand as they ascend, which leads to a cooling rate of 5.5°F for every 1,000 ft (9.8°C for every kilometer). Descending areas of dry air warm at the same rate because they compress as they fall. A thermal will rise if its cooling rate is less than that of its surroundings, that is, less than the ELR. When an air bubble is

POLLUTION PLUME
Plumes of water droplets from cooling towers and chimney stacks sometimes flatten underneath an inversion layer some distance above the surface.

warmer at each level of the atmosphere than its environment, it is said to be unstable. At a certain height, the temperature will reach the air's dew point, condensation will begin to form, and a cumulus cloud develops. The cloud can then only grow to the height at which its temperature is the same as that of the surrounding air. The higher it grows, the higher the chance of rain.

EFFECTS OF STABLE AIR

Sometimes, the ELR increases with height. This inversion creates stable air because any air bubbles will always be cooler than the surrounding air, so

will not rise. Such a situation occurs during clear, calm nights when the ground cools the air above it.

Descending air in an anticyclone creates a "subsidence" inversion above the surface. This stable layer caps any cumulus clouds in the unstable layer beneath, flattening them and turning them into stratocumulus.

TYPES OF LAPSE RATE

The Environmental Lapse Rate is the rate of change in air temperature through the atmosphere, as recorded by a weather balloon's instruments. The rate of change in temperature in ascending or descending bubbles or layers of air is known as the Adiabatic Lapse Rate, and varies depending on whether the air is dry or saturated.

STABLE CLOUDS
A temperature inversion, such as this one near the top of the Grand Canyon, creates a layer of stable air that acts as a "lid" to prevent the vertical development of cumulus clouds.

Climate change

THE EARTH'S CLIMATE HAS VARIED A GREAT DEAL OVER THE FOUR AND A HALF BILLION YEARS OF ITS EXISTENCE. HOWEVER, THE EFFECTS OF HUMAN ACTIVITY ON THE ATMOSPHERE'S COMPOSITION MEAN THAT THE CLIMATE IS NOW CHANGING AT AN ACCELERATING RATE. CLIMATE CHANGE WILL BE THIS CENTURY'S GREATEST CHALLENGE.

As the Earth's primitive atmosphere evolved, the planet's climate changed. When the continents divided and drifted, it changed again. Scientists today have a great deal of knowledge about past climates. They know that fluctuations of the planet's temperature over the last few hundred thousand years are linked to long-term variations in the Earth's orbit. The timing and intensity of the climate changes that occurred in different phases of the most recent ice age are also better understood, gained from the painstaking work of atmospheric scientists, glaciologists, geologists, and other specialists.

CHANGING MIGRATIONS
The timing of the annual migration of many birds, such as geese, has altered in response to changes in the timing of the seasons.

Climatic conditions are now monitored right across the world. The widespread deployment of scientific weather instruments over the last century means we can now reliably measure where, and how large, recent changes in climate have been. Global and regional annual and seasonal mean temperature changes

SHRINKING LAKES
Drought has become more frequent in some regions over recent decades, as seasonal precipitation patterns have changed in response to warming.

are caused by the Sun, but can be altered in various ways, including, for example, by large volcanic eruptions, which inject huge volumes of volcanic particles into the atmosphere. Natural factors alone are insufficient to explain some of the changes over the last century, however. Detailed scientific studies point to an increase in global temperature since the early 20th century. Moreover, in the last four decades the Earth has warmed at an accelerated rate, and has seen changes in other aspects of the climate, including the intensity and distribution of precipitation in some areas.

Climate science not only demonstrates that climate change is taking place, but that its cause is mostly down to human activity. It can also provide responses to the challenges that will ensue. Global and regional climate models can predict likely scenarios for the coming decades and century—an essential tool that will allow governments and business to assess the risks of climate change and to help them adapt to any change that does occur.

THE CLIMATE SYSTEM

The Earth's climate is determined by interactions between the land, ocean, and atmosphere—known as the climate system. Many influences on this system are natural, but human activities, such as burning fossil fuels, also affect global weather patterns.

Solar energy warms land and ocean

Emitted greenhouse gases, such as CO_2, trap outgoing infrared energy

Clouds reflect sunlight and trap outgoing infrared energy (heat)

Melting sea ice affects ocean circulation

Oceans absorb, store, and release heat and CO_2

NATURAL FACTORS

Solar radiation is the main external influence on climate. Variation in the intensity of the Sun at different latitudes and seasons—due to the Earth's tilt on its axis—sets the atmosphere and ocean in motion. Other influences include changes in the Earth's orbit over hundreds of thousands of years, which have resulted in ice ages. Volcanoes also affect the climate when they eject massive amounts of sulfate aerosols into the atmosphere, blocking out the Sun. Some large volcanic eruptions have cooled global temperatures for more than a year.

MANMADE FACTORS

The concentration of greenhouse gases in the atmosphere is crucial to determining the Earth's climate. These gases, which occur naturally, include water vapor, carbon dioxide, and methane. They absorb some of the heat that would otherwise escape to space, radiating it back to the surface and atmosphere, and, although present only in small quantities, account for the Earth being 54°F (30°C) warmer. Increases in concentrations of greenhouse gases due to human activity, such as burning fossil fuels and deforestation, have changed the balance of energy entering and leaving the climate system.

Aerosols are tiny particles suspended in the atmosphere and have both natural and artificial origins. They tend to cool the climate by blocking radiation, and also increase the number of particles that clouds can condense onto.

SECONDARY CAUSES

Clouds greatly affect the climate. They reflect some of the incoming solar radiation and absorb some outgoing terrestrial radiation. Factors such as where clouds occur, how thick they are, whether they are composed of droplets

AEROSOL CLOUDS
Large-scale forest fires, such as this one in Central America, emit huge amounts of aerosols into the atmosphere, causing temperatures to cool.

Volcanoes add aerosols to atmosphere, reflecting solar energy back into space

Bright surfaces, such as ice, reflect solar energy back into space

Clouds release rainfall

GLOBAL CLIMATE SYSTEM

The Earth's climate is determined by a delicate balance between the land, ocean, and atmosphere, powered by the Sun. Human activities are having a greater effect on climate than ever before.

Vegetation and soil absorb CO_2 from the atmosphere

Melting land ice raises sea level and affects ocean circulation

Deforestation and biomass burning release CO_2 into atmosphere

Evaporation from land and ocean creates cloud

JAMES LOVELOCK

British scientist and inventor James Lovelock (1919–) developed the Gaia hypothesis. This suggests that the Earth functions as a single organism—the living and non-living parts, including the climate, work together in a complex system. Lovelock believes that the Earth's biosphere regulates the climate in order to sustain life.

VOLCANIC AEROSOLS
Large eruptions from volcanoes can throw sulfate particles high into the stratosphere, where they spread around the globe.

or ice crystals, and how high they are, affect the radiation balance and therefore the climates of atmosphere and surface. Global warming may affect clouds – but exactly how is still not known. Melting ice also affects the balance by reducing the Earth's reflectivity, which further warms the climate.

INTERNAL VARIABILITY

The Earth's climate varies naturally due to factors external to the climate system, such as the Sun and volcanoes. Internal variability also arises due to, for example, complex interactions between the ocean and atmosphere, such as the El Niño Southern Oscillation.

Reconstructing past climates

Direct measurements using instrumentation cover only a tiny fraction of the Earth's climate history. Finding out what climates were like in the distant past involves a host of techniques that identify the major fluctuations in temperature and atmospheric composition.

OCEAN EVIDENCE

The world's oceans contain a climate record buried in the sediment that covers vast areas of the sea floor. Vertical cores are extracted from the sediment by ocean-going research vessels, and analyzed in different ways. For example, by studying the distribution of the fossil remains of tiny sea animals that were sensitive to sea-surface temperature change with sediment depth, and therefore time, scientists can work out the changes in past sea-surface temperatures. The length of the vertical cores is limited by the equipment used, so how

STORING ICE CORES
Ice cores taken from continental ice sheets are kept at temperatures below 5°F (-15°C) to prevent cracks. Storage areas are built deep under the ice sheets.

far the record stretches back depends on how fast the sediment accrued: a rate of ¾ in (2 cm) per 1,000 years enables "viewing" over millions of years, while a rate of 4 in (10 cm) per 1,000 years limits the "view" to about the last 10,000 years.

FROZEN RECORDS

Ice cores extracted from the continental ice sheets of Greenland and Antarctica also have evidence of past climate changes locked within them. Every year, fresh snow is gradually compacted into glacial ice. Oxygen trapped in the snow as it falls remains in the ice down to great depths, so the oxygen can

PAST DROUGHT AND FAMINE
Human records give clues about past climate, although they do not produce precise data. This Egyptian carving from about 2100BCE shows people starving because the Nile River failed to flood for several years, and farmers could not irrigate crops.

be analyzed to discover temperature levels when the snow fell. Breaking the analysis down to annual temperatures is possible only in the very topmost section of the core. Analysis of the deeper core produces a poorer time "resolution." Annual dust layering throughout the core aids dating, as do major, known volcanic eruptions. The cores can be up to 2 miles (3 km) in length and offer information about climate fluctuations from 800,000 years ago. Differing concentrations of greenhouse gases trapped in the glacial air bubbles also provide invaluable information on past climate changes.

THE PAST IN PLANTS

The growth of trees depends mainly on temperature, rainfall, soil moisture, and the age of the tree. Dendroclimatologists —scientists who study tree rings to determine past climate—try to select trees from areas unaffected by anything but climate. Tree rings have an annual resolution—generally they are narrower in cool or dry

STRADIVARIUS VIOLINS

Italian instrument maker Antonio Stradivari (1644–1737) was famed for the superb sound of his violins. The period of manufacture occurred during a minimum of sunspot activity, which may have caused tree growth to slow over a period of years. The density of the Alpine wood used may explain the sound quality, which defies reproduction.

years, and wider in warmer, wet growth years. Rings from living trees can be "overlapped" with those of dead trees to create a record going back thousands of years. However, tree-ring analysis can only be used to reconstruct a relatively local climate.

Fossilized pollen and seeds can also be studied with powerful microscopes to identity the past temperatures in which certain types of plants flourished.

POLLEN GRAIN RECORDS
The frequency of tree pollen grains taken from cores, such as those taken from bogs, can offer evidence of past climates stretching back 10,000 years.

Early climate records

The scientific observation of weather—with measurements averaged over months, seasons, and years to form the basis of climate study—stretches back more than 300 years in some places. Reliable global climatic records, however, are available only from the mid 19th century.

WEATHER LOGS

As early as the Middle Ages, a handful of enthusiastic individuals in scattered areas of the world were keeping descriptive records of the daily weather. Marine weather logs that were kept routinely and conscientiously became widespread between the 15th and 19th centuries —the Age of Sail— while there was a growing network of private observers on land. Climatologists can use such daily logs to improve and extend climatic records.

SAMPLING SEA TEMPERATURE
Buckets for measuring sea-surface temperature have evolved over time from wood and canvas, to rubber and plastic with an built-in thermometer.

ADVANCES IN INSTRUMENTATION

The development of reliable scientific instruments in the 17th century means that some climatic indicators can, with a measure of uncertainty, be known as far back as that period. The world's longest instrumental record of climate is the Central England Temperature time series, which began in the 1660s and is still updated regularly. With a series so long, it is essential to know the exact type of thermometer used, and how it was exposed, to correct any potential biases.

WEATHER JOURNAL

High-quality daily weather records with instrumental values and detailed commentary, such as this 18th-century example, provide reliable data sets over relatively short periods.

GLOBAL NETWORK

The first detailed recording of wind data at sea began in the 18th century. Early records were based on the wind scale devised by Admiral Sir Francis Beaufort (see pp.228–29), and permitted a gradual improvement in knowledge of the maritime wind climate. Additionally, observations of sea-surface temperatures, taken from shipping lanes for several centuries, provide a long series that is essential to climate change studies. Climate scientists must adjust the figures to account for errors introduced by the different ways in which sea-surface temperature is measured. Some vessels measure the temperature at the intake where sea water is used for engine cooling, which biases the value to a little warmer than the actual sea-surface

value. Others throw a bucket over the side, then haul it up to the deck to measure the water temperature. This tends to underestimate the real value because the water loses heat depending on the type of bucket used, whether it be wood, canvas, or some other material. Modern buckets are made with insulating materials that minimize heat loss.

RECONSTRUCTING TIME SERIES

The work of reconstructing time series for any long-period record of wind, temperature, or pressure, is a painstaking exercise. In addition to details of any changes in instrument type, it is vital to know the nature and timing of changes to its surroundings. Vegetation growth, or building development over time, will influence a site's wind flow, temperature, and precipitation catch.

REMOTE WEATHER STATIONS

Over the last 100 years, monitoring has become truly global, and remote stations, such as this one off the Labrador coast of North America, transmit measurements from automated instruments by radio.

Climate monitoring

The rapid pace of technological change has transformed climate monitoring. The most remote regions of land and sea have automatic, radio-linked weather stations, and orbiting weather satellites provide global mapping of indicators such as sea temperatures and ice cover.

SATELLITE MONITORING

A new era for climate observation dawned in April 1960, with the launch of the first weather satellite. Today, there is a network of geostationary and polar orbiting satellites monitoring climates and how they change with time (see pp.190–91). They provide data on indicators such as cloud cover and surface temperature. These are taken from the intensity of reflected solar radiation, and of emitted terrestrial radiation. They also measure temperature and humidity through the depth of the atmosphere.

Readings from satellites are used to form a long-term data set for climate change research. Variations in cloud

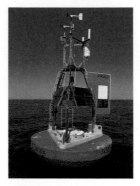

OBSERVING THE OCEANS
Over a thousand buoys take measurements from the atmosphere and the oceans.

cover and the height of clouds are potential indicators of climate change. Satellite images also provide an up-to-date picture of pollution levels, forest fires, snow cover, and the extent of glaciers and continental ice sheets. Land-use changes, such as deforestation, are also sensed by higher-resolution land-surface imaging satellites.

Sea-surface temperature is monitored frequently. Satellites measure the "skin" temperature of the ocean surface in cloud-free conditions, complementing the measurements taken by ships and buoys (see pp.242–43) to provide a truly global picture.

DIRECT OCEAN MONITORING

The global network of drifting and fixed buoys has expanded over recent decades. Buoys monitor atmospheric variables,

MAPPING THE CRYOSPHERE
The frozen components of the Earth's environment, known as the cryosphere, are mapped by satellites that monitor changes in ice and snow cover.

MONITORING PRECIPITATION
The frequency of torrential downpours and the incidence of floods are both measures of possible change that are monitored by climate observers.

such as air and sea-surface temperature, by relaying their data in real time via satellite. Ocean floats sink down to 3,300 ft (1,000 m), and measure salinity and temperature at different depths as they are carried along by ocean currents. This aids the study of changes in the oceanic heat budget and circulation as the Earth warms (see pp.60–61). Buoys also provide a range of data on wave height that can be used, over longer time spans, to assess the degree of storminess at sea, and how this changes over time.

FULLY AUTOMATIC
A meteorologist checks an automatic weather station on Antarctica. It collects basic data on wind speed, daylight hours, humidity, and temperature. Results are relayed by satellite to a base station.

SEASONAL MONITORING

Climate scientists are not only interested in the extent of thermal change—they look to other indicators that might arise from such change. With long series of data from climate stations, it is possible to detect trends in the number of days with snowfall, frosts, maximum temperatures exceeding a critical threshold, or precipitation levels above a significant total. Events involving more extreme precipitation are likely to be part of the global warming story, as are the incidence of dry spells or droughts in some areas.

There is now proof that the growing season is lengthening in some parts of the world, adding further evidence of a change in the Earth's climate.

Evidence of global warming

In the hundred years from 1906 to 2005, the global average surface temperature rose by 1.3°F (0.74°C). A substantial part of this rise occurred in the last 50 years. Scientific evidence has shown beyond doubt that our world is warming.

WARMING LAND AND SEA

From 1995 to 2007, the world experienced 12 of the 13 hottest years on record (although one year, 1998, is known to have been influenced by an El Niño, so cannot solely be attributed to global warming). The rate of warming varies across the planet. The land is heating up roughly twice as fast as the oceans partly because much of the warmth is mixed down into the water, spreading the impact of warming into the depths. Higher northern latitudes are warming at twice the rate of the global average. Ice and snow in Greenland and the Arctic Ocean make this area more sensitive to warming than other parts of the Earth. This is because any decrease in snow or ice, which are highly reflective, exposes darker surfaces, such as open water or rocks. These surfaces absorb heat, which adds to the warming. Other evidence for global warming includes a decrease in the number of frosts, and an increase in warm days and nights in many parts of the world. The most recent decades have also seen longer-lasting heatwaves in many areas, including southern Europe.

THE FROZEN COMPONENT

Most of the world's glaciers are retreating. Arctic sea-ice cover has reduced by an average rate of 2.7 percent each decade since the late 1970s. At the end of the summer season of 2007, it had shrunk to its smallest

SHRINKING GLACIERS
Mountain glaciers, such as Grinnell Glacier in Montana, are in steady retreat around the Earth as a result of global warming.

Grinnell Glacier, 1933

Site of Grinnell Glacier, 2004

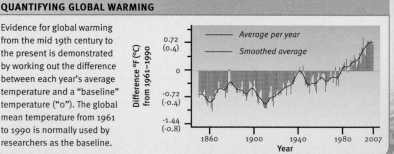

QUANTIFYING GLOBAL WARMING

Evidence for global warming from the mid 19th century to the present is demonstrated by working out the difference between each year's average temperature and a "baseline" temperature ("0"). The global mean temperature from 1961 to 1990 is normally used by researchers as the baseline.

Difference °F (°C) from 1961–1990

— Average per year
— Smoothed average

0.72 (0.4)
0
-0.72 (-0.4)
-1.44 (-0.8)

1860   1900   1940   1980 2007
Year

ERODING COASTLINES
Increases in global temperatures have led to a greater frequency of extreme weather, such as storms. This, along with higher sea levels, is causing severe erosion along some coasts.

extent since records began. Around the edges of Greenland and Antarctica, the continental ice sheets are melting, and massive icebergs are breaking off. The ice cap at the center of Greenland is, conversely, thickening due to an increase of snowfall across this region. Areas of permafrost (permanently frozen ground) are now temporarily thawing to a greater depth in many places, including Siberia.

RISING SEA LEVELS

Evidence from long-term tide records and recent satellite observations shows that sea levels are rising. The melting of continental ice sheets and glaciers is adding to sea levels, but melting sea ice does not contribute to rising levels because it is already displacing its own weight in water. The rate at which sea levels rise may increase further as the edges of some ice sheets destabilize and ice slips into the ocean. The biggest factor causing sea levels around the world to rise, however, is the expansion of the water in the oceans as it warms.

MELTING ICE SHEETS
As the continental ice sheet around Antarctica breaks up, this leads to the "calving" (formation) of giant icebergs. In 2000, an iceberg the size of Connecticut calved from the Ross Ice Shelf.

The human contribution

The greenhouse effect is a natural phenomenon that makes the Earth habitable, but human activity—agricultural and industrial— has enhanced the effect. Particles produced by industrial combustion offset warming, while manmade greenhouse gases enhance it.

ENHANCED GREENHOUSE EFFECT

There is strong evidence that the Earth's greenhouse effect has been strengthened as a result of human activity over the last 250 years or so. Observations confirm that the concentration of carbon dioxide has increased by more than 35 percent since the start of the Industrial Revolution in the mid 18th century. During the same period, concentrations of two other important greenhouse gases have increased because of human activity—methane has more than doubled, and nitrous oxide has increased by about 20 percent. These rates of increase are very unusual— levels of all three gases were more or less constant for thousands of years before the Industrial Revolution, but are higher today than they have been for hundreds of thousands of years. The impact these

INDUSTRIAL POLLUTION
Industrial furnaces emit smoke particles into the atmosphere, along with gases and water vapor in plumes of steam from cooling towers.

gases have on climate varies, depending on their lifetime, abundance in the atmosphere, and potency. Carbon dioxide (CO_2) is the most abundant manmade greenhouse gas. A molecule of CO_2 released into the air will last

TRAFFIC FUMES
The engines of vehicles, ships, and aircraft emit both carbon dioxide and nitrous oxide, which further increases global greenhouse gas concentrations.

CHARLES KEELING

US scientist Charles Keeling (1928–2005) trained as a chemist and spent most of his career at the Scripps Institute of Oceanography in California. Keeling discovered that a fraction of the carbon dioxide produced by industrial activity remains in the atmosphere, rather than being completely absorbed by the oceans and vegetation, thus proving that human activity is increasing carbon dioxide concentrations in the atmosphere.

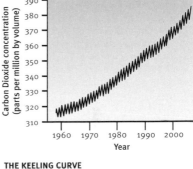

about 100 years, while methane has a lifetime of about 12 years and is much less abundant, but one molecule is about 30 times more potent than one of CO_2. Water vapor is the most abundant greenhouse gas, but its concentration is not directly affected by human activity.

Greenhouse gases absorb outgoing terrestrial radiation and re-emit it in all directions—some of it back toward the Earth to increase temperatures in the lower atmosphere. Concentrations of CO_2 have increased over the last few centuries due to the burning of fossil fuels and land-use changes, including large-scale deforestation. Concentrations of methane have risen due to biomass burning, landfill, and increased cattle and rice farming; those of nitrous oxide due to fertilizer use and biomass burning.

AEROSOL PARTICLES

Artificial aerosols, such as sulfates, are injected into the atmosphere by industry. The tiny particles reflect incoming solar radiation, so offsetting the influence of greenhouse gases. Action to reduce industrial pollution will lessen the "masking" effect that aerosols have on global warming. It is these particles that are reducing the intensity of sunlight

THE KEELING CURVE
Keeling expressed the annual increase in CO2 in a simple graph. The saw-tooth effect occurs because plants absorb more CO2 in the northern hemisphere summer when plant growth is higher than in winter.

reaching the Earth's surface—known as global dimming. Contrails from jet aircraft both reduce incoming radiation and absorb outgoing radiation. Their net effect is to warm the atmosphere.

DEFORESTATION
Large-scale clearance of rain forests, such as Amazonia, increases CO2 levels through logging and burning.

Climate modeling

The modeling of the climate has greatly improved in recent years, thanks to the advent of supercomputers. Their immense calculation power, along with rapidly improving data and understanding, is used to simulate the complex interactions that affect the Earth's climates.

ADVANCES IN CLIMATE MODELING

In the same way that computer models are used to compile weather forecasts (see pp.186–87), climate models are designed to solve complex equations that express the physical laws governing the behavior of the atmosphere, land, and oceans.

The climate system is extremely complicated, involving a range of interactions and feedbacks between its components. Different types of cloud, for example, have different influences on climate. As understanding of this complexity has improved, representation in climate models of the processes involved has become more comprehensive. At the same time, rapid advances in computing power have transformed modeling from the simplified atmosphere simulations used in the 1970s. Contemporary climate models include "interactive" clouds that grow and dissipate in a realistic manner, ocean currents and temperatures, the full range of land surfaces with their distinctive climates, and aerosols from industry.

EARLY CLIMATE MODELING

The first climate models, developed in the 1970s, used a very simple simulation of the atmosphere. Precipitation was included but clouds were not, and while carbon dioxide and its role in the thermal balance of the atmosphere was included, the result was only a partial picture.

CO2

Rain

Natural and industrial aerosols reflect incoming solar radiation

Agricultural developments release methane

Plants and soil exchange moisture and Co2 with the atmosphere

Manmade greenhouse gas emissions trap heat

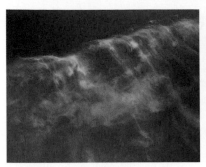

CLIMATE FACTORS—HIGH CLOUDS
Cirrus clouds, including contrails, reflect some solar radiation but trap more outgoing terrestrial radiation, with a net warming effect.

CLIMATE FACTORS—LOW CLOUDS
Low cloud tends to reflect a large amount of incoming solar radiation and trap less long-wave radiation, with a net cooling effect.

LONG-TERM THINKING

Unlike weather models, which can produce widely varying forecasts depending on the initial conditions (see pp.198–99), climate models are not driven by short-term changes in the weather. Climate is influenced by the balance between incoming and outgoing radiation. Over seasons and years, oceans and land surfaces play a key role in shaping the nature of climate, while over longer time scales (a decade to a century), greenhouse gas concentrations dominate.

Clouds reflect sunlight and trap infrared radiation

The amount of ice cover affects the amount of solar radiation that is reflected

Melting ice affects sea temperature and ocean circulation

Ocean circulation distributes heat and CO_2

Ocean and atmosphere exchange heat and CO_2

CLIMATE MODEL VARIABLES

A typical climate model divides the world into grid spaces of 84 miles (135 km), with 38 levels in the atmosphere and 40 under the ocean's surface. The phenomena and processes represented in such a model include:

Clouds—affect the level of heating and cooling of the atmosphere, and may produce precipitation.

Oceans—act as vast thermal stores of heat and CO_2, transporting them around the world.

Land surfaces—various factors, such as topography and reflectivity, determine the degree of heat loss and absorption.

Aerosols—particulates in the atmosphere generally have a cooling effect on climate and can change the properties of clouds.

Chemistry—changes in greenhouse gas concentrations are related to warming, and are caused by changes in the biosphere, such as deforestation and expansion of farming.

COMPLETE CLIMATE MODEL
Climate models are increasingly sophisticated. They include a rich range of governing factors, including complex interactions between the land, oceans, and atmosphere.

Modeling recent change

Records show that there has been a significant warming in the Earth's climate over the last 100 years. By running simulations that take account of different factors affecting climate, scientists can determine which changes are due to humans and which are natural.

PROVING THE CASE

Before attributing a cause to climate change, scientists first had to demonstrate conclusively that it was indeed taking place. Global observations of various climate variables, such as temperature and rainfall, have been made for over a century and a half. Scientists painstakingly monitor the climate using data from stations across the globe that deploy a host of different instruments. Careful analysis of the data has enabled scientists to show how climate has changed.

From year to year, temperatures can show a certain amount of variability. However, over the period for which global records exist as a whole (from about 1850), global temperatures show a distinct upward trend, leading scientists to conclude that the world is warming.

TRACKING SOLAR OUTPUT
Changes in solar output can cause climate change, but the levels of energy reaching the Earth from the Sun have been very stable over the past 50 years.

This warming has largely taken place in two distinct phases—during the early to mid 20th century and, most dramatically, over the last 40 years. There have also been short periods of cooling within the 150-year period.

MODELING THE CAUSES

In a 2007 report, the Intergovernmental Panel on Climate Change (IPCC) very clearly attributed a cause to recent climate change, stating that "it is very likely that anthropogenic greenhouse gas increases caused most of the

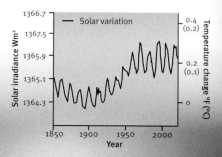

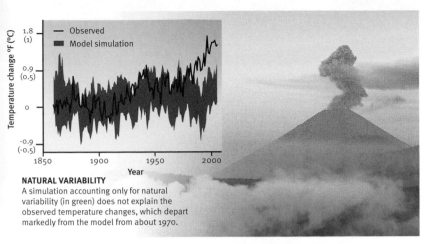

NATURAL VARIABILITY
A simulation accounting only for natural variability (in green) does not explain the observed temperature changes, which depart markedly from the model from about 1970.

observed increase in global temperatures since the mid 20th century." Climate models play a key role in revealing the causes of this change. Simulations can be run with different variables that affect climate, and these can be compared with observed data. For example, changes in manmade greenhouse gases and aerosols can be omitted to see how they affect temperature. In this way, it is possible to see whether the increase in temperature can be explained by natural variability—such as changes in solar output, volcanic activity, and internal variability—or by human interference in the climate system. If, when all plausible factors are included, the match with observed data is good, this gives confidence that the model is accurate.

INTERPRETING THE MODELS

The models show the probable causes of the warm and cool phases during the last 150 years. The cool period from the 1880s to the 1920s coincided with a number of volcanic eruptions that injected aerosols and ash into the stratosphere. A warm period in the mid 20th century is likely to have been caused by an increase in solar output and greenhouse gases. A stable period from about 1945 to 1975 was in part due to significant amounts of anthropogenic aerosol in the lower atmosphere. Since about 1980, clean air acts have reduced aerosol levels, while levels of greenhouse gases have increased, and this has coincided with a period of rapid global warming.

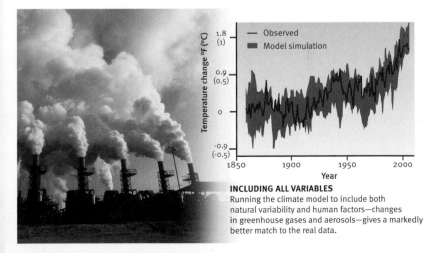

INCLUDING ALL VARIABLES
Running the climate model to include both natural variability and human factors—changes in greenhouse gases and aerosols—gives a markedly better match to the real data.

"CLIMATE IS A FUNCTION OF TIME. IT VARIES. . . IT HAS A HISTORY."

Emmanuel Le Roy Ladurie

Predicting future climates

Observations indicate that the climate is changing—and at a rapid rate. Most scientists are more confident than ever that these changes are the result of human activities, and the question is not whether the global temperature will continue to increase, but by how much.

TEMPERATURE AND PRECIPITATION

All climate-prediction models forecast an increase in global temperature, but its magnitude will depend upon industrial growth and change over the coming century. Even if the emission of greenhouse gases were stabilized at current levels, the increased emissions of recent years are already enough to produce warming over the next two decades. Over that period, about 50 percent of the predicted warming of 0.7°F (0.4°C) will be due to gases already emitted. The oceans delay the rate of increase by storing large amounts of heat in their slow, deep-water circulation.

The Intergovernmental Panel on Climate Change (IPCC) report of 2007 indicated that the likely range of global warming by the close of this century is 3.2°F (1.8°C) to 7.2°F (4°C), depending on emissions. Land surfaces are expected to warm more than the oceans. High northern latitudes will warm most rapidly,

INCREASING DROUGHT
Climatologists predict that precipitation across the subtropics will decrease over the coming century, leading to more frequent droughts.

because of a greater proportion of land mass and, as Arctic ice melts, the reduction in surface reflectivity will amplify the warming.

Mean global precipitation is predicted to increase, as higher temperatures cause greater evaporation. Although

CLIMATE PREDICTION ONLINE

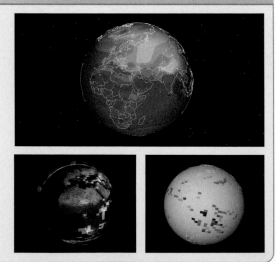

Anyone with a computer can volunteer it for use in climate prediction at www.climateprediction.net. This study produces climate forecasts for the century by using spare capacity on about 100,000 machines worldwide. The network's unique advantage is that a many-thousand-member ensemble can be run to study the simulation's response to small changes to its starting conditions. Forecasts include temperature (top), cloud cover (bottom left), and precipitation (bottom right).

TEMPERATURE CHANGE AND FUTURE EMISSIONS

The UK Met Office Hadley Centre's climate-prediction models are based on a range of possible future emission scenarios. A1F1 represents a fossil-fuel-powered world of rapid economic growth. A2 represents a less globalized economy than A1F1. B2 shows slower population growth than A2, alongside diverse technological changes. B1 shows the world moving toward a service-based economy and low-carbon technologies.

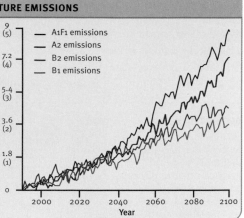

— A1F1 emissions
— A2 emissions
— B2 emissions
— B1 emissions

Global temperature rise °F (°C)

9 (5)
7.2 (4)
5.4 (3)
3.6 (2)
1.8 (1)
0

2000   2020   2040   2060   2080   2100
Year

precipitation is highly variable in space and time, an increase is expected to occur across high latitudes and a decrease over the subtropics between about 20 and 40 degrees latitude. Warming oceans may cause areas affected by oceanic weather systems to experience more torrential rain.

WARMING OCEAN AND LAND

Sea level is predicted to increase due to the expansion of warming oceans, coupled with meltwater from land-based ice. These two factors are forecast to lead to an increase of sea level between 8 in (0.2 m) and 2 ft (0.6 m) by the end of the century. However, this range does not include the potential impact of accelerating ice flow as ice sheets become destabilized by warming.

The rate of Arctic sea-ice melt is predicted to increase to the extent that by the end of this century, there will be virtually no ice left at the end of each summer. Polar snow cover is expected to decrease and permafrost will thaw each year to a much greater depth, which will both expose darker, more absorptive surfaces, leading to further warming.

Warmer land and oceans are likely to absorb less carbon dioxide, leading to a higher concentration in the atmosphere. This change to the global carbon cycle could create positive feedback (tending to increase temperatures still more) and have as yet uncertain consequences on the global climate.

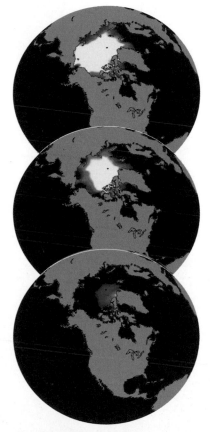

PROJECTED ICE CAP SHRINKAGE
Computer-prediction models simulate the reduction in average August-to-October Arctic sea ice concentration from 1885 (top), 1985 (middle), and 2085 (bottom).

Extreme events

The evidence indicates that future climate change will bring an increased number of extreme weather events, such as floods or drought. A relatively small increase in average temperatures can have a significant effect on the frequency or intensity of severe weather.

DEFINING EXTREMES

An extreme weather event is defined as an event that rarely occurs at a particular time or place—an extreme event in one part of the world would not necessarily count as extreme in another. Temperatures associated with a heatwave in northern Europe, for example, might not be unusual for Africa. Extremes include tropical storms, intense rainfall, droughts, and maximum and minimum temperatures.

HURRICANE SEASON
June to November 2005 was the most active storm season on record in the North Atlantic. There were 28 tropical storms, of which 15 developed into hurricanes, including the destructive Katrina.

HEAT AND PRECIPITATION LEVELS

Over the last 50 years, the number of hot days and nights worldwide has increased, and the number of cold days and nights has decreased, with fewer frosts. This observed trend is predicted to continue in the future, with a greater frequency of heatwaves, such as the record-breaking European heatwave of 2003. There has been a notable decrease in the number of frost days over many mid-latitude regions.

As the atmosphere warms, it is able to hold more moisture, which leads to more rainfall globally. However, there

FLOODING AND MIGRATION
Sea level rise combined with stronger storm surges could lead to increased flooding and migration in regions including Bangladesh.

are local variations in the amount and intensity. Mid-latitudes, for instance, have seen greater increases of intense precipitation over this period.

Changes in the duration of drought can be detected by analyzing monthly precipitation totals and temperature averages. The evidence points to a drying trend across much of the northern hemisphere's land areas in the last 50 years—including southern Eurasia, Canada, and northern Africa —due to both decreased precipitation and enhanced evaporation caused by greater surface warming.

TROPICAL CYCLONES AND STORMS

Unraveling the impact of global warming on tropical cyclones is difficult as their frequency and intensity vary greatly from year to year. In addition, El Niño events are known to affect Pacific and North Atlantic cyclones.

Climate models predict that tropical cyclones could become less frequent, but their intensity is expected to increase.

A number of studies have shown an increase in the number and intensity of extratropical storms over the last 50 years. There has also been a poleward migration of storm tracks. Models suggest a future poleward shift of storm tracks in both hemispheres, particularly the southern.

EXTREME DROUGHT
Overall, global precipitation is rising, but certain regions of the world, such as North Africa, are experiencing an increased incidence of drought, which kills livestock and destroys crops.

SYDNEY ENGULFED
Increased drought is likely to lead to dangerous bush fires encroaching on Australian cities more frequently, such as the bush-fire smoke that engulfed Sydney in 2002.

Dangerous, sudden change

Over the coming decades, global warming and climate change are
likely to progress gradually. Scientists predict, however, that certain
changes may happen suddenly if some features of the climate system
reach a critical "tipping" point, and many changes may be irreversible.

OCEAN CIRCULATION CHANGE

The global circulation of
the oceans—known as the
thermohaline circulation,
which is driven by
differences in temperature
and salinity—is an important
means of transporting heat
from the tropics to higher
latitudes. Scientists believe
that the increasing supply
of fresh water to the
northern North Atlantic,
from melting ice sheets

STORES OF METHANE
Methane clathrate is formed
when water molecules
freeze around a molecule
of methane gas.

and increased rainfall, could influence
the ocean circulation. Less dense fresh
water at the surface may lead to the
slowing, or even shutting down,
of this important system of heat
transportation. This could result in
the cooling of the climate in large parts
of Europe, although scientists do not
believe this will occur this century, and
a total shutdown is very unlikely.

CHANGING THERMOHALINE CIRCULATION
The transportation of heat to Europe by the North
Atlantic ocean circulation may decline or even stop
if there is a substantial increase in freshwater.

METHANE RELEASE

Methane clathrate is an icy
solid buried in sediments at
the bottom of the ocean.
There is a huge store of this
compound under the oceans
today, and it is thought that
the substance may have
caused rapid climate changes
in the past. Warmer sea floor
temperatures may result in
the melting of this icy solid,
causing a rapid increase in
the number of methane
bubbles rising through the oceans and
being released into the atmosphere.
Methane is a powerful greenhouse
gas, and a jump in its concentration
in the atmosphere could result in
sudden climate change.

MELTING PERMAFROST

Permanently frozen soil, known as
permafrost, lies under large tracts of
land in the high-latitude regions of the
northern continents, accounting for
between 20 and 25 percent of the
Earth's land surface. In recent years,

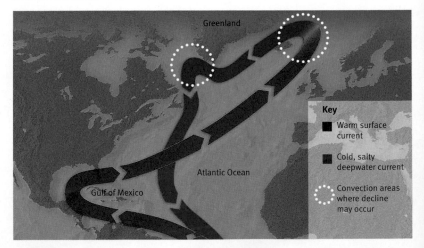

Greenland

Key
- Warm surface current
- Cold, salty deepwater current
- Convection areas where decline may occur

Atlantic Ocean

Gulf of Mexico

MELTING PERMAFROST
Warming across high, northern continental areas has led to the thawing of permafrost. As a result, buildings have been damaged and stored methane has been released into the atmosphere.

warming has led to more widespread thawing of the upper layers in some places. As a result, some buildings have collapsed and pipelines have fractured. More importantly, thawing has caused the release of methane into the atmosphere, accelerating global warming.

MELTING ICE SHEETS
The world's continental ice sheets—over Greenland and Antarctica—are melting around the edges. Climate scientists have shown that a warming of about 8.1°F (4.5°C) in Greenland could lead to significant shrinking of the ice sheet. If this trend continues, the rate at which sea levels are rising will increase significantly from today's rate of 0.12 in (3 mm) each year.

The most vulnerable parts of ice sheets are thought to be the "marine" ice sheets, which rest on rock that is below sea level. Marine ice sheets sitting on bedrock that slopes downward inland are unstable, and warming above a certain critical temperature could cause them to collapse in a very short space of time. The largest remaining marine ice sheet is in west Antarctica. Scientists are monitoring coastal glaciers in the region. If the glaciers' movement speeds up, this is an indication that the ice sheet may be on the verge of collapse. If that happens, the sea level will rise by 20 ft (6 m) over the next few centuries.

-30 days   -15 days   0   +15 days   +30 days

GREENLAND MELT-DAY ANOMALY
The Greenland melt-day anomaly map shows the difference between the number of days on which melting of the ice sheet occurred in 2007, compared to the average annual melting days from 1988–2006. If the entire 0.68 million cu miles (2.85 million cu km) of ice were to melt, global sea levels would rise by 23.6 ft (7.2 m).

AMAZON FOREST DAMAGE
Some climate models suggest that a warming climate could cause shifts in the atmospheric circulation around Amazonia, which would lead to frequent droughts similar to those seen in 2005. This would increase the risk of fire and add to the impact of deforestation. It is even possible that rainfall could drop below the level necessary to support rain forest, which would accelerate climate change by releasing more CO_2 into the atmosphere.

DEFORESTATION
The destruction by humans of large areas of forest, such as Amazonia, could lead to changes in the carbon cycle.

Impact on life on Earth

Climate change is already affecting the natural and human environment. As the Earth continues to warm, impacts will vary widely across the globe. Vulnerability will depend not only on the nature and level of climate change, but on the capacity of systems to adapt.

WATER RESOURCES

As the world's population rises, the stress on water resources is increasing. Climate change will add to this stress as rising temperatures lead to increased evaporation and changes in precipitation patterns. (Plants may conserve more water as CO_2 in the atmosphere increases, however, partly offsetting this.) While some areas will suffer drought, others will be affected by flooding. Water availability is predicted to decrease by 10–30 percent in some dry, mid-latitude and tropical regions, but in higher latitudes and parts of the humid tropics, it will increase by up to 40 percent.

As global temperatures rise above a certain threshold, agricultural production is expected to fall. A warming over the coming century of 1.8–5.4°F (1–3°C) is likely to improve crop productivity across higher latitudes, but a greater increase would be harmful.

EXTINCTIONS

The golden toad, native to Costa Rica, was declared extinct in 1992, as a consequence of climate change-related disease.

Golden toad

At lower latitudes, in the dry tropics, even a small change in temperature will reduce crop yields. Some African countries that depend on rain-fed agriculture rather than irrigation could see a reduction of up to 50 percent by 2020. In the meantime, drought and floods can also impact on yields. Combined with an increasing human population, malnutrition will be a growing problem, particularly for child health and development.

More than one-sixth of the world's population depends on melt water from snow and glaciers. Melt water from the Himalayas may lead to increased flooding in the region by 2030, but later in the century the

ENVIRONMENTAL DESTRUCTION

The vivid colors found in coral reefs are produced by tiny unicellular algae called zooxanthellae, which live symbiotically with the coral. Extreme sea temperatures kill the algae. In turn, the coral and the fauna that lived in it also die.

MASS MIGRATION
In 2005–06, east Africa suffered its worst drought in 50 years. As crops fail, increasing numbers will migrate away from arid areas, leading to humanitarian disasters.

reduction in the volume of water stored in ice and snow will decrease the water available for human consumption.

SPECIES EXTINCTION

If the mean temperature increases by 1.8–4.5°F (1.5–2.5°C) above 1990 levels, it is estimated that 20–30 percent of plant and animal species assessed so far will be at an increased risk of extinction. Polar bears are one of many particularly vulnerable species, as they hunt seals on Arctic sea ice, which is already disappearing. Many coastal ecosystems are sensitive to climate change. An increase of just 2°F (0.9°C) could bleach many coral reefs.

CHANGING FISH STOCKS
As the Pacific Ocean grows warmer, salmon are changing their migration routes in search of colder water. Fishermen must move with them.

NATURAL DISASTERS

Disease and natural disasters are likely to increase in some areas as heatwaves, floods, drought, and wildfires become more common. Disease-carrying insects could migrate to regions where they were previously not present. The spread of malaria will depend on practices such as swamp drainage and spraying.

Approximately 23 percent of the global population lives near the coast. These communities will become more vulnerable as sea levels rise, exacerbated by the expected increase in coastal population. Some deltas are expected to see more flooding by rivers swollen by increased rainfall and glacial melt.

TACKLING CLIMATE CHANGE

Climate change is a global problem that requires a global solution. This was recognized as early as 1992 when, at the UN Earth Summit in Rio de Janeiro, more than 150 countries expressed a desire to stabilize greenhouse gas emissions. However, emissions continue to rise, and we must now plan to deal with future changes.

MITIGATION

The reduction of greenhouse gas emissions—by cutting fossil-fuel use or by increasing the removal of such gases from the air—is known as mitigation. Such measures range from switching off a light when not needed to replacing coal-fired power stations with nuclear-powered ones.

At a meeting of international representatives at Kyoto, Japan, in 1997, the Kyoto Protocol, an agreement setting out targets for greenhouse gas reductions, was adopted. Binding targets were set for the developed nations because they are better placed economically to reduce emissions and historically they have been the major

SAVING ENERGY
Standard light bulbs convert just 5 percent of their energy into light. Energy-saving bulbs produce the same amount of light using 80 percent less electricity.

source of the problem. Some poorer nations were permitted to increase their output to promote economic growth.

For the Protocol to have binding legal status, a majority of developed nations had to ratify it. This occurred in February 2005. By 2008, 182 nations had ratified the Protocol, including the whole of the EU. Of these, 137 nations—including China, which is now the largest producer of carbon dioxide, Brazil, and India—had, for the moment, agreed only to a monitoring and reporting role. The world's second-largest producer of carbon dioxide, the US, had refused to ratify the Protocol.

IMPROVED SEA DEFENSES
As sea levels rise, flood defenses around low-lying coasts will need to be rebuilt. Areas already at risk of flooding will need extra defenses, and some harbors or marinas may have to be abandoned.

No matter what action is taken over the coming 20 years, inertia in the climate system means that some change is inevitable. It takes a long time for the oceans to warm up and to cool down, so there will be a time lag of several years after greenhouse gas emissions have been cut before any benefits will be felt. Changes in the way we do things now will not significantly affect developments over the next two decades. This means some adaptation is already necessary, from increasing rainwater storage in urban areas to the development of drought-resistant crop strains.

The concept of a personal or collective "carbon footprint" has raised awareness of the impact of individual and group activity on the environment, and schemes such as carbon trading have been proposed to provide an economics-based solution. However, great challenges face the world community as overall carbon emissions continue to increase. Richer nations still consume fossil fuels at a very high rate per capita, and as poorer countries strive to industrialize and raise the living standards of their people, their carbon footprints grow ever larger. The Kyoto targets fall short of what is required to stabilize climate, but they are seen as an important first step in tackling climate change.

ADAPTATION

Preparing for and protecting against the impacts of climate change will involve varying levels of adaptation. This will range from improving ventilation in homes to cope with more extreme summer temperatures to extending flood protection schemes. Rising sea levels mean that low-lying coasts are at increasing risk of inundation. Governments need to decide whether to invest money in coastal defenses or, in some cases, to give up relatively unproductive land.

THE BALI CONFERENCE

The Kyoto Protocol expires in 2012, and the UN Framework Convention on Climate Change was convened in Bali in December 2007 to discuss a new pact to replace it. Negotiations were protracted due to the politically sensitive nature of the proposals, and took their toll on the Executive Secretary of the Convention, Yvo de Boer, who broke down at one point. At the end, more than 10,000 delegates from 189 nations agreed to the "Bali Road Map," which will establish a new negotiating process to tackle climate change.

Lobbying for change

As the evidence for human-induced climate change has grown, scientific bodies have used this new information to lobby governments and compel them to tackle the problem. Crucial to their work are the improved data on climate, and the technology used to obtain it.

THE ROLE OF THE IPCC

The Intergovernmental Panel on Climate Change (IPCC) was established in 1988 by the World Meteorological Organization and the United Nations Environment Program to "provide decision makers with an objective source of information regarding climate change." The IPCC is a unique world body, which carefully assesses and synthesizes a vast body of scientific climate research. The involvement of scientists worldwide and from diverse disciplines ensures that the science is thorough and balanced.

Assessment Reports published by the IPCC informed the crucial UN summits on climate change in Rio de Janeiro in 1992, Kyoto in 1997, and Bali in 2007. On December 10, 2007, the IPCC and former US Vice President Al Gore were awarded the Nobel Peace Prize "for their efforts to build up and disseminate greater knowledge about manmade

PUSHING THE CAUSE
The IPCC convened in Budapest in April 2008 to discuss the role of its task force bureau, which was charged with raising awareness of climate change.

climate change, and to lay the foundations for the measures that are needed to counteract such change."

INCREASED CONFIDENCE

As more research is undertaken, and as the time series of climate data grows, scientists are becoming more confident in their results. The most recent IPCC scientific assessment report, published in 2007, stated that, "it is *very* likely that anthropogenic greenhouse gas increases caused most of the observed increase in global average temperature since the mid 20th century." This can be compared to the previous report in 2001 in which the assessment was that it was *likely*. These terms are quantified: "likely" is greater than 66 percent probability; "very likely" is

greater than 90 percent probability.
Scientific confidence has grown
as a result of new and better
data, improved methods of analysis,
and a better understanding of
the physics of climate and its
representation in climate models.

FINER RESOLUTION IN PREDICTION MODELS
Improved resolution allows a better representation
of climate processes in computer models. The new
higher-resolution prediction of temperature change
(right) shows more detail than the older one (left).

BETTER MODELING

Improving climate
models help to resolve
atmospheric features,
including clouds, ice
sheets, vegetation, land
use, and topography,
and thus to enhance
the quality of the
prediction. Increased
computing power has
made it possible to
design finer-resolution
models with more levels

INCREASED COMPUTER POWER
The processing speed of supercomputers
is growing yearly, providing the power to
produce models in much finer resolution.

through the atmosphere and oceans.
Fine detail is very important. It enables
scientists to make regional forecasts from
climate models that are used to predict
global patterns. Any
increase in resolution
is limited by computing
power. Reducing the
size of each grid square
by half and doubling
the number of
atmospheric levels,
which increases the
accuracy of the model,
would require a
15-fold increase in
computer power.

MODELING UNCERTAINTY

Like weather forecasts, some climate
predictions use the ensemble technique to
judge uncertainty in predictions for the years
ahead (see pp.198–99). Below are four out of
hundreds of runs that were made of a model
depicting the range of possible precipitation

anomalies across the world by the end of
this century. Ensembles like this are used by
scientists to present probability predictions of
future climate to policymakers, who can then
build appropriate risk management measures
into their adaptation and mitigation strategies.

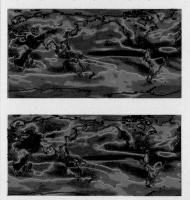

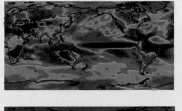

Sustainable energy

The global economy is heavily reliant on fossil fuels to provide energy, but these resources are a major cause of global warming and are vulnerable to security issues. The governments of many countries are now investing in energy sources that are sustainable and locally derived.

SOLAR POWER

Harnessing the global potential of solar power could theoretically satisfy all our energy demands. However, it has major drawbacks. Solar radiation is unevenly distributed across the planet, and it would be necessary to cover an impossibly large area with solar cells to generate the required output.

Nevertheless, even relatively cloudy, high-latitude locations can generate solar power using solar cells. These are made of silicon, whose atoms lose electrons when they are bombarded with photons from sunlight. Conductive wires draw the free electrons away from the cells, generating electricity. Cells can be mounted on domestic roofs to provide power for the home, or on business premises to generate electricity for commercial use, although commercial usage is limited at higher latitudes.

Solar-heating panels are being fitted on the roofs of more and more buildings around the world. They harness the Sun's energy to heat water, which is used to heat rooms. Installation of solar water heating has become the norm in countries with an abundance of sunshine, such as Israel and Greece. Following an energy crisis in the 1970s, the Israeli government passed a law

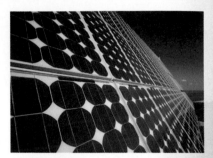

SOLAR PANELS
Industrial or domestic solar panels are angled toward the Sun for maximum efficiency. Some even track the Sun's daily movement across the sky.

requiring the installation of solar water heaters in all new homes. Israel is now the world leader in the use of solar energy.

Solar-heating panels are used on an industrial scale in some parts of the world with reliable sunshine, such as California and Spain, where solar-heating plants use the heat they capture to generate electricity. Solar-powered stoves are also being introduced in parts of Africa and India to reduce reliance on burning wood.

GEOTHERMAL POWER

Heat generated beneath the Earth's surface through volcanic activity can be used as an environmentally safe energy source. Steam and hot springs have been used for centuries for bathing and heating, but it was not until 1904 that the first geothermal power generator was

GEOTHERMAL STATIONS
Iceland has high levels of geothermal activity, and 87 percent of homes there are now powered by geothermal stations.

OFFSHORE FARM
Offshore wind farms usually generate more power than land-based farms because winds reach higher speeds over water. They are also less controversial, as they are sited away from populated areas.

tested at the Larderello dry steam field in Italy. Geothermal power is generated in more than 20 countries, and has good potential for expansion in regions such as Iceland and New Zealand, which have high levels of geothermal activity.

WIND POWER

Turbines driven by the wind are becoming more common in many areas and are usually most productive offshore or on exposed uplands, where average wind speeds are higher. The building of wind turbines is sometimes controversial, as they are often sited in scenic areas. Nevertheless, many nations are investing in wind farms. Although wind currently produces only about 1 percent of electricity worldwide, it accounts for approximately 20 percent of electricity production in Denmark, 10 percent in Spain and Portugal, and 5 percent in Germany and Ireland.

The disadvantage of wind power is that the strength of the wind varies from season to season and day to day, so that there will be periods when little power is generated. In some cold conditions, there can often be little wind, when electricity for heating is needed most.

TURBINE TECHNOLOGY

The mechanical energy generated by many sustainable sources is converted into electricity by turbines, with blades that are driven by a fluid flowing across them. In wind turbines, the wind rotates three blades linked to a shaft whose rotation generates an electrical current. Hydroelectric turbines are driven by water streaming from a dam.

Low-carbon solutions

As the world becomes more energy-hungry, clean forms of fuel that do not contribute to greenhouse gases are urgently needed. However, many of the alternatives to fossil fuels are beset by their own issues, both environmental and economic.

HYDROELECTRIC AND TIDAL POWER

Hydroelectric power supplies 19 percent of the world's electricity. It is able to satisfy fluctuations in demand by using storage reservoirs from which water can flow to drive turbines when necessary. However, the construction of huge dams, such as the Three Gorges Dam in China, may involve the destruction of sensitive ecosystems and the compulsory movement of large numbers of people.

Tidal power is most suitable in areas with strong tidal currents, or large tidal ranges. Tidal-barrage plants generate electricity using turbines as water flows in and out. Controversially, tidal plants can have a detrimental effect on fish populations and the wider ecosystem.

BIOFUEL PRODUCTION

The term "biofuel" refers to solid, gas, or liquid fuels that can be produced from biological sources of carbon, usually

HYDROELECTRICITY STATIONS
Energy produced by hydroelectric stations does not release carbon dioxide or other greenhouse gases. Such stations are a "clean" source of power, but impact significantly on the local environment.

plants. Crops are converted into liquid fuel, which is used mainly to power vehicles. Ethanol can be produced from sugar crops, such as sugar cane and beetroot, or from corn by fermentation. Oils from plants such as oil palm and soybean can be used directly in diesel engines or processed to produce biodiesel.

Increased production of biofuels has led to conflict between the demand for low-carbon fuel and the need to feed the world. Land that could be used to grow food crops is being used to grow biofuels, leading to food shortages. Rain forests are being stripped in places such as the Amazon to make way for sugar cane, possibly accelerating global warming. Biofuel can also be generated from

FIELDS OF FUEL
More and more agricultural land is being used to grow crops such as canola for biofuels, using space that would otherwise be used for food crops.

waste. Landfill sites generate methane and other gases that can be used for domestic heating. While biofuel from plants is renewable and sustainable, landfill generation of methane is not, and this method of waste disposal is becoming less common.

NUCLEAR POWER

The usual method of producing electricity from nuclear reactions is nuclear fission, in which the nuclei of atoms are split. This generates energy that is then used to boil water, producing steam that turns turbines.

Nuclear power has been used for more than 50 years to generate electricity. After a fairly rapid rise in

NUCLEAR REACTORS
More than 15 percent of world energy demand is supplied by nuclear power. France and the US are the world's main producers.

CARBON CAPTURE

Carbon capture or "sequestration" is a method for reducing carbon emissions by preventing the carbon dioxide produced by fossil-fuel power plants from entering the atmosphere. One scheme proposes to extract the carbon dioxide from fumes produced by power plants and store it securely in the empty oil and gas fields under the North Sea. It is estimated that carbon capture could reduce carbon dioxide emissions from power plants by 90 percent.

global output, production has slowed since the 1980s. This was partly due to fears of a repeat of the major disasters at Three Mile Island, in Pennsylvania in 1979 and Chernobyl, Ukraine, in 1986. Nevertheless, the advantages of nuclear energy as an alternative source of energy are now seen by some to outweigh the dangers, especially as newer, safer nuclear technologies are developed.

Geoengineering

A way of lessening the impact of global warming may be to mitigate its effects using technology. A number of untested techniques have been proposed to modify the environment to maintain habitable conditions. However, such methods may have unforeseen detrimental effects.

DEFLECTING RADIATION

Several techniques for deflecting the Sun's radiation away from the Earth have been proposed. One involves launching large-scale, orbiting space mirrors that would reflect sunlight back into space and reduce the radiation entering the Earth's atmosphere. This technique is problematic because it would not affect the levels of greenhouse gases in any obvious way. There may even be detrimental environmental consequences, such as increasing acidification of the oceans due, to the fact that CO_2 is absorbed more strongly with decreasing temperatures.

A simpler technique would be to "seed" clouds—making them reflect more incoming radiation by spraying seawater into them. Another proposal is to cool the atmosphere using aerosols, which block incoming solar radiation and play a role in offsetting global warming. One way of enhancing their role may be to launch sulfate aerosols into the stratosphere.

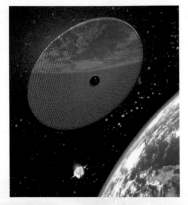

SPACE MIRRORS
Very large mirrors – up to 62 miles (100 km) in diameter –would be needed to reflect even a fraction of the incoming solar radiation, but would cool the region in their shadow.

BIOENGINEERING

Not all techniques aim to block incoming radiation. One method proposes to encourage the growth of phytoplankton in the oceans by

FIRING SULFUR PELLETS
Sulfur pellets could be launched into the atmosphere from warships. Increasing aerosol concentration in the lower stratosphere would, some scientists believe, offset warming by reflecting more of the incoming solar radiation.

PLANKTON GROWTH
Fertilizing the oceans with urea would encourage the growth of large "blooms" of phytoplankton, which may help to absorb CO_2.

introducing nitrogen-rich compounds. These would increase the absorption of CO_2 but may affect the oceans' ecosystem in unforeseen ways.

RADICAL SOLUTIONS
Halting deforestation and carbon emissions from industry is the best way to reduce greenhouse gas concentrations,

CLOUD SEEDING

The most reflective clouds are thick and made of water droplets. "Seeding" clouds over the ocean by spraying them with sea water produces more droplets and extends the area of the cloud, which then reflects more incoming radiation. However, this may have the side-effect of trapping the radiation that is reflected from the Earth.

but a radical geoengineering option may one day have to be considered if global warming becomes irreversible. However, the techniques are untested and it is difficult to know which would have measurable results. It would be hard, for example, to gauge the effect of the techniques designed to block radiation, given the natural variability of cloud cover. Any geoengineering solution could have unforeseen knock-on effects on the climate that may be highly undesirable.

Glossary

Accretion The process of supercooled water droplets freezing on contact with ice crystals to produce snowflakes.

Adiabatic The process by which air cools or warms by expansion or compression, without transfer of heat between the volume of air and its surroundings.

Aerosol Microscopic solid and liquid particles suspended in the atmosphere.

Air mass An extensive region of air that has broadly uniform temperature and humidity.

Albedo The percentage of solar radiation reflected by a surface.

Altocumulus Mid-level cloud composed of regularly arranged small elements.

Altostratus Mid-level layer cloud through which hazy sunshine may appear.

Anabatic wind Local airflow up a slope heated by sunlight.

Anemometer An instrument for measuring wind speed.

Aneroid barometer An instrument without liquid for measuring pressure.

Antarctic continental An extremely cold, dry air mass restricted to Antarctica.

Anticyclone A region of high pressure. It features clockwise flow in the northern hemisphere and counterclockwise flow in the southern.

Banner cloud Stationary cloud attached to an isolated mountain peak, extending downwind.

Barometer An instrument for measuring air pressure.

Barograph A self-recording barometer. A strip chart within the barograph displays a week's worth of data.

Beaufort scale A means of estimating wind speed by observing sea state and other criteria, such as swaying trees.

Blizzard Seriously reduced visibility due to heavy snow and high winds.

Bomb An extreme frontal depression, deepening by at least 24 hPa in 24 hours.

Breeze A wind of moderate strength.

Buys-Ballot's law A rule relating the distribution of highs and lows to wind direction, which states that when standing with one's back to the wind in the northern hemisphere, low pressure is to the left and high to the right.

Cell Large-scale patterns of air circulation in the atmosphere. Also used to describe separate areas of circulation within a cloud.

Clear air turbulence (CAT) Choppy airflow in cloud-free air.

Cirrocumulus Thin, high, ice-crystal cloud in the form of delicate ripples and small patches.

Cirrostratus High, ice-crystal cloud in a thin veil that often produces halos.

Cirrus Thin, high, ice-crystal cloud, often in the form of filaments or tufts.

Cloud An aggregate of water droplets, ice crystals, or both, suspended in the atmosphere.

Cloudhead A distinct, large, curved feature in the cloud pattern of a bomb.

Coalescence The process by which cloud droplets merge by colliding with each other.

Cold front The leading, elongated edge of a cold, dry air mass.

Condensation The change of state from water vapor into liquid water, releasing latent heat in the process.

Conduction A means of heat transfer by physical contact.

Contrail Condensation trail—a line of ice crystals produced by jet engines at high altitude.

Convection The process of heat transfer by the currents within a fluid.

Convergence A flowing together of air streams, linked to upward and downward motion.

Conveyor belt The ascending flow of moist air through the warm sector of a frontal depression.

Coriolis effect An apparent force that explains the deflection of the air or ocean currents on the rotating Earth.

Corona A series of colored rings around the Sun or Moon produced by diffraction of light through water drops.

Cumulonimbus Very tall, precipitating cloud with a low, flat base and fibrous, icy upper region, often with lightning and thunder.

Cumulus Detached, low cloud with a flat base and bulging upper surface.

Cyclone A region of low pressure. It features counterclockwise flow in the northern hemisphere and clockwise in the southern. Also a name for tropical storms originating in the Indian and southwest Pacific oceans.

Depression See cyclone.

Dew A deposition of water droplets, either from soil or from the air, onto a surface whose temperature has cooled by radiation to below the dew point of the air in contact with it.

Dew point The temperature to which the air must cool to be saturated with water vapor.

Divergence A spreading apart of airstreams, linked to upward and downward motion.

Doppler radar An instrument that senses the location of rain and maps the speed of the drops' movement toward and away from the instrument, to locate areas of convergence and divergence.

Drizzle Liquid precipitation of very small droplets produced in shallow, low-layer cloud.

Dropsonde A sensor package released from aircraft to provide pressure, temperature, humidity, and other data during its descent.

Dry adiabatic lapse rate The fixed rate of cooling or warming experienced by ascending or descending unsaturated air respectively.

Dry-bulb temperature The air temperature measured by a mercury-in-glass thermometer.

Dust-devil A whirlwind that carries dust or sand aloft by convection from a hot surface.

El Niño An occasional, pan-equatorial Pacific phenomenon involving migration of warm surface water eastward across the ocean, changing atmospheric circulation and producing anomalous dry or wet conditions over a larger area.

Electromagnetic spectrum The entire range of wavelengths of radiation, from the shortest (gamma rays) to the longest (radio waves).

Ensemble forecast A forecast method that accounts for the chaotic nature of the atmosphere by running a number of different forecasts with initial conditions simultaneously.

Environmental lapse rate The change of temperature or humidity with height as sensed by a balloon-borne instrument package.

Evaporation The change of liquid water or ice into water vapor; the change from ice is also known as sublimation.

Eye The calm centre of a hurricane, typhoon or cyclone, typically 9–15 miles (15–25 km) across.

Ferrel cell A large-scale, troposphere-deep circulation cell in mid-latitudes where flow is parallel to lines of longitude.

Fog Horizontal visibility of less than 3,300 ft (1 km) caused by suspended water droplets.

Front A sloping boundary between different air masses.

Frontal depression A traveling low-pressure system associated with different air masses.

Frost Icy deposits that occur when the temperature of a surface is below 32°F (0°C) and the adjacent air is below the dew point.

Frost hollow A localized, bowl-like surface into which cold air can accumulate in katabatic flow, leading to more frequent frosts.

Fujita scale A scale that expresses the severity of tornadoes based on the damage they inflict.

Funnel cloud Tubelike cloud that protrudes from the base of a parent cumulonimbus cloud, marking the potential for a tornado.

Gale A wind speed of between 34 and 40 knots, or force 8 on the Beaufort scale.

Geostationary orbit A satellite track above the equator that takes 24 hours to complete one orbit, so "hovers" above the same location.

Greenhouse effect An elevation in the Earth's surface temperature caused by greenhouse gases absorbing some outgoing long-wave radiation and re-radiating it back down. Without it, the lower atmosphere would be about 55°F (30°C) colder.

Greenhouse gases Gases that absorb and re-radiate some of the Earth's outgoing long-wave radiation, such as carbon dioxide and ozone.

Gridpoint Points of intersection on the latitude-longitude network used in weather and climate models.

Gust A very short-lived increase in wind speed, often related to interference with air flow by manmade or topographical features.

Hadley cell A large-scale, troposphere-deep circulation cell in the tropics, running parallel to meridians.

Hail Solid precipitation in the form of hard, mainly spherical pieces of ice produced within deep convective clouds.

Halo A circle around the Sun or Moon produced by refraction of light through ice crystals, commonplace in cirrostratus.

Haze A suspension of very small, dry particles, such as smoke and dust, reducing visibility.

HectoPascal (hPa) A unit of barometric pressure, equal to one millibar.

High A region of high barometric pressure; also known as an anticyclone.

Hoar frost Thin ice crystals in the form of scales, feathers, or needles, that are deposited on surfaces cooled by radiation.

Humidity The water-vapor content of the air.

Hurricane An intense tropical cyclone in the tropical north Atlantic.

Hygrometer An instrument for measuring relative humidity.

Ice pellets Solid precipitation that is neither hail nor snow, formed from freezing raindrops or melted snowflakes.

Infrared radiation A type of long-wave radiation emitted from relatively cool bodies, such as the Earth and atmosphere.

Instability An atmospheric state in which a small disruption, such as heating, will lead to a displacement of the warmed air.

Inter-Tropical Convergence Zone (ITCZ) The boundary between northeasterly and southeasterly trade winds across the equator.

Inversion An atmospheric layer in which the temperature (or humidity) increases with increasing height.

Iridescence Patches of color sometimes observed on high clouds, produced by diffraction of sunlight by small cloud particles.

Isobar A line joining places of the same barometric pressure.

Isotherm A line joining places with the same temperature.

Jet stream A long, snaking belt of strong winds, mainly in the upper troposphere.

Katabatic wind A flow of air down slopes on nights when the air is chilled by radiation.

Köppen classification The first method used to classify world climates based on vegetation cover and including non-vegetated regions.

La Niña A condition across the equatorial Pacific Ocean in which central and eastern areas have much cooler than average sea-surface temperatures, leading to seasonal anomalies.

Land breeze A gentle nighttime flow of air offshore on days when sea breezes have occurred.

Lenticular cloud Lenslike cloud formed most often to the lee of hills and mountains.

Lightning Huge electrical discharges associated with thunderstorms.

Long-wave radiation In meteorology, radiation emitted by relatively cool bodies, such as the Earth and atmosphere.

Low A region of low barometric pressure; also known as a cyclone.

Mammatus Bulbous protuberances on the underside of a cloud.

Maximum temperature In weather observation, the highest value of dry-bulb temperature within a Stevenson screen, usually over a 24-hour period.

Mercury barometer A standard, wall-mounted barometer that measures pressure by the height of a mercury column.

Mesocyclone A rotating column within a supercell storm. Mesocyclones are often associated with tornadoes.

Mesopause The upper boundary of the mesosphere roughly 50 miles (80 km) above the Earth.

Mesosphere The atmospheric layer between about 30 miles (50 km) and 80 km (50 miles), in which temperature decreases with height.

Methane A greenhouse gas produced mainly by biological decay.

Minimum temperature In weather observation, the lowest value of screen (or ground) dry-bulb temperature, usually over a 24-hour period.

Mist Impaired visibility of more than 3,300 ft (1 km), due to microscopic water droplets, with relative humidity greater than 95 percent.

Monsoon A seasonal reversal of winds associated with distinct wet and dry seasons.

Nacreous cloud Rare, possibly lenticular, stratospheric cloud observed at high latitudes.

Net radiation The difference between solar or terrestrial incoming and outgoing radiation.

Nimbostratus Extensive, thick, gray layer cloud from which precipitation falls.

Noctilucent cloud Luminous night cloud observed at high latitudes during summer, occurring at heights near the mesopause.

North Atlantic Oscillation (NAO) The fluctuation, between winter seasons, of the difference in pressure between the high-pressure center in the Azores and the low-pressure center around Iceland.

Nowcasting Very short-term weather forecast, most often of precipitation.

Occlusion A front in which warm, humid air is lifted away from the surface, usually accompanied by a narrow band of cloud and precipitation.

Orographic cloud Cloud produced by air cooling as it ascends hills or mountains.

Orography The study of large-scale mountainous regions.

Ozone Tri-atomic oxygen created and destroyed naturally in the stratosphere by ultraviolet radiation.

Ozone hole A region in the Antarctic stratosphere where ozone is depleted every spring by the presence of artificially produced gases.

Permafrost Soil that is permanently frozen.

Polar cell A troposphere-deep circulation cell that dominates the highest latitudes.

Polar continental A dry, cold air mass formed across the extensive wintertime continents of the northern high latitudes.

Polar low A relatively small-scale depression that forms in polar air over wintertime high-latitude oceans.

Polar maritime A mild, damp, showery air mass that has been modified by a long track across the sea.

Polar orbit The track of satellites over or nearly over both poles, producing a striplike image swathe.

Precipitation Solid and liquid water particles that fall from the atmosphere.

Pressure A measure of the downward force at a certain point exerted by the atmosphere above.

Pressure gradient The rate of change of atmospheric pressure between two points.

Psychrometer An instrument for measuring relative humidity, using wet-bulb and dry-bulb thermometers.

Radar Remote sensing instrument for mapping the location and intensity of precipitation.

Radiation A means of transporting energy by electromagnetic waves that involves no medium.

Radiosonde A balloon-borne instrument set that measures and transmits pressure, temperature, and relative humidity.

Rain Liquid precipitation in the form of drops with a diameter greater than 0.02in (0.5mm).

Rain gauge An instrument for measuring precipitation, usually daily.

Rain shadow A dry region to the lee of hills or mountains.

Rainbow An arch of spectrally colored bands produced by refraction and internal reflection of sunlight through raindrops.

Relative humidity The degree to which air is saturated with water vapor, expressed as a percentage.

Rime White, rough ice crystals (frost) deposited from supercooled water droplets that grow upwind on solid objects.

Saffir-Simpson scale A classification of hurricane intensity determined by wind strength and storm surge.

Sea breeze Inland penetration of cool, humid air from the sea.

Sensible heat Heat transferred by air motion from warmer to cooler bodies.

Short-wave radiation In meteorology, radiation emitted by the Sun.

Shower A short-lived burst of precipitation.

Smog Fog that has been partly formed by smoke or some other pollutant.

Snow Solid precipitation in the form of small hexagonal plates or snowflakes.

Southern Oscillation A fluctuation in the pressure difference between the southeast Pacific high and low pressure north of Australia; a small difference is linked to El Niño.

Specific humidity A measure of the mass of water vapor in a mass of air.

Spiral rain-band An inward-curving line of deep shower clouds, running toward the center of intense tropical cyclones.

Stability A state of the atmosphere in which a small disruption, such as moving over a hill, will lead to the air returning to its original position, to the lee of the hill.

Stevenson screen A white, slatted-side weather screen that houses maximum-temperature, minimum-temperature, wet-bulb, and dry-bulb thermometers.

Sting jet A damaging "jet" of accelerating air descending from the cloudhead of a "bomb."

Storm A general term for a windy, wet-weather disturbance, usually linked to a deep low.

Storm surge Elevated ocean-water surface produced by doming up underneath a traveling low-pressure system; can produce serious inundation along low-lying coasts.

Stratocumulus Low, usually non-precipitating cloud in extensive sheets that are formed of cumuliform patches.

Stratopause The upper boundary of the stratosphere at roughly 30 miles (50 km).

Stratosphere The very dry, stable layer of the atmosphere between about 6–11 miles (10–18 km) and 30 miles (50 km) above the surface, in which temperature increases with height.

Stratus Low-layer cloud in extensive sheets with a monotonously gray base.

Sundogs Bright spots either side of the Sun when it is near the horizon, caused by refraction of sunlight through ice crystals; also known as a "mock sun."

Supercell A severe-weather, rotating cumulonimbus cloud lasting many hours.

Temperature A measure of the heat content of a substance.

Tendency The rate of pressure change over a specified period of time, often three hours.

Thermal A warmed bubble of cloud-free air formed in unstable conditions.

Thermohaline circulation Ocean circulation that is determined by the combined effect of water temperature and salinity on density variation.

Thermometer An instrument used for measuring temperature.

Thermosphere A region of the atmosphere above 50 miles (80 km) where temperatures can reach 27,000°F (15,000°C).

Thunder The sound produced by the instantaneous, intense heating and expansion of the air by lightning.

Tornado A narrow, rotating column of air that reaches the ground from a parent cumulonimbus, marked by a funnel cloud or debris.

Trade winds Markedly constant winds that blow out from subtropical anticyclones toward the Inter-Tropical Convergence Zone.

Tropical continental An air mass that originates across hot, dry continental areas.

Tropical cyclone A term defining tropical rotating, traveling, low-pressure systems.

Tropical maritime A mild, damp air mass that originates from the subtropical oceanic highs and flows generally poleward.

Tropical storm A category of tropical cyclone in which the system is named; one category below tropical cyclone.

Tropopause The thin layer that tops the troposphere, above which temperature is constant or increases with height.

Troposphere The lowest layer of the atmosphere, within which temperature normally decreases with height. It contains virtually all the Earth's weather.

Typhoon The regional name used for intense tropical cyclones in the northwest Pacific.

Virga Streaks of precipitation falling from a cloud but not reaching the surface.

Visibility A measure of horizontal clarity of the atmosphere, defined as the greatest distance an object can be seen and recognized with the unaided eye.

Visible radiation The narrow waveband of radiation to which the eye is attuned.

Walker cell Troposphere-deep circulation, stretched along the equator with ascending and descending limbs, linked to upper- and low-level westerlies and easterlies.

Warm front A very gently sloping, leading edge of warm and damp air in a frontal cyclone, characterized by extensive cloud, widespread precipitation, and wind shift.

Warm sector A region of tropical maritime air in a frontal cyclone between the warm and cold fronts.

Water vapor The gaseous form of water, the concentration of which defines the air's humidity.

Wet-bulb temperature The temperature sensed by a thermometer that has a permanently wet muslin wick over its bulb. Wet-bulb temperature indicates the air's humidity.

Wind shear A change in wind speed in the horizontal or vertical direction.

Wind vane A flat-plate instrument that indicates wind direction.

Vortex A mass of rotating air or ocean, ranging in scale from a dust devil to an anticyclone.

Useful resources

NATIONAL WEATHER SERVICES

The following national weather services have useful websites:

National Weather Service
www.nws.noaa.gov

National Severe Storms Lab
www.nssl.noaa.gov

National Hurricane Centre
www.nhc.noaa.gov

National Storm Prediction Centre
www.spc.noaa.gov

Environment Canada
www.weatheroffice.gc.ca

Chinese Meteorological Agency
www.cma.gov.cn

Japanese Meteorological Agency
www.jma.go.jp/jma/indexe.html

SOCIETIES AND ORGANIZATIONS

These national societies offer up-to-date, authoritative data:

American Meteorological Society
www.ams.edu

National Weather Association
www.nwas.org

Canadian Meteorological and Oceanographic Society
www.cmos.ca

World Meteorological Organisation
www.wmo.int

GENERAL ONLINE WEATHER RESOURCES

The following organizations offer a range of resources, including latest forecasts:

CNN
www.cnn.com/WEATHER

USA Today
www.usatoday.com/weather/wfront.htm

CBC
www.cbc.ca/weather/map.jsp

World cities weather forecast and climate data
www.worldweather.org

SATELLITE IMAGERY

Some of the following satellite imagery sites have links to real-time satellite views of the Earth:

GOES (Geostationary Operational Environmental Satellites)

http://goespoes.gsfc.nasa.gov/goes/index.html
http://rsd.gsfc.nasa.gov/goes/text/hotstuff.html
http://wwwghcc.msfc.nasa.gov/GOES
http://198.122.199.231/GOES/goeseastconusir.html

SPECIALIST SITES

These sites focus on specialist aspects of weather phenomena, including tornadoes, hurricanes, and storm prediction:

The Tornado Project
www.tornadoproject.com

NOAA Storm Prediction Center
www.spc.noaa.gov

NOAA National Hurricane Center
www.nhc.noaa.gov
www.elnino.noaa.gov
www.elnino.noaa.gov/lanina.html

CLIMATE-CHANGE RELATED SITES

These sites have the latest scientific information and news on climate change:

NOAA National Climatic Data Center (NCDC)/Climate Extremes
lwf.ncdc.noaa.gov/oa/climate/severeweather/extremes.html

EPA Global Warming Site
www.epa.gov/globalwarming

NASA's Global Change Master Directory
gcmd.gsfc.nasa.gov/resources/learning/index.html

Environment Canada/Climate Change
www.ec.gc.ca/climate/home-e.html

Intergovernmental Panel on Climate Change
www.ipcc.ch

Index

Acknowledgments

Publisher's acknowledgments

Dorling Kindersley would like to thank Farrar, Straus & Giroux for use of the quotation from *Times of Feast, Times of Famine: A History of Climate Since 1000* (1988) by Emmanuel Le Roy Ladurie on p.255; the Maltings Partnership for artworks on pp.122–123, 136–137, and 238–239; the Apple Agency for the artworks on p.250; Kieran Macdonald for editorial help; Chris Bernstein for the index, Simon Tuite for development work, and Simon Gilbert, Barry Gromett, Helen Chivers, and Dave Britton at the Met Office.

PICTURE CREDITS

The publisher would like to thank the following for their kind permission to reproduce their photographs:

(Picture Key: a = above; b = below/bottom; c = center; f = far; l = left; r = right; t = top)

TOP BAR IMAGES
DK Images: Courtesy of the National Maritime Museum, London / James Stevenson 21-47; **Dreamstime.com:** Burcu Arat Sup 237-273; Jerry Horn 83-141; **NASA:** Jacques Descloitres, MODIS Land Rapid Response Team / GSFC 51-79.

© **ECMWF:** 78t, 201t, 203t; akg-images: 8br, 35tr, 104bl; British Library, London 18-19t; **Alamy Images:** Aerial Archives 247tr; Bryan & Cherry Alexander Photography 86cra; Archivberlin Fotoagentur GmbH 171tr; Bill Brooks 59b; Alan Campbell 103cl; Ashley Cooper 63cla, 111br, 261tr; Neil Cooper 267tl; Dalgleish Images 71t; Michael Dwyer 244c; Mary Evans Picture Library 27tl, 31cb, 31clb, 31crb; David R. Frazier Photolibrary, Inc. 58br; Robert Harding Picture Library Ltd 118b; Images of Africa 133c; Israel Images 141br; Lebrecht Music and Arts Photo Library 241tr; Ern Mainka 135tr; Ryan McGinnis 107c; Medical-on-Line 221c; Mountain Light / Galen Rowell 135br; Nepal Images 230bc, 230bl, 230br, 230-231b, 231bc, 231bl, 231br; Pablo Paul 224br; Phototake Inc. 195r; Frances Roberts 47t; tbkmedia.de 97br; Visual Arts Library, London 36b, 40cr; Richard Wareham Fotografie 212bl; **Ancient Art & Architecture Collection:** Private Collection 31tr; **The Art Archive:** Society of Apothecaries / Eileen Tweedy 32-33b; Tate Gallery, London / Eileen Tweedy 36cra; Turkish and Islamic Museum, Istanbul / Gianni Dagli 21; Eileen Tweedy 22-23b; **The ASTR Project:** 173cra; **The Bridgeman Art Library:** Yale Center for British Art, Paul Mellon Collection, USA 27b; **Bureau of Meteorology, Australia (www.bom.gov.au):** 188bl, 200b; Courtesy of **Climateprediction.net:** 256br; **Corbis:** 75b; Dennis di Cicco 226cra; Pierre Colombel 28ca; Dallas Morning News / Irwin Thompson 258c; DPA / Frank May 220b; DPA / Michael Hanschke 14cr; EPA / Jon Hrusa 215cra; EPA / Mast Irham 267br; EPA / Mick Tsikas 206cra; EPA / Moonwha Daily News / Str 217b; Lindsay Hebberd 181t; Hulton-Deutsch Collection 74bl; Kim Kulish 196bl; LA Daily News / Gene Blevins 133br; David Lees 34bc; Barry Lewis 259cr; Michael S. Lewis 202-203b; Charles Mauzy

141tl; Mediscan 241c; Christopher J. Morris 181br; Jehad Nga 263t; Charles O'Rear 57br, 234-235t; Reuters / Finbarr O'Reilly 165t; Gianni Dagli Orti 240bc; Louie Psihoyos 267c; Carl & Ann Purcell 80t, 148b; Jim Reed 119t; Jim Reed Photography / Mike Theiss 9t, 125tl; Reuters / Daniel Aguilar 61cr; Reuters / Daniel Leclair 121b; Reuters / David Gray 212t; Reuters / Jorge Silva 229r (12); Reuters / NASA 173tl; Reuters / Paulo Whitaker 217cra; Reuters / Rafael Perez 229r (9); Reuters / Tim Wimborne 105tl; Reuters / Toby Melville 208-209; Reuters / Vincent Laforet 124-125bc; Rob Sanford 103br; Paul Souders 234-235b; Stapleton Collection 32cra; Jim Sugar 249tr; Sygma 139t; Telegram Tribune / Jason Mellom 167cr; Ultimate Chase / Mike Theiss 103tr; Visuals Unlimited 197t, 204br; Doug Wilson 22ca; ZUMA / Earl Cryer 177b; **DK Images:** Courtesy of the Community Collaborative Rain, Hail and Snow Network 225br; Brian Cosgrove 64cra, 77cl, 88, 88bl, 89br, 94br, 95b, 96c, 99tr, 100, 101cr, 106cr, 231cl, 232cra, 251tl, 251tr; Modelmaker: David Donkin 25cl; Rowan Greenwood 226-227b; Judith Miller / Carlton Antiques 44ca; Courtesy of the National Maritime Museum, London / James Stevenson 12; Courtesy of the Norwegian Maritime Museum / James Stevenson 31ca; Rough Guides / Michelle Grant 29tr; Courtesy of the Royal Museum of Scotland, Edinburgh / Andy Crawford 29bc; Satellite Image Map © 1919-2003 Planetary Visions 56bl; **Dreamstime.com:** Rod Adcock 152-153bs; Wolfgang Amri 262bl; Noam Armonn 156br; Arsty 65tl; Can Balcioglu 60-61bs; Mark Bond 264b; Bridgetjones 134c; George Burba 158cra; Ron Chapple Studios 172c; Olga Chernetskaya 219clb; Paul Cowan 46b; Dehew 26br; Pier Delune 229r (7); Willem Dijkstra 271tl; Diomedes66 24bc; Djb31st 172-173bs; Eraxion 25br; Feblacal 218cr; Ferderich 50; Kre Geg 156c; Domenico Gelermo 229r (1); Maksym Gorpenyuk 77tr; Peter Hazlett 178cl; Jerry Horn 132cr; Grondin Julien 239cr; Martin Krause 73cra; Ryszard Laskowski 63br; C. Mapuk 160cl; Aril Mellul 221t; Will Moneymaker 117c; Mylightscapes 106bl; Nicolette Neish 63cra; Pakhnyushchyy 48-49t, 77cr; Greg Payan 229r (10); Pomortzeff 115cl; Sergey Anatolievich Pristyazhnyuk 159tl; Armin Rose 63cl, 73tl, 79c; Dmitry Rukhlenko 252bl; Weldon Schloneger 229r (4); Sedmak 102b; Nico Smit 157cl; Kamil Sobócki 10b, 269t; Petr Stalbovskiy 229r (3); Pavalache Stelian 229r (2); Alexander Studentschnig 229r (0); Sunnyfrog 110br; Dan Talson 176b; Aravind Teki 229tl; Tiero 56cra; Vitaly Titov 101cla; Imants Urtans 229r (5); Angie Westre 231tr; Ximagination 236; drr.net: UPI Photo / Carlos Gutierrez 2-3; **ESA/CNES/ARIANESPACE:** 191bl; Eumetsat 2002 58cr; **FLPA:** Frans Lanting 142-143b; **Getty Images:** AFP / Frederic J. Brown 214cr; AFP / Jamie Razuri 245t; AFP / José Jordan 206bl; AFP / Nicolas Asfouri 215tl; AFP / Philippe Lopez 220cra; AFP / Romeo Gacad 259tr; AFP / Simon Maina 215crb; AFP / Steve Jaffe 139crb; AFP / STF 140cra; AFP / STR 168bl, 264; AFP / Yoshikazu Tsuno 229r (6); All Canada Photos / Thomas Kitchin & Victoria Hurst 248c; Allsport / Adam Pretty 127tr; Allsport Concepts / Ryan McVay 226; Aurora / Jerry Dodrill 112-113; Aurora / Joanna B. Pinneo 263br; Daniel

Berehulak 27tr, 202cr, 258-259b; China Photos 207t; Gallo Images / Anthony Bannister 79tr; Hedgehog House / Colin Monteath 175b; Hulton Archive 44crb; Hulton Archive / Central Press 117br; Iconica / Eric Meola 10-11t, 232-233b; The Image Bank / Bruno Morandi 253tr; The Image Bank / Macduff Everton 222-223b; The Image Bank / Patti McConville 221br; The Image Bank / Terje Rakke 105c; MOD 44-45b; National Geographic / James P. Blair 78-79b; National Geographic / Joel Sartore 180b; National Geographic / Peter Carsten 138b; Scott Olson 204t; Panoramic Images 5; Photographer's Choice / Frank Cezus 17t; Photographer's Choice / Hiroyuki Matsumoto 6-7; Photographer's Choice / Michael McQueen 182-183b; Photographer's Choice / Richard Price 210ca; Joe Raedle 123br, 184, 205clb; Reportage / Christopher Pillitz 141bl; Reportage / Per-Anders Pettersson 207br; Riser / A.J. James 227r (8); Riser / Jack Dykinga 175tl; Riser / Lorentz Gullachsen 256cra; Science Faction / Fred Hirschmann 4; Science Faction / Jim Reed 130-131b; Science Faction / Norbert Wu 144; Science Faction / Seth Resnick 128cra; Sebun Photo / Shigeki Kawakita 63tr; Sebun Photo / Tadao Yamamoto 270; Stone / Art Wolfe 116b; Stone / Chip Porter 82; Stone / Eddie Soloway 132bl; Stone / James Balog 211cr; Stone / James Stillings 107br; Stone / Jerry Alexander 179t; Stone / Lorne Resnick 85t; Stone / Paul Chesley 80-81b; Mark Thompson 214b; Time Life Pictures / Time Inc. 75tc; Ian Waldie 167cl; John Warwick Brooke 38cl; **Hong Kong Observatory:** 213cr; **iStockphoto.com:** 51, 94cr, 135bl, 151t, 155bl, 158b, 201b, 242-243b, 266ca, 268bl; Steven Allan 28b; Maria Barski 110cr; Don Bayley 145, 195bl; Eric Bechtold 218b; Vera Bogaerts 159cr, 175cr; Chris Boychuk 77tl; Daniel Cardiff 90cra; David Ciemny 165c; Rachell Coe 216bl; Daniel Cooper 127b; Parker Deen 227r (11); Anthony Dodd 171cla; John Flewin 25t; Greg Gardner 216t; Eric Gevaert 237; Julien Grondin 24c; Izabela Habur 71br; Alexander Hafemann 160-161b; Yuri Hnilazub 13; Timothy Hughes 90b; Björn Kindler 154cl; Matt Knannlein 63crb; Roman Krochuk 53bl; Liz Leyden 179br; Daniel Loncarevic 30br; Adrian Matthiassen 73cl, 268cra; Matteo Evangelista Mazzenga 171cra; Kenneth McIntosh 149c; Jouke van der Meer 9c, 54ca; Hans F. Meier 116tr, 233t; David Parsons 248br; Andrey Pavlov 162-163; Chad Purser 121tl; Dave Raboin 9br, 92-93b; Brian Raisbeck 271tr; Sean Randall 142-143t, 153tr; Giovanni Rinaldi 69crb; Juergen Sack 164b; Roberto A. Sanchez 148ca; Richard Schmidt-Zuper 269br; Christian Schöps 231cr; Jon Sharp 191cr; Jo Ann Snover 63clb; Michel Uytterbroeck 150b; Maurice van der Velden 155cr; Stefan Williams 227cr; John Woodworth 155t; Ling Xia 67b; **Kenneth G. Libbrecht:** 83, 108c, 108ca, 108cr; **Library Of Congress, Washington, D.C.:** L. Prang & Co. 33t; Charles Turner 37bl; **NASA:** 161c, 196cra, 261c; Jesse Allen, Earth Observatory / MODIS Rapid Response Team 149crb; Image copyright BYU, 2000 1t, 205br; Jacques Descloitres 174cla; Image Courtesy GOES Project Science Office 68cl; International Space Station 48-49b; Johnson Space Center 54b, 57tr; JPL 150ca, 152cra, 178br; JPL Ocean Surface Topography Team 166cra; Langley Research Center 198; MODIS Rapid Response Team 273tl; Jacques Descloitres, MODIS Land Rapid Response Team / GSFC 120bl,

120crb, 122cra; National Hurricane Center 119br; NSSTC Lightning Team 131t; Hal Pierce and Steve Lang (SSAI / NASA GSFC) 191br; SeaWiFS Project / Goddard Space Flight Center and ORBIMAGE 224b, 238bl; SeaWiFS Project / Goddard Space Flight Center, and ORBIMAGE 120clb; SEAWIFS Project, GSFC and ORBIMAGE 177tr; Donna Thomas / MODIS Ocean Group / GSFCC SST product by R. Evans et al, U. Miami 61tl; **National Meteorological Library And Archive:** 199cl, 199cr, 199tr, 242c, 265b, 265t; Crown Copyright 95tr, 185, 186cl, 204bl; John Hammond 98b, 99br, 114; **NERC Satellite Receiving Station, University of Dundee:** www.sat.dundee.ac.uk 127c; **NOAA:** 123br, 213dl; Carol Baldwin, NOAA OMAO 231tl; Lieutenant Mark Boland, NOAA Corps 164cr; David Burdick 262br; Central Library 72br; Climate Program Office, NABOS 2006 Expedition 23cr, 101b; GFDL 257br; Dr. Joseph Golden 137tl; George E. Marsh Album 39tl; National Weather Service Collection 42cl, 92cr; PD-USGOV 124c; Satellite and Information Service 120br, 120cb, 129b, 129cb, 129crb; Captain Albert E. Theberge Jr., NOAA Corps (ret.) 99cl; Treasures of the NOAA Library Collection 20, 41b, 41c; **Oceanweather Inc.:** 210b; Image courtesy of **Oregon Scientific (UK) Limited:** 224c; **Panos Pictures:** G.M.B. Akash 16-17b; Crispin Hughes 169b; Gerd Ludwig 261br; Espen Rasmussen 47br; Dieter Telemans 254-255b; **Photolibrary:** AlaskaStock 211t; Chad Ehlers 249br; Index Stock Imagery / Paul Katz 109tr; Jiri Jiri 108b; OSF / Warren Faidley 136cra; **Mr William S. Pike:** 97c; **Rex Features:** 205cra; Newspix / Alan Pryke 271br; Stock Connection / Chad Ehlers 253bl; **Rutgers State University of New Jersey:** C. Grant Law 170cra; **Science & Society Picture Library:** Science Museum, London 34ca, 35bl, 85br; **Science Photo Library:** American Institute of Physics / Emilio Segre Visual Archives 199br; British Antarctic Survey 245cr; Eurelios / Massimo Brega 241b; Dr Tim Evans 260ca; Gustoimages 223tl; Victor Habbick Visions 272c, 272-273b; NRSC Ltd 126; Paul Rapson 193c; MIke Theiss 140b; University of Dundee 96br; Courtesy of **SOHO/EIT Consortium**. SOHO is a project of international cooperation between ESA and NASA: 52c; **SST, Royal Swedish Academy of Sciences, LMSAL:** 52bc; **Still Pictures:** Biosphoto / Ittel Jean-Frédéric 246crb; Biosphoto / Ittel Jean-Frédéric & Association Morain 246clb; Biosphoto / J.-L. Klein & M.-L. Hubert 14-15b; Nigel Dickinson 129tl; Mark Edwards 169tl; R. Gerth 147tl; W. Holzenbecher 111tr; Frans Lemming 46cl; Luiz C. Marigo 188c; S. Meyers 115b; A. Rose 247b; Kevin Schafer 181cl; **U.S. Navy:** 43b; Cpl. Alicia M. Garcia, U.S. Marine Corps. 69tr; Photographer's Mate 3rd Class James R. McGury 189t; Senior Chief Aviation Structural Mechanic Andrew Stack 115cr; **U.S. Air Force:** 55tr; Lockheed-Martin 45cra; G.A. Volb 45tl; **USGS:** 240c; **Wikipedia, The Free Encyclopedia:** 18-19b, 26ca, 35br, 38-39b, 43tr, 68-69b, 70bl, 89tr, 91b, 91tr, 93cra, 102cr, 109b, 118cra, 147br, 151crb, 182-183t, 197br, 219t, 239bl, 262ca, 273cra; C. Goodwin 131c; Orbital Sciences Corporation 190cra

All other images © Dorling Kindersley
For further information see: **www.dkimages.com.**